Increase and Multiply

Governing Cultural Reproduction in Early Modern England

David Glimp

MINNESOTA

University of Minnesota Press
Minneapolis
London

Sections of chapter 3 appeared in "Staging Government: Shakespeare's *Life of King Henry the Eighth* and the Government of Generations," *Criticism* 41, 1 (winter 1999): 41–65; reprinted with permission from Wayne State University Press. Sections of chapter 5 appeared in "Paradisal Arithmetic: *Paradise Lost* and the Genesis of Populations," *Modern Language Quarterly* 60, 1 (March 1999): 1–31; copyright University of Washington; reprinted with permission from the Modern Language Association and Duke University Press.

Published by the University of Minnesota Press
111 Third Avenue South, Suite 290
Minneapolis, MN 55401-2520
http://www.upress.umn.edu

Library of Congress Cataloging-in-Publication Data

Glimp, David.
Increase and multiply : governing cultural reproduction in early modern England / David Glimp.
p. cm.
Includes bibliographical references and index.
ISBN 0-8166-3990-6 (HC : alk. paper) — ISBN 0-8166-3991-4 (PB : alk. paper)
1. English literature—Early modern, 1500–1700—History and criticism. 2. Population in literature. 3. Sidney, Philip, Sir, 1554–1586—Views on population. 4. Shakespeare, William, 1564–1616—Views on population. 5. Milton, John, 1608–1674—Views on population. 6. England—Population—History—16th century. 7. England—Population—History—17th century. 8. Demography—England—History—16th century. 9. Demography—England—History—17th century. I. Title.
PR428.P66G58 2003
820.9'355—dc21 2002013314

Printed in the United States of America on acid-free paper

12 11 10 09 08 07 06 05 04 03 10 9 8 7 6 5 4 3 2 1

Increase and Multiply

For Lisa Claire Boyle

Contents

Acknowledgments

I am pleased to have the opportunity to thank the many people whose kindness and intelligence made this book possible. Jonathan Goldberg, first and foremost, deserves the greatest thanks for his painstaking response to many early drafts of this work and for his kind guidance at every stage of this project. I continue to be inspired by his critical rigor, his scholarly acumen, and his gifts as an advisor and teacher. I am grateful as well to John Guillory for his important feedback, and to Mary Poovey for her encouragement and her thoughtful response to various sections of this work in their earliest stages. Margaret Williams Ferguson first prompted me to ask the questions that through profoundly circuitous routes led to this book; for this and much else besides, I am in her debt.

Over the years of this book's composition, many friends and colleagues have been generous with their time, knowledge, and suggestions. During my time at Johns Hopkins University, I profited from the demanding readings of and invigorating conversations with Scott Black, Dan Denecke, Robert Matz, Elizabeth Pittenger, Jennifer Summit, and William Weaver. Forrest Tyler Curtain also has my enduring gratitude for his input and for his abiding friendship. Since arriving at the University of Miami, I have had the good fortune of finding an equally supportive and equally challenging intellectual community. Leslie Bow, Kathy Freeman, Frank Palmeri, Catherine Judd, John Paul Russo, Michael Rothberg, Jeff Shoulson, and Mihoko Suzuki either read and generously responded to parts of this work or asked key questions that helped me clarify my thinking on many points. Russ Castronovo and Tassie Gwilliam deserve special mention for their patience in reading more drafts of more chapters than collegiality would demand; I am deeply thankful for their friendship and intellectual generosity. I am grateful to the University of Miami Research Council, which provided valuable support in the form of two Max Orovitz Summer Awards in the Arts and Humanities and funding for research trips to the Folger Shakespeare Library and the British Library.

Portions of this work have been presented to audiences at Johns Hopkins University, Florida State University, Kansas State University, the University of Miami, and Stanford University, as well as at annual meetings of the Modern Language Association, the Shakespeare Association of America, and the Group for Early Modern Cultural Studies. Members of the audiences at these events provoked me to clarify and rethink my argument in many ways, and the argument is better for their ideas.

Thanks are due as well to the kind folks at the University of Minnesota Press, especially to Richard Morrison for his interest in this project and to Paula Friedman for her artful and expert copyediting. Two readers for the Press, Jonathan Crewe and an anonymous respondent, provided important direction for revision, and I remain indebted to them for their incisive feedback.

My parents, Shirlie and Hudson Glimp, and my sister, Ammie Jo Busby, have my love and deepest gratitude for their affection and support, which have never wavered, even in the face of my perhaps unexpected vocational turns. I especially look forward to the response of Genevieve Katherine Glimp, whose delightfully ungoverned presence has graced the final stages of this project. Lisa Claire Boyle made this book possible in more ways than I can say; her intelligence, sense of humor, compassion, and clarity of perspective have sustained me throughout its composition. Such as it is, this work is for her.

Introduction

In his 1798 *Essay on the Principle of Population,* Thomas Malthus asserts the by now familiar thesis that history is driven by the mismatch between resources and population. Offering an example of how these imbalances determine humanity's progress through various stages of social organization, Malthus describes the unsettling changes brought about by the relative "ease," mobility, and safety of shepherd societies. The very abundance that allowed these people to flourish removed obstacles to reproduction, yielding the "natural and invariable effect" of population growth and then misery. "Want pinched the less fortunate members of society," Malthus explains,

> and, at length, the impossibility of supporting such a number together became too evident to be resisted. Young scions were then pushed out from the parent-stock and instructed to explore fresh regions and to gain happier seats for themselves by their swords. "The world was all before them where to choose."[1]

There is something breathtaking about Malthus's quotation from the close of *Paradise Lost.* The allusion to Adam and Eve making their reluctant way out of Eden implicitly rewrites the Fall as the unavoidable—indeed natural—result of the imbalance between numbers of persons and means of subsistence. The Fall was thus no fall at all; it was but a moment in the inevitable transition among modes of social organization. Although Malthus was himself a parson, and although there are theological dimensions of the *Essay,* this reference so obviously and jarringly dislocates Adam and Eve from Milton's conceptual framework that one (at least one inclined to look) has to wonder what discursive and practical resources Malthus utilizes, modifies, displaces, or reconfigures as he develops his theory. Implicit in Malthus's allusion is a massive revision and reorganization of the conceptual vocabularies and the governmental techniques through which people come to be subjects implicated in larger collectives. *Increase and Multiply* seeks to describe crucial aspects of this revision and reorganization by detailing the ways numbers of people are comprehended as objects and agents of government in early modern England. My attention to the allusive presence of Milton in Malthus's work synechdochically signals my interest in understanding what accounts of human aggregates have to do with sixteenth- and seventeenth-century English literature. This book examines how early modern literary practice acknowledges, contributes to, resists, or disavows the dynamics that have as their unanticipated and unplanned outcome the development of population as a theoretical and practical construct.

In its most general terms, the argument of *Increase and Multiply* is this. Sixteenth- and seventeenth-century England witnessed an intensified interest in registering and counting people. Although forms of census and human registration were by no means invented during these years, it was then that parishes, cities, and royal officials began systematically to record marriages, births, and deaths, to gauge the numbers of poor and indigent, to estimate the numbers of immigrants, to count those dead from the plague. These disparate practices signal decisive shifts in how people understand what it is that governments do and the phenomena for which government can be held responsible. Both documenting and contributing to these changes, a considerable array of pamphleteers, academics, officials, and counselors develop conceptual vocabularies that render people thinkable and hence governable in new ways. This reconfigured scrutiny of the stability, vitality, activity, and size of the populace creates profound urgency around the project of reproduction. The objective organizing this urgency is never simply to add more people, though, but to make more of the *right kinds* of people and to foreclose the possibility of creating the *wrong kinds*. Merely producing offspring is not enough to guarantee that people will reinforce order and will contribute to the objectives of a given institution or collectivity. Biological reproduction requires practices of cultural reproduction, and the efforts of families, churches, schools, armies, and city officials, to name only the groups and institutions discussed in this book, come to be understood as playing a prominent role in the manufacture of family members, good Christians, intelligent and serviceable graduates, warriors, and good citizens of the commonwealth. To the extent that humanist pedagogy constitutes a condition of possibility for much Renaissance literary production, literature is implicated in these reproductive imperatives as well; indeed, an array of poets and playwrights formulate their endeavors in precisely such reproductive terms. Focusing primarily on Sir Philip Sidney, William Shakespeare, and John Milton, this book demonstrates how these authors claim for their work a capacity to achieve the governed creation of men and women to shape the future of the polity. At the same time, their texts reflect upon the scope of these procreative claims, interrogate the objectives an ideal of regulated cultural fecundity would seek to secure, identify and explore the potential failures of generative practices to achieve their governmental designs.

No doubt, taking Malthus as a starting point risks imposing upon this study a false teleology by suggesting that somehow all roads lead inexorably to his vision of the population. Although this book resists such an understanding of history, gesturing toward Malthus at the outset does help to acknowledge what might be called an attenuated neo-Malthusian dimension of recent criticism of early modern English literature. As one scholar has recently written, "population growth" because of its "real and quotidian influence . . . needs to be studied as a basis of the culture and cultural production of Renaissance England."[2] Though not always so explicitly, a number of materialist scholars have drawn attention to the ways population growth and mobility impacted daily existence, cultural production, or more specifically the formation of markets for literary goods.[3] The present study is sympathetic to the impetus driving the appeal to what Fernand Braudel calls "the weight of numbers," both the evidence provided by the extraordinary work of historical demographers and the concrete effects of population changes.[4] However, its intention is also to raise some questions about the obviousness of the evidence grounding claims about population impact. The difficulties arise when the numbers are taken to speak for themselves. The scholar quoted above writes, with respect to London, that "the city often encoded in its cultural self-representations what the population table gives in statistics."[5] Where early modern artists "encode," contemporary demographic historians simply "give." This suggests that statistics provide a transparent view of the real, give a gift of facts that, once received, provides the critic with a tool with which to "decode" plays, to winnow the chaff of the "ideal"—misrecognitions, interested misrepresentations, mistakes, oversights—from the kernel of materiality within any given text.

Without discounting the claim that population changes impacted daily existence and thus, in however mediated a form, influenced cultural production, it seems worthwhile to step back from the hermeneutic model advanced above and to reflect on the status of the facts we are being asked to consider as transparently descriptive of the material world. To inquire into the status of our knowledge about the population is to undertake an exercise in what Lorraine Daston and Mary Poovey have called "historical epistemology," a "history of the categories that structure our thought, pattern our arguments and proofs, and certify our standards for explanation."[6] Such an approach to the production of knowledge seeks to understand the conceptual and practical conditions of possibility for making true and false statements about the world and thus for conceptually organizing and interacting with it. With respect to the appeal to the work of historical demographers, we may observe that it is possible to reconstruct "population table[s]" for sixteenth- and seventeenth-century England only because, as noted above, efforts to enumerate people proliferated considerably during this time. Although much useful information can be derived from parish registers, censuses of the poor and immigrants, and bills of mortality by employing the sophisticated tools of analysis and statistical "back projection" afforded by historical demography, a study interested in questions of historical epistemology requires that we pursue another set of queries.[7] What if we asked why we have these sources at all? How did registering and enumerating people come to be so widespread? What forms of personhood do these practices utilize and in turn make available for others to use? With what understandings about the work and scope of government can such practices be associated? What may the intensified interest in numbers of people have to do with literary production? Does literature simply "encode" the demographic facts? Or may there not be other ways of imagining the relation between literary practice and these early efforts to record and to count people?[8]

To be sure, this series of interrogatives defines an expansive field of study and raises more issues than can be addressed in a single work. It will therefore be worthwhile to spell out the organizing principles and concerns that structure my own effort to answer these questions. *Increase and Multiply* pursues three interrelated agendas. First, as is evident in my remarks about Malthus and the neo-Malthusian dimensions of recent materialist literary criticism, this book contributes to a genealogy of the population as a governmental concept. Second, the chapters that follow describe how practices of cultural reproduction are construed as central to the project of imagining, constituting, and ruling human aggregates. Finally, as a way to emphasize what specifically literary production takes from and contributes to the practical and conceptual dynamics I trace, this book addresses the activities of writers who both claimed and reflected on the reproductive effects of their literary endeavor—and who in some cases were taken to be a part of a population problem in their own right. In its survey of these concerns, this introduction seeks to spell out as concisely as possible the methodological assumptions guiding this study, to specify more precisely the interrelations of the three emphases, and to clarify what is at stake in the arguments the book advances.

In contributing to a genealogy of the population, I draw on and elaborate the work of Michel Foucault, which provides considerable resources for thinking about the population as a historically specific object of knowledge and focus of governmental reflection and action. According to Foucault, the constitution of the population as an empirically accessible level of reality, "both as an object of analysis and as a target of intervention" invested with its own internal logic and regularities, discursively authorized and provided the conceptual resources for a new dispensation of government.[9] "One of the great innovations in the techniques of power in the eighteenth century," he argues,

> was the emergence of "population" as an economic and political problem: population as wealth, population as manpower or labor capacity, population balanced between its own growth and the resources it commanded. Governments perceived that they were not dealing simply with subjects, or even with a "people," but with a "population," with its specific phenomena and its peculiar variables: birth and death rates, life expectancy, fertility, state of health, frequency of illnesses, patterns of diet and habitation. (25)

Enabled and bolstered by the spread of descriptive technologies of statistical enumeration and classification, this understanding of the population anchored the formation of what Foucault calls a "biopolitics of the population" (139).[10] Biopolitics sought to measure and regulate persons in the aggregate, to differentiate and specify their capacities and limitations, to diagnose the pathologies draining their productivity, to subject them to a medico-moral regimen of social hygiene, economic optimization, and eugenic invigoration. Biopolitically conceived practices of governance advanced both totalizing and individualizing objectives. That is, even as a biopolitics of the population sought to produce regulative effects on the population as a whole, it also worked on, and through, each constituent member of that population. The imperative to produce knowledge about the population attempted to coordinate the activities of individuals—including, centrally, their sexual practice—with the needs and demands of a larger order, to enlist and to invest people in the present health and future viability of the population. As Colin Gordon explains, biopolitics represented a means of governing "all and each," a dispensation "in which issues of individual sexual and reproductive conduct interconnect[ed] with issues of national policy and power."[11] The population provided not only a set of objectives for national government—it was to be managed, invigorated, strengthened, augmented, utilized, channeled, protected—but also a horizon of governmental reflection for both individuals and states. The population became a factor to be considered when gauging the implications of personal action or governmental intervention.[12]

The approach just outlined does not take sides in the debate about the status of population changes as last-instance determinants of economic and social transformation.[13] Neither does it rest on claims about changing patterns of mortality and fertility. Rather, Foucault's concern is to understand the very terms and practices through which the population comes to be available as a way of understanding the world, and as a way of conceptualizing the work of government. This way of characterizing Foucault's account seeks to make clear its connections to his work on "governmentality," work that he understood to be in part a contribution to a genealogy of biopolitics. Foucault's comments, dispersed through lectures and interviews in the late 1970s, sketched out a research agenda pursued, elaborated, and refashioned by Graham Burchell, Peter Miller, Nikolas Rose, Mitchell Dean, Giovanni Procacci, and Ian Hacking, among other scholars.[14] What links their work is an effort to understand how historically specific practices of government utilize and rely upon practices of knowledge production to structure our worlds, to impact what it is possible for us "to think, do, say, be, and feel."[15] The definition of government informing this work is functionally expansive. "'Government,'" Foucault asserts, with respect to sixteenth- and seventeenth-century Europe,

> did not refer only to political structures or to the management of states; rather it designated the way in which the conduct of individuals or of groups might be directed: the government of children, of souls, of communities, of families, of the sick. It did not only cover the legitimately constituted forms of political or economic subjection, but also modes of action, more or less considered and calculated, which were destined to act upon the possibilities of action of other people. To govern, in this sense, is to structure the possible field of action of others.[16]

Defining governance in this way draws attention to practices that might be associated with domination or oppression, but are not reducible to such strategies of rule. Foucault emphasizes the structure of agency, the efforts (never guaranteed in advance) to define and to delimit the kinds of actions people may take. Government in this sense is action upon potential actions, the endeavor to anticipate and to channel how people will behave in the future, to define what is thinkable and hence possible for them to do in any given situation. Government approaches people as rationally knowable and manipulable objects, certainly, but it also posits their agency, their ability to decide how to act within a range of "possibilities," and even their capacity under certain circumstances to call into question the authority, techniques, severity, and objectives of those who rule.[17]

This account of government qualifies an abiding narrative of political analysis that would reduce all power relations to the monolithic and voraciously aggrandizing force of the state. "[M]aybe, after all," Foucault writes somewhat tendentiously, "the state is no more than a composite reality and a mythicized abstraction, whose importance is a lot more limited than many of us think."[18] Although Foucault's comments intervene in a localized debate, his polemic retains its relevance for us in light of the considerable importance the state continues to have in Renaissance literary criticism. This bracing statement, taken with the passage cited earlier, does not dismiss completely any focus on the state; rather, it simply invites more nuanced accounts of the institutions, departments, councils, practices, techniques, and forms of knowledge production and distribution that we have come to treat as a unified agent—how they cohere or not, the kinds of agencies they possess, enable, or disallow, their scope and effectivity, their limits and internal conflicts.[19]

The definition of government advanced above also insists on the need to situate such an assemblage in relation to other forms of governmental activity not easily subsumed beneath, or reducible to, the state. Contrary to a view that would see government as a concern ultimately only for the prince (a monarch who stands above his or her territory) or a putatively monolithic and omnicompetent bureaucratic apparatus, Foucault insists that the "conduct of conduct"[20] is not a unified activity, and cannot be located within a singular institutional site. Construed in this way, government encompasses "a massive domain between the minutiae of individual self-examination, self-care, and self-reflection, and the techniques and rationalities concerned with the governance of the state."[21] As Foucault observes, during the sixteenth and seventeenth centuries, which he identifies as a time of considerable intensification of concern about government, "one speaks . . . of 'governing' a household, souls, children, a province, a convent, a religious order, a family."[22] Of course, in officially Protestant early modern England not everyone would associate convents or Catholic religious orders with regulated conduct; indeed, the fact that many (though certainly not all) would consider these organizations a threat to government compels us to modify Foucault's Francocentric perspective to accommodate the specificities of early modern England. Even so, Foucault's definition usefully foregrounds the ways a wide array of activities were understood to be forms of governance. Government constitutes an activity and objective pursued in many domains, the sites of problems and, thus, arenas for the production of knowledge on how best to rule and to be ruled: the relation of a sovereign to his or her subjects or the care of a father (or, in some cases, parents) for a family, of a pastor for a congregation, of a tutor for his pupils, of an individual for him- or (in some cases) herself.

Dismantling a notion of the state as a unified agent, and dispersing government across many domains, changes the kinds of questions it is possible to ask about the state. Rather than analyze how (or, as is more frequently the case, simply assume that) the state amasses ever more power to itself, and in the process consciously works to the economic interest of some members of the population at the expense of others, Foucault opens up the possibility of a different kind of inquiry, one that interrogates how the state came to take the economy and population as its primary objects. How did such governmental constructs as the economy and the population come to define what it was possible for governments to do or not do? And how did these totalizing constructs enable individualizing strategies of rule? That is, how did the task of governing "all" facilitate or rely upon the government of "each" person? Of course, these questions do not preclude the important concerns of Marxist analysis; they do seek to complicate the kinds of stories it is possible to tell about government by historicizing the standard categories of social history and by disrupting the transhistorical self-evidence of the interpretive matrices offered by political economy. Of most relevance for this study is Foucault's suggestion that the development of a dispensation of rule organized in the nineteenth century around the population may be traced to the intensified concern about government that he locates in the sixteenth and seventeenth centuries. The imperative to rule with greater efficiency and effectiveness prompts the refinement and application of governmental techniques and vocabularies to spheres of existence beyond their initial use—for example, the adaptation of the model of household government to the domain of national rule as a way of conceptualizing appropriate forms of political action, or the appeal to the model of pastoral care, a shepherd's vigilant attention to each member of his flock, to understand the project of administering national existence.[23] These developments eventually make it possible to conceptualize the population as a governmental totality, a "sector of reality" with its own internal laws, principles of coherence and regulation, anchoring and authorizing practices of knowledge production, forms of expertise, standards of "normality" and "deviance," and efforts to modify the behavior of individuals.

These comments and the shift in emphasis enabled by the work on "governmentality" are relevant as well to the considerable critical attention given by literary scholars to the development of early modern English nationhood.[24] The central organizing concern within these studies is the question of inclusion and exclusion. English national identity is approached either as an exclusive cultural form, constituted through the more or less violent exclusion of abjected others, or as a totality constructed through attempts at defining or imposing an inclusive consensus about what England and Englishness represents. Of course, these two approaches are not entirely separable. Britain may be viewed less as a collection of discrete, coherent, and unified national identities and more as a space of negotiation between necessarily incomplete and unstable identities, unstable and open for redefinition and contestatory rearticulation because they are defined by, and thereby logically require, that which they are not.[25] These are extremely important insights, and I shall draw on them below; for example, chapter 1 identifies the constitutive lines of inclusion and exclusion structuring sixteenth-century efforts to define the national community as a "common weal." However, alongside this aspect of nation formation, it seems useful to give greater attention than is usually provided to the governmental forms into which one might be included or from which it was possible to be excluded, and to inquire into the governmental implications of exclusion or inclusion.[26]

As indicated by this book's subtitle, the emphasis of what follows will be upon how the governmental forms I study—households, churches, schools, vocations, genders, polities, poetry, theaters—seek to impact reproduction. I use this latter term expansively to encompass not only giving birth but also an array of practices that contribute to the making of persons. Foucault's work emphasizes how procreative activity comes to be constituted as an object of knowledge and a target of governmental intervention; biopolitics renders individual fertility a factor with national, if not global, ramifications and incites people to comprehend a functional relation between their procreative activity and the future of the population, its vigor and continued or improved health.[27] The present study certainly focuses on procreative activity, how it gets constituted as an object of governmental concern, and how people are made to feel responsible for their fecundity prior to a fully consolidated biopolitical dispensation. But as the act of procreation is never enough to make a person, I also focus on an array of activities widely understood to be central to the task of creating people. The frequent attribution of generative effects to the acts of a sovereign, a military leader, a colonial administrator, a pastor, a teacher, or to a poem or play, constitutes an evocative way of imagining the person's or thing's future impact on the community, parish, nation, or faith. Characterizing any endeavor as reproductive likewise calls people to task for their actions, insists that they are obligated to conduct themselves and others in a responsible manner so that what they do will stabilize rather than disrupt families, communities, the church, or the polity.

My focus is thus upon a field of reproductive practices, a field that encompasses both biological fecundity and cultural activity. I develop this focus in two related directions. First, I work to clarify some of the more important ways generating persons comes to be a matter of urgency prior to an operative concept of the population. What ends render reproduction necessary, a vital imperative? What relationships or hierarchies do writers seek to secure under the promise of generating numbers of persons? Alternatively, what specific dangers are attached to the specter of propagating numbers of people out of control? The emphasis here is on the large-scale outcomes linked to generation—how any given reproductive practice impacts, for example, the English church in its agon with the Pope and Satan, or the monarchy or nation in its effort to expand, to maintain stability, to gain advantage militarily or through trade. Second, I attempt to define the ways reproductive claims seek to authorize government. That is, in sixteenth- and seventeenth-century England, how do various cultural domains justify and assert the necessity of their governmental activities through investing them with procreative effects? Conversely, in what ways does the figure of generation provide a means to stigmatize forms of cultural activity perceived as threatening? My focus is on the kinds of legitimacy granted to any activity—teaching a child, reading a poem, performing a play, supervising a parish, preparing for war, ruling a nation—when it is described as capable of making persons. As the title of this book suggests, a crucial distinction is that between cultural reproduction that is governed and cultural reproduction that is ungoverned, between practices of government said to yield stable and stabilizing generative effects and those construed as producing unregulated numbers that topple order, destabilize, and devastate.

A primary emphasis of this book is upon the ways early modern literature is implicated in these dynamics of cultural reproduction. Poetic claims to a capacity for producing reproductive effects derive in large measure from the pedagogic dimensions of literary practice, both its growth out of forms of rhetorical and linguistic training in grammar schools and universities, and its own claims to educational impact. My points along these lines are indebted to the considerable attention brought to bear upon the ways pedagogic endeavor works to produce and reproduce social relations. To take one prominent instance, Pierre Bourdieu and Jean-Claude Passeron have argued powerfully that education is never simply a matter of transmitting information, but instead represents a form of symbolic violence that confirms and perpetuates the hierarchies and hegemonic relations constitutive of any society.[28] Generally indebted to this approach, *Increase and Multiply* also follows in the wake of important work that demonstrates the socially reproductive aspects of Renaissance humanist educational practice.[29] Advocates of humanism often asserted that exposure to the texts of antiquity could redeem the nation from bestial ignorance; an important version of this argument was that humanist pedagogy constituted a kind of lettered birth, a means for making ideal persons.[30] Sir Philip Sidney, William Shakespeare, and John Milton, among numerous others, give voice to and explore the limits of generative claims central to English humanist practice. These authors make frequent appeal to such a generative capacity (to create well-governed and well-governing people) as a way to authorize their work. Sidney's vision of a procreative aesthetics, in which poets propagate "many Cyrusses" by providing ideals of proper conduct to be imitated by readers, is taken up and reworked throughout the period. This engagement with the objectives of humanist generation constitutes one prominent way that the authors studied attempt to contribute to imagining and securing personal, familial, civic, religious, and/or national futures.

Although governed cultural reproduction represents a widely shared objective, generative success is not guaranteed. Neither does governmental optimism imply that all activities characterized as generative necessarily contribute to the same unified project.[31] In this regard, Stuart Hall's caveat against the possibility "of an endlessly successful, functionally unfolding, reproduction . . . without either end, contradiction, crisis or break" is especially relevant.[32] The focus I propose offers a means of gauging the relations of antagonism and contest among persons, practices, and institutions, and implicitly locates sites where cultural reproduction threatens to fail. An important instance here, touched upon in one way or another in each of the chapters that follow, is the potentially contestatory relation between the birth that generally takes place within, and seeks to perpetuate, family structures, and the kind of generation effected by schools or through literature. Bourdieu and Passeron take the fact that pedagogic institutions are referred to in terms of parenting as simply an indication of the priority of family structures in the arena of educational reproduction. They note:

> the relation of pedagogic communication . . . is often experienced or conceived along the lines of the primordial relation of pedagogic communication, i.e., the relationship between parents and children, or, more generally, between generations. The tendency to re-establish with any person invested with [pedagogic authority] the archetypal relationship with the father is so strong that anyone who teaches, however young, tends to be treated as a father.[33]

The immediate point is well taken. Within their expansive definition of "pedagogic action," which is dispersed throughout society, not confined to a single institution or system, a child's education begins from his or her earliest moments as he or she learns the language, bearing, and dispositions of those nearby. But, as Bourdieu and Passeron also insist, pedagogic authority, the cultural legitimacy of the educational practice of any given person or institution, accrues within relations of competition. While the above passage argues that treating the pedagogue like a father (and we can note the parthenogenetic fantasy underwriting the displacement of both parents by the paternal figure) simply illustrates the "primordial" basis of all education in the family, the existence of Goffmanian "'total' institutions," those that attempt the complete "de"- and "reculturating" (44) of the pedagogic subject (such as boarding schools or convents, to name two of their examples), implies that families are imbricated within these relations of contest. This is especially so in early modern England, where family structures could not be said to have consolidated fully into a recognizably modern form. Humanist education in England is frequently defended as vital through an explicit or implicit argument that noble families are failing properly to educate their children, and consequently that England is populated by beasts rather than humans. As I argue in my penultimate chapter, John Milton insists upon the need for his program of educational reform, sketched in his brief pamphlet *Of Education*, by emphasizing the failure of parents—both the first parents, Adam and Eve, and England's contemporary parents who have allowed their children to be miseducated. Conversely, even as some defend poetry and drama as capable of making well-governed persons, others excoriate them for producing a dissolute spawn that threatens domestic economies and thus the nation as a whole. This book traces the implications of these relations of coordination and contest, and details the ways early modern authors respond to, elaborate, and intervene in the tensions among forms of generation, and are thereby compelled to acknowledge and to try to think through the limits of their own reproductive claims.

These are the more or less abstract concerns that inform this book. I turn now to providing a more concrete overview of each chapter. Chapter 1, "'Making Up People': The English Commonwealth and the Writing of Populations," establishes a frame of reference for the readings that follow by exploring the ways that numbers of people come to be a matter of concern in early modern England. The analysis focuses on Sir Thomas Smith's *Discourse of the Common Weal,* an important contribution to the "commonwealth" writings of the sixteenth century. An advisor to Edward VI and Elizabeth I, Smith helped forge a complex and elaborate set of terms for imagining the objective of government vis-à-vis the populace as a whole. This chapter explores the administrative, ethical, and political languages Smith and other scholars, royal counselors, and pamphleteers advance for conceptualizing rule in the wake of the profound social unrest of the sixteenth century. Their emphasis is less upon dominance of an inherently ungovernable "many-headed monster" and more upon carefully managing the balance between England's resources and its people. Humanism plays a crucial role in this redefinition of the scope and aims of rule, since, as Smith argues, its access to, and focus on, moral philosophy renders it the activity most concerned with personal, domestic, and national government.

The second chapter, "Defending Poetic Generation: Sir Philip Sidney and the Aesthetics of Educational Reproduction," begins to examine how concerns about population are central to the cultural work that literary texts were understood to perform. Sidney's *Defence of Poesie* responds to detractors of the arts by investing the poet with the capacity to generate well-governed and well-governing men for the commonwealth. These aspirations for poetry exist alongside a contemporary set of anxieties about what amounts to a flooded job market, a sense that educational institutions are producing *too many* learned people and hence that humanist training can potentially destabilize English society. Sidney broaches these fears by expressing contempt for the multitudes of incompetent artists, mere "rhymers" besetting the nation with abusive poetry, detracting from the good name of "poet" with their disordered verse. Although, in his *Defence,* Sidney distinguishes his ideal of regulated poetic fecundity from what amounts to poetry's promiscuous generative potential, his *Arcadia* illustrates the difficulties of maintaining such distinctions. The central male figures, Pyrocles and Musidorus, for example, imitate one of the standard Renaissance exemplars, Hercules; however, they imitate the hero at a less than exemplary moment of his career, when he cross-dresses to win the love of the Amazon Omphale. Spending most of the long prose romance in women's or peasants' garb, the princes undermine the ideals of masculinity they were trained as children to embody. Their transgressive behavior links them to the reviled figure of Clinias, who, although a "scholar" and an "actor in tragedies," causes rebellion in Arcadia, inciting the masses of local artisans and farmers to attempt to slaughter their king and to lay waste to the royal household and nation. Consequently, while Sidney seeks to produce narrative pleasure through depicting the actions of the princes, he also acknowledges and attempts to manage this connection between enjoyable and dangerous mimetic excesses by severely limiting the circulation of what he describes as his own poetic offspring, if not by destroying it altogether. Biographers accounting for Sidney's poetic activity seek to recuperate the potentially damaging instabilities in Sidney's poetic work by enlisting it in projects of pedagogic generation, though neither the success of such projects nor the exemplarity of Sidney's life as a model can be fully guaranteed.

Chapter 3, "Staging Government: Shakespearean Theater and the Government of Cultural Reproduction," focuses on the appeal to the notion of poetic generation in both assaults against, and defenses of, the popular theater. Those who wrote in support of the stage argued that it was valuable because it produced ideal men for the nation; those who feared the theater's effects on the nation argued that it was dangerous because it generated multitudes out of control, numbers that would destroy the kingdom. This chapter argues that Shakespeare does not so much take sides in this debate as interrogate its central terms. *Love's Labor's Lost* at once presents fantasies of learned generation and parodies them, a dynamic that informs the play's destabilizing treatment of both status and gender. The *Henriad* explores how Henry V's development and rule hinge on practices of mimetic pedagogy. Capitalizing on recent work that emphasizes these plays' relation to England's colonial endeavor in Ireland, I argue that Hal's reproductive efforts ultimately seek to resolve a problem inherent in "colonial governmentality," a challenge faced by both England in Ireland and Henry in France: How can a few people achieve dominance over many? Where Henry IV worried on his deathbed that, under his son, England would be invaded and misruled by a crew of Falstaffian "ruffian[s]," Henry V turns the tables on this vision by generating an army of men like himself to defeat the French, a reproductive ideal that incorporates—rather than rejects—Falstaff's voracity and unlicensed fecundity. My discussion of *Henry VIII* locates the contingencies of this reproductive vision by reading the ways in which the birth of Queen Elizabeth disrupts the fantasy of self-sufficient male generation. Through these representations of pedagogic fecundity, Shakespeare works to establish the cultural authority of the stage as a relatively autonomous site of potentially disruptive (and hence, from a stage perspective, potentially pleasurable) generation.

Where, in chapter 3, a theological perspective underwrites the strident critique of the stage's allegedly dangerous fecundity, in chapter 4 I note an important instance when the tables are turned, where the Church of England itself comes under scrutiny for its potential for ungoverned generation. "The Educational Genesis of Men: Puritan Reform and John Milton's *Of Education*" takes as its focus John Milton's prose writings of the 1640s, primarily his interventions against the hierarchy of the Church of England and his *Of Education,* a published letter of advice to the Puritan reformer Samuel Hartlib. Milton excoriates prelates for depopulating the nation, driving faithful English men and women abroad through, among many reasons, the prelates' educational incompetence and irresponsibility. In the same texts, he lambastes them for producing hordes of unprincipled, effeminate, and hollow persons through an abusive pedagogy. *Of Education* answers both the fear of losing well-governed numbers and the specter of prelatical abuse threatening to destroy the nation with a demonic hyperfecundity. The work does so by outlining what Milton asserts is a more rationally ordered, and hence efficient, educational regimen that effectively produces good men for the commonwealth. Although Milton's objectives align him with Hartlib's other correspondents, his pamphlet cannot be collapsed into the project of the Puritan reformers; where Jan Amos Comenius, for example, imagined a more disciplined Christian existence through universal childhood education, Milton's work registers desires for distinction from what he construes as the ungovernable English multitudes.

The final chapter, "Paradisal Arithmetic: *Paradise Lost* and the Genesis of Populations," relates Milton's epic to William Petty's *Political Arithmetic*, a roughly contemporary text frequently taken to be the founding document of modern demographics. Petty's work builds on and elaborates the views of the sixteenth-century commonwealth writers, emphasizing especially their administrative vision of manipulating the national populace, which he understands to be a component of England's wealth. While *Paradise Lost* endorses Petty's equivalence between people and wealth—Adam, Eve, and their offspring are figured on several occasions as treasure—this account raises troubling implications for God's dominion, implying that the future stability of his rule depends on Adam and Eve procreating. The poem resolves this difficulty by granting privilege to another account of why generating offspring is important, one that places considerable emphasis upon Eden's agricultural superabundance and Adam and Eve's daunting task of keeping this superabundance in check. From this perspective, reproduction comes to be an imperative not because God needs their offspring to bolster the strength of his kingdom, but because their children will help prevent Eden's produce from going to waste. Milton's dislocation from Petty's demographic and administrative efforts is evident in another respect as well. Political arithmetic responds to the midcentury rebellion by attempting to remove theological questions from the field of administrative calculation; by contrast, Milton's celebration of "wedded love," and his own desire to place himself among the angelic chorus singing God's praises, embraces what Petty would have considered theological "enthusiasm" as crucial for the project of living a well-governed life.

This study concludes by returning briefly to Malthus's *Essay* to underscore the unevenness and historical discontinuities constitutive of "the population" as a concept. Malthus does not simply endorse and elaborate Petty's vision of the populace as an administratively manipulable component of national wealth. Although political arithmetic enables Malthus's account, the latter places the onus of reproductive responsibility not on national legislators but precisely where Milton places it—squarely on the shoulders of married couples.

According to E. A. Wrigley and R. S. Schofield, in their pathbreaking effort to construct a viable estimate of England's population before the modern census, the number of people in England increased drastically from around three million to just over five million in the century between 1550 and 1650.[34] Population growth of 66 percent in a century could not but have had drastic effects on social structure and standard of living, as many social historians have demonstrated.[35] The chapters that follow suggest the value of stepping back momentarily from the facts and asking a set of questions about the bases of demographic knowledge, the governmental concerns associated with this knowledge, and the ways Renaissance aesthetics and literary texts intersect with these concerns. Even as we acknowledge the impact that numbers of people had on early modern culture, it seems important to question where we get our statistics, to understand the modes of intelligibility that rendered people available for thought and action during this period, and to investigate how literary practices relate to these governmental dynamics. As the above overview indicates, *Increase and Multiply* pursues primarily the latter concerns. Focusing on issues of reproduction, broadly defined, it contributes to a genealogy of the population as a concept, a genealogy that helps us understand how early modern writers actively participated in the complex processes through which human aggregates and individuals were constituted as both objects and agents of government.

CHAPTER ONE

"Making Up People"

The English Commonwealth and the Writing of Populations

In his study of statistical inquiry and the methods of social science, Ian Hacking argues that acts of description effectively "make up people." This unusual phrase foregrounds Hacking's point that forms of knowledge condition our ways of thinking about and acting upon others and ourselves. When "bureaucrats" or "students of human nature" set out to enumerate or to describe people, he contends, they do not provide an empirically neutral account of a somehow transparently accessible reality. Rather than simply being "recognized," categories of personhood are fabricated, and subsequently come to feel like a natural way to think of oneself or others: "a kind of person came into being at the same time as the kind itself was being invented."[1] Hacking's largest point is that the evidentiary technologies and conceptual forms through which people are "made up" are crucial to the work of government. Description enables action—the action of government authorities upon people, but also of people upon themselves and others. Government, in its expansive, Foucauldian sense, is not an activity undertaken in relation to subjects who exist outside of the various domains in which they might be implicated. Instead, government operates precisely through the complex and potentially conflictual processes through which forms of personhood become available for thinking about and acting upon and in the world.

This chapter outlines important ways people were "made up" in sixteenth- and seventeenth-century England. Consistent with the perspective advanced by Hacking, what follows works to specify the conceptual vocabularies through which the English populace was made thinkable, and to locate the agendas and effects with which these vocabularies can be associated. Descriptive practices of "making up people" in early modern England both prompt and respond to concerns about the size and stability of England's population, which in turn fuel a sense of urgency around the task of creating more people. Specifying different kinds of people, I argue, is a crucial aspect of the manner in which behavior that may be said to be generative—"generative" in a sense including but not restricted to biological procreation—comes to be formulated as governable, available for reflection and potential action. The argument to follow centers on *A Discourse of the Commonweal* (1581), a dialogue among several representative members of the English polity, published anonymously but most likely written in 1549 by Sir Thomas Smith, a prominent Tudor intellectual and advisor to Edward VI and Elizabeth I.[2] Among the many reasons for choosing this text is the explicit manner in which it names and locates itself within the conceptual totality, the commonwealth, that organized a host of efforts to formulate and to clarify the nature and ends of government, the scope of what government was capable of accomplishing, and the extent of the phenomena for which government was responsible. The elaborate and complex discussion about how best to insure the well-being of the nation advanced a set of terms for imagining the English people, both collectively and individually, as objects and agents of government. Smith, in *A Discourse,* enables us to view the administrative, ethical, and political aspects of the conceptual vocabularies through which people and various kinds of reproductive behavior were made available for reflection and governmental action in Renaissance England.

The question of how to govern people gained considerable urgency in sixteenth-century England in large part from widespread concern among dominant groups about popular unrest. Although these fears often ran well in excess of actual chances for rebellion, a general awareness of hardship and dissatisfaction among the people, and of the movements and activities of dislocated persons forms a crucial theme in contemporary writings. Smith's text offers a case in point. Each participant in the conversation that constitutes *A Discourse*—the Capper, Merchant, Husbandman, Knight, and Doctor Pandotheus—emphasizes the profoundly unsettled nature of the English populace, commenting on the "wild and unhappy uproars amongst us" (49), the "commotion" of the "poor commons" (87), the "great tumult and disorder in the Commonweal" (50).[3] A dominant tendency within early modern scholarship has been to focus on such moments as evidence of a pervasive fear of the "many-headed monster," a recalcitrant mass that threatens the dominant classes.[4] Such an approach demonstrates the manner in which the metaphorics of the people as monster works to justify and to legitimize the most horrific violence; if the people constitute a monstrous threat to property and status, then, precisely because of their monstrosity and irrationality, the authorities possess few options for responding to disorder or insurrection beyond the most brutal of reprisals. And indeed royal, parish, and civic officials frequently acted as if they were guided by just such a representation. When the actions of crowds were perceived to be too great a threat to the status hierarchies, institutions, and structures of deference, obligation, and mutual dependence making up a community, then authorities instituted martial law, imposed capital punishment, and brutally quelled dissidence.

As compelling as this account is, and despite its ability to explain much early modern reaction to "tumult and disorder," slaughter was not the only possible way of addressing unrest. Although in other contexts Smith himself counseled violent response to dissidence,[5] in his writing he, like numerous other writers, constituted "uproar" not simply as the ominous limit of government, but as an indication of the need to reform government. For example, when the Knight complains about the disruptiveness of the members of the cloth industry who riot when their trade is impaired, and suggests that the country would be better off without them, Doctor Pandotheus responds by asserting that such an attitude misses the whole point of government. Certainly, rule is difficult, the Doctor concedes. "Yet were it but a mean policy either for a prince to diminish his number or for a master of a house to put away his servants because he would not have any trouble with the governance of them" (88). Although Smith subtly acknowledges the account of England's populace as an inherently turbulent challenge *to* government, he also contends that it is a challenge *for* government—not only its limit, but also its pretext. For any governor to attempt to avoid the "trouble" required to rule people effectively makes about as much sense as a head of household dissolving the domestic economy because he does not want the difficulty of governing it. To get rid of people—perhaps to deport the most difficult, or perhaps to execute the most intransigent (the Knight is tactfully silent about precisely what he has in mind)—is not to govern, but risibly and irresponsibly to avoid the hard work of governance.

What follows works to understand more precisely how Smith, along with his contemporaries, comprehends the hard work of governance, the challenges faced by governors, the means available for responding to the crises besetting England, the objectives of rule, the modes of authorizing governmental activity, and the conceptual vocabularies through which governance becomes thinkable at all. Such a project seeks to displace the dominant critical approach to the work of Smith and his peers. Although Smith's pamphlet addresses a truly stunning array of topics—ranging from agricultural production to geopolitical relations, from chronic unemployment to the devaluation of currency, from the decay of towns and of the country's infrastructure to educational policy and the state of the church—scholars frequently read the governmental program of *A Discourse* solely in terms provided by the discipline of economics. Smith and his contemporaries are either failed economists,[6] or fair-to-middling economists,[7] or much better economists than we realize.[8] Certainly economic analysis possesses the capacity to render everything intelligible, even retroactively, to times before such modes of analysis were available. (Indeed, our contemporary moment might be described as that in which economic modes of intelligibility have come to claim an ability to explain all human phenomena.) However, such an approach elides the historically specific governmental objectives guiding Smith's and others' efforts to understand and shape the world, the specific discourses in which they participate, and the manner in which they work to constitute a field of governmental agency and intervention.[9]

From the perspective of a genealogy of governmental discourses and practices, the discipline of most relevance to Smith's work as a governmental intervention is not economics but one of its precursors, moral philosophy. Although an economic approach requires one to look beyond, to qualify, or to dismiss Smith's "largely moral vocabulary,"[10] *A Discourse* understands moral philosophy to be the the privileged discipline for thinking, talking about, and formulating the work of government.[11] "What part of the Commonweal," the Doctor asks,

> is neglected by moral philosophy? Does it not teach first how every man should guide himself honestly? Secondly, how he should guide his family wisely and prophetically, and thirdly it shows how a city or a realm or any other Commonweal should be well ordered and governed both in time of peace and also war. (29)

Doctor Pandotheus claims here for moral philosophy discursive and practical terrain that in the eighteenth and nineteenth centuries will come to be divided much differently, reconfigured within the discipline of political economy in addition, for example, to the fields of theology, psychology, sociology and (in the twentieth century) home economics.[12] The facts we take to be legible from the perspective of self-evidently distinct disciplines are here formulated within a single intellectual enterprise, authorizing and organizing an intellectual practice oriented toward the government of several kinds of conduct—of self, family, city, and realm. Smith names this collection of governmental domains the "commonwealth," which he understands to be both a specific site of governmental activity and a governmental totality that unifies all the rest. It is both a political structure linking self, family, city, and nation, and an objective secured through the proper conduct of existence in these domains.

Although Smith's definition of moral philosophy can be traced back through scholasticism to Greco-Roman antiquity,[13] his effort to establish it as the discipline and intellectual practice most suitable to the proper government of the *commonwealth* signals the quite contemporary stakes of his assertion. To see how this is the case, it will be worthwhile briefly to consider how this term comes to occupy the forefront of moral philosophical reflection in sixteenth- and seventeenth-century England. The term had been operative in continental Europe and England at least since the Middle Ages, and derived in part from Roman conceptions of the polity as "res publica." Ernst Kantorowicz has argued that the concept of "res publica" was crucial for the elaboration in medieval England of a "sphere of supra-personal continuity," a fiscal entity that exceeded the scope or authority of any individual, and that possessed a temporal duration extending beyond the limits of a single life, even that of the monarch.[14] The royal *fisc*, or treasury, came to be conceived of as a common possession, representing the wealth held in trust by the king in behalf of king and people, present and future; the task of governing under such a dispensation was understood to be a matter of caring for this wealth and of acting in accord with the "public utility."[15] This model of the "common wealth" provided a means for people to comprehend their relation to this ideally stable order; it represented a totality "touching everyone," in which everyone supposedly was invested, and to which everyone was obligated and ideally committed.[16]

In subsequent centuries, this medieval conceptual framework was adapted and reworked for new purposes, taken up and reconfigured to meet new challenges. Several important studies have emphasized the ways the commonwealth came to function as a central term in a wide array of efforts to rethink the scope and impact of national government in the later Middle Ages.[17] David Starkey argues that a redefined understanding of the "commonweal" anchored a "new language of politics" in the fifteenth century, one that provided powerful and compelling resources for insisting upon the need to reorganize court institutions, for demanding that the crown undertake financial reforms, and more generally for clarifying and recasting the relation between the monarch, counselors, nobility, and people.[18] In the sixteenth century, the focus of this "revitalized notion of the commonwealth"[19] changed somewhat—shifted, according to Starkey, from its emphasis upon court institutions and formal relations between crown and people to privilege questions of (what we would now define as) "*social* improvement and reconstruction."[20] A refined and elaborated understanding of the commonwealth provided an ideal of stability reinforced by active governmental intervention, against which current crises could be measured, and which could lend urgency to calls for civic, religious, legal, or monarchical authorities to address these crises. A host of writers (clerics, academics, royal advisors, and anonymous pamphleteers) developed and disseminated terms for comprehending the changes taking place in the sixteenth century and the problems that beset the polity. This is to say that these writers provided intellectual tools for recognizing an array of phenomena *as problems available for governmental action.* As Arthur B. Ferguson argues, Tudor England's "articulate citizens" came to share the sense "that society constituted an area of experience capable of being investigated rationally [. . .]; that the 'ills' of society could be diagnosed and their causes determined within the context of observable fact." This insistence on the capacity to know the causes of England's problems advanced alongside efforts to constitute these problems as susceptible to governmental intervention. Commonwealth writers assumed that "it was possible by intelligent policy to remove" the causes fueling the many crises, "and so restore the community to health, perhaps even to reshape it to meet the challenge of change itself."[21] So doing, they attempted to produce a sense both of the capacity and of the obligation of governmental authorities to address the underlying causes disrupting the polity.

This chapter focuses on one aspect of commonwealth writers' efforts to know the world and to render it actionable—how numbers of people come to be constituted as objects of knowledge, as individual or collective entities capable of exercising governmental agency, or as targets of governmental intervention. I outline below three closely related ways Smith and his contemporaries "make up people." First, I discuss how the understanding of the commonwealth contributes to an apprehension of human aggregates as administratively manipulable. Second, I describe the ethical dimension of commonwealth discourse, the forms of personhood it makes available or alternatively seeks to render unviable; where it might be customary to treat administrative rationalities as inherently hostile to individual autonomy or ethical considerations, I emphasize the interrelation and overlap of these concerns. Third (consistent with this emphasis), I detail how commonwealth discourse seeks to authorize participation in the conduct of national existence by constituting forms of political agency at once expansive and highly limited. As a way to specify the link between this chapter's concerns and those of the chapters that follow, I conclude by focusing upon humanism as the institutional context within which the commonwealth vocabularies were consolidated, as a source of governmental expertise, and as a population problem in its own right.

Administering People

To develop our focus on what I refer to as the "administrative aspect" of commonwealth writings, we may take a more detailed look at the exchange between the Knight and the Doctor. Recall that the Knight has complained of disruptive clothiers and has suggested the benefits of being rid of them. The Doctor responds:

> Surely, whosoever has many persons under his governance shall have much ado to govern them in quiet, and he that has a great family shall have sometimes trouble in the ruling of them. Yet were it but a mean policy either for a prince to diminish his number or for a master of a

> house to put away his servants because he would not have any trouble with the governance of them. He that would so do might be well resembled to a man that should sell his land because he would not be troubled with the account of it. (87–8n8)

A key element of the Doctor's call to governmental responsibility is the functional comparison between national government and domestic government, between commonwealth and *oikos* (the Greek word for "household"). Foucault emphasizes the analogy as of great importance for the transformation he traces in government. "The art of government," he writes, "is essentially concerned with answering the question of how to introduce economy—that is to say, the correct manner of managing individuals, goods and wealth within the family (which a good father is expected to do in relation to his wife, children and servants) and of making the family fortunes prosper—how to introduce the meticulous attention of the father towards his family into the management of the state."[22] Such an account renders the Doctor's statement legible as an instance of the "economizing" of rule, in which the model of the household becomes applicable to larger totalities. The Doctor's rejoinder to the Knight's dismissive attitude towards popular dissidence gains its force from the implied understanding of what constitutes proper conduct of a domestic economy which has become the standard against which proposed actions at the national level can be gauged.

Of course, the oeconomic analogy has a long history. What, then, is specific about this appeal to the household as a model? Although it might be tempting to answer this question by invoking a standard narrative about the "rise of the state," the latter conceived of as an entity steadily amassing to itself ever more power over the centuries, I appeal instead to a more complex model of the development of governmental rationalities as the condition of possibility for the rule of large territories. The intensified reliance upon the household model, which constitutes rule as a painstaking activity requiring detailed attention to the minutiae of national existence, enables a profound rethinking of precisely what government does, its objectives, its means of operation, its authority, and its limits. Crucial here is the notion of "policy" invoked by Doctor Pandotheus. The term "policy" forms a cognate of a crucial governmental concept, "police," a word that has narrowed in meaning considerably over the last five hundred years or so. In this period "'good police'…

signified the general objectives of good government, these being good order and happiness"[23]—what comes to be defined in England as the "common weal." In addition to a state of order, happiness, or prosperity, "police" signifies the administrative action taken to produce such conditions. The "aim" of police, according to Gerhard Oestreich:

> was to produce a well ordered civic or territorial community. This conception of "police" soon gave rise to the claim on the part of the ruling authorities to a general competence in the combating of all social disorders for which law and custom did not provide a remedy. The object was to provide regulations for the "common benefit" and to establish a "well ordered republic."[24]

This understanding of "police" accounts for the English usage of the term "policy" to mean any political structure or system as well as governmental action or endeavor. One important resource for such an account of policy is early modern humanists' active rereading of Aristotle, which contributed to and lent philosophical credibility to the reconceptualization of existence in this world as a rationally accessible realm of being and as a worthwhile domain of human activity.[25] Detailing the impact of Aristotelian thought on Italian and English political theory, J. G. A. Pocock underscores the manner in which policy responds to unprecedented or unanticipated events in the life of the political entity. Policy, he argues, employs "prudence and experience" in the task of "coping with the unique, the contingent, and the unfor[e]seen" occurrence, addressing "the fluctuations of times and seasons, events, circumstances, and human wills," the uncertainty built into the job of government. Prudence, as here defined, is the ability to apply a specialized knowledge and a workable grasp of past experiences to the present in order to direct the polity towards a stable and healthy future. As such, it represents the intellectual capacity that enables those who govern to provide intelligent and inventive responses to the challenges facing the commonwealth.[26]

Although "police science" never developed in England to the extent it did in Germany, especially in Prussia, the discursive and practical emphasis on "policy" suggests comparable effects. Consistent with Oestreich's account, in the fifteenth and sixteenth centuries in England, the field of governmental action and responsibility expanded considerably, and larger areas of existence came to be apprehended as sites for positive human agency. Problems hitherto not recognized as concerns for government became visible as both opportunities for governmental intervention and responsibilities of administrative authorities.[27] The sixteenth century alone witnessed an extraordinary array of policy initiatives, ranging from proposals for financial reform, urban redevelopment, improvement of national infrastructure, poor relief, and reorganization of church government, to encouragement of education, discouragement of predatory market practices, regulation of prices, limitations on enclosure, management of food supply, control of international trade, and promotion of domestic industries and enterprises.[28] This breadth of governmental discussion and, occasionally, administrative action indicates the extent to which policy and the implicit claim of governmental "competence in the combating of social disorders" constitutes an expanded and redefined space of existence as available to prudential reflection and as appropriate for governmental action. Commonwealth writers offer both a way of describing the terrain of this governmental action and a way of defining its objective; the increased emphasis upon the common weal reinforces government through *policy*, authorizes and prompts the operation of ameliorative agencies upon what are thus defined as actionable problems besetting the national domestic economy.

Of course, in the latter sixteenth century and into the seventeenth century, "policy" accrues a number of pejorative meanings: craftiness or subterfuge, acts of ambition, self-centered duplicity, or the manipulative pursuit of self-interest.[29] These meanings by no means displace the understanding of policy as a vital mode of administrative action. They do, however, register the reaction in England to developments within European governmental thought, a reaction strongly influenced by the conceptual vocabulary organized around the ideal of the commonwealth examined thus far—namely, the formulation and dispersal of what comes to be known as "reason of state." In the context of the Italian city-states, *ragion di stato* represents a set of techniques and knowledges geared toward "attaining power and using public institutions for private purposes."[30] "Interest" is the watchword of this understanding of governmental endeavor, which comes to be understood as the pursuit of individual or group interest against the interests of others. As reason-of-state arguments find their way into English governmental discussion in the seventeenth century, "interest" comes to assume prominence as a basic criteria of governance only so long as the interest of the polity as a whole—that is, the common weal, the *salus populi*—takes priority.[31] In England, at least, the commonwealth, and not the interest of any individual or group, ideally constitutes the ultimate horizon of governmental reflection.

Smith's text demonstrates the extent to which sixteenth-century commonwealth writers established the terms for such an emphasis. The Doctor's oeconomic analogy suggests that the king is not simply a lord over his territory, ruling arbitrarily, with either incompetence or capricious indifference to the larger effects of his actions. The oeconomic context implies that the monarch must behave in a certain way, manage carefully the resources in his domain, rule in such a fashion as to optimize resource use and contribution to the whole. Certainly there are obvious limits to this analogy; no prince could ever achieve this kind of comprehensive managerial control over his or her realm. (For example, Smith argues that there are inherent limits to a nation's ability to regulate trade activity, unaccounted for by the oeconomic analogy. While a household has one gate, a nation has many, which makes careful scrutiny or control of the flow of goods impossible [47–48].) These limits notwithstanding, the equivalence between the government of the nation and the government of the household insists that the people of the commonwealth require "policy," active and careful management with an eye less on maintaining control or expanding authority over a territory than on ensuring the security, welfare, and health of the whole.

With this understanding of the commonwealth as requiring and enabling policy, it is possible to turn to the issue of human aggregates, and to examine the ways numbers of people come to be constituted administratively as objects of knowledge and as potential targets of governmental intervention. During the sixteenth century, the imperative to enumerate persons, actions, and things takes on palpable urgency. The establishment of parish registers in 1538, designed to record every christening, death, and marriage, is only the most prominent instance of a striking proliferation of efforts to count people. This proliferation includes: municipal attempts to inventory persons and food (for example, in Coventry in 1520); local and national initiatives to register the poor and indigent (Norwich in 1570 and the entire country in 1572); orders by the Privy Council discreetly to census the "strangers" in various municipalities (for example in 1573, 1574, and 1592); and the grim undertaking of recording the numbers of the dead in London's weekly bills of mortality (beginning in 1592).[32]

The diverse efforts to register or enumerate people look forward to, but do not yet constitute anything as coherent or unified as, what William Petty will propose in his *Political Arithmetic*, published in the latter part of the seventeenth century. Petty asserts (as I elaborate in this book's final chapter) the necessity of a systematic reasoning upon numbers as an essential technology of government, one vital to the task of determining England's strength vis-à-vis its trading partners and international rivals. The instances of human registration and enumeration noted above are far too ad hoc, dispersed, and specifically formulated to constitute a single project. What this list does illustrate, though, is one way that sixteenth-century writers and administrators contribute to the intellectual and practical conditions of possibility for political arithmetic and, beyond that, for a governmental dispensation eventually organized around populations. Recording births, deaths, and marriages, enumerating the poor, counting "strangers," or listing the dead all reinforce a growing sense that detailed information about particular circumstances is necessary for effective policy, for confronting the "unique, the contingent, and the unfor[e]seen" events faced by governments.[33] Under the imperative effectively to govern the commonwealth, techniques of recording and registration make it possible to comprehend particular details of a wide array of problems for which parish, civic, and national governments were not hitherto considered responsible, or for which they are being held responsible in new ways. Evidentiary technologies contribute significantly to constituting phenomena as problems available for governmental reflection and action. The ability to know things about people, the availability of epistemological and practical tools to render people into discourse, helps make people possible subjects of government.

In the context of policy proposals, commonwealth writers display a biblically sanctioned bias (one that will need to be qualified somewhat) towards having the largest populace possible. Proverbs 14:28 is cited with considerable frequency in the literature of reform: "In the multitude of people is the king's honor: but in the want of people is the destruction of the prince." Consequently, encouraging the generation of more persons becomes an important and urgent objective in the eyes of many writers. Thomas Starkey, for example, one-time chaplain and advisor to

Henry VIII, made a number of suggestions designed to achieve "the increse of chrystan pepul":[34] allowing "secular prestys to mary at theyr lyberty," encouraging gentlemen not to keep so many retainers who are unable, because of their service, to marry (99), providing tax breaks for those who have five or more children, and providing financial penalties for men of specified portions who remain unmarried (100). The next section will say more about the way reproductive behavior comes to be invested with governmental significance; for now, we can note that other kinds of policies are advanced and defended in terms of how they effectively generate people by enabling increase of the nation's numbers. The anonymous author of the 1549 tract "Policies to reduce this realme of Englande unto a prosperus wealthe and estate" promised that the proposals he offered would render the "realme . . . Populus."[35] Similarly, Smith claimed that his suggestions about the regulation of enclosures, the proper management of the currency, immigration policy, and the establishment of domestic industries to provide employment would effectively "replenish the realm [with] people able to defend it and also save and win much treasure to the same" (91).

However, the idea that more is better is only part of the story. Indeed, as evidenced in the cases of poor-registration and counting "strangers," which imply anxiety about having too many people, the objectives of policy with regard to the size of the populace are somewhat more complex. This complexity has two interrelated aspects, which I shall treat separately, for clarity. The first concerns the coordination of people and resources, the second the manner in which policy addresses, and constitutes, specific kinds of people. The first difficulty surfaces in the King James translation of Proverbs 14:28 quoted above, stating that "in the want of people is the destruction of the prince." I have emphasized an understanding of "want" as a lack of people, but "want of people" also signifies a state in which the people themselves lack something, like food, employment, or a place to live. Starkey's *Dialogue* is helpful here, to the extent that it articulates the operative assumptions informing the work of certain writers (including Smith). According to Starkey, the body politic can have either too many or too few people. To have too few people is like the disease of "consumptyon" (96) and prevents the proper utilization of the nation's agricultural resources and the adequate staffing of the crafts necessary to the healthy functioning of the commonweal. By contrast, having too many people overburdens the country and the nation's capacity to produce food. In Aristotelian fashion, Starkey's ideal rests in the mean between these two extremes, a careful match between resources and persons. The optimal number of people in any given country, Starkey refers to as a "convenyent multytude." Even "yf the cuntrey be never so rych fertyl & plentyful of al thyngys necessary & plesaunt to mannys lyfe," Starkey argues,

> yet yf therbe of pepul other to few, or to many or yf they be as hyt were etyn away dayly devouryd & consumyd by commyn syknes & dysease, ther can be no ymage nor schadow of any commyn wele, to the wych fyrst ys requyryd a convenyent multytude & convenyently to be nuryschyd ther in the cuntrey. (32)

A "convenyent multytude" is one in which there is a due proportion between the people of a nation and the capacities of their land. As Starkey elaborates, just as the land must support the people, the people must be of adequate quantity and enterprise to be equal to the task of ensuring that the land is "wel tyllyd & occupyd" and that trades are "wel & dylygently exercysyd" (32). There is a relation among people, geographical capacities, and cultural activity, and this relation has its own due harmony or proportion, a "convenyence," upon which depends the "commyn wele." The objective of policy is to produce this convenience, or to provide "convenient remedies" (95), as Smith puts it, to imbalances that beset the nation; conversely, this ideal provides a kind of benchmark against which one may judge the potential effectiveness or advisability of any given policy initiative.

The standard of convenience is of course hortatory, and calling attention to problems is much easier than fixing them. Perhaps Elizabeth's Privy Council under the direction of Burghley, or the city fathers of London or of any of England's municipalities, or parish officials aspired to this capacity to manage details, but the fact is that England possessed no institutional structure capable of gathering all of the relevant information, or undertaking all of the minutely calibrated administrative actions, necessary to achieve a convenient balance of people. A variety of institutions and governmental domains are asked, and attempt, to know and manage sections of the populace. These efforts are scattershot, ad hoc, improvisational responses to specific challenges or crises. It may be that, in some cases, local authorities were successful in producing "convenience"; more usual was what might be termed "inconvenience," actual imbalances of people and resources that resulted in deprivation, social dislocation, and popular unrest.

There is perhaps a more conceptual point to be made here, as well. Nikolas Rose and Peter Miller have asserted that "[g]overnment is a congenitally failing operation."[36] By this they do not mean that governmental activities produce no effects, but that there is an imperfect match between governmental aspirations and governmental outcomes. Government meets with resistance; the objectives and practices of one domain interfere with those of another; they produce unwanted or "unexpected consequences."[37] Although governmental officials in England may have sought to produce "convenience," and thereby to augment the commonwealth, their reach consistently exceeded their grasp.

One example of the distance between policy planners' optimism and the outcomes of their actions will help demonstrate the importance both of an implied standard of "convenience" and of the inherent difficulties in administratively achieving balance between people and resources. Some two decades after the composition of *A Discourse,* Smith received authorization to establish a "plantation" in Ireland, in the region of County Antrim.[38] As specified in the contract undertaken by Queen Elizabeth, Smith, and his son (also named Thomas Smith), the objective of this settlement was "to have [Ireland] peopled with good and obedient subjects" available to serve "to repress all rebels and seditious people and be an occasion by their example to bring the ruse [sic] and barbarous nation of the wild Irish to more civility of manner."[39] The plantation Smith proposed promised not only to subdue, by civilizing, the Irish populace, but also carried benefits for England, which was overburdened with too many people. "England was," he wrote, "neuer that can be heard of, fuller of people than it is at this day."[40] Where England had been in need of "replenish[ing]" with people, now there were apparently too many, and colonial Ireland represented a safety valve for these excess numbers.[41]

Smith's ambitions and optimism met with abject failure. Upon receiving word of his success in mustering as many as eight hundred men to join his expedition in the spring of 1572, the colonial administration in Ireland became alarmed enough at the potential for Smith's enterprise to destabilize an already volatile situation that they convinced Queen Elizabeth to delay his departure until midsummer. This move was enough to defuse enthusiasm for the plantation, and by the time he arrived in

Ireland, Smith's son (who supervised the undertaking) had only around one hundred men, about whose mettle and resolve there was much concern. Once they arrived, the younger Smith did in fact meet with substantial armed resistance, and was eventually murdered by some of his Irish servants. Reinforcements were sent in 1573, but the ship never arrived. Undaunted by the loss of his heir, Thomas Smith the elder tried again, this time sending his brother and several nephews to head up the plantation in 1574. This effort at settlement met with similar difficulties, was beset by deep conflicts among the leaders of the plantation, and eventually failed completely. No doubt the Antrim plantation foundered on incompetence, poor planning, and inexperience, but this is to oversimplify a very complex story about the challenges built into policy, the inherent difficulties of both colonial and domestic government. Government aspires to perfect administrative effectiveness, but people resist, accidents happen, unanticipated situations arise, officials differ about how to proceed or even about what the objectives of governance should be. "Convenience" is an ever-receding goal with respect to the government of a populace, at once defining the terms for policy formation and serving as a gauge for the inadequacies of governmental intervention.

Commonwealth Ethics

The account advanced thus far might suggest that policy apprehends people in relatively undifferentiated terms, but this is decidedly not the case. Smith's project of colonial expansion provides a place to begin thinking about how commonwealth writers distinguish forms of personhood. Perhaps the most obvious distinction Smith advances is between the "civil" colonizers and the "barbarous" colonized. A less obvious aspect of his colonial proposal and endeavor comes into relief when placed alongside the Doctor's desire voiced in *A Discourse* to undertake policies that would "replenish" the realm with people; this latter objective would seem to run counter to the stated urgency surrounding the project of finding an outlet for the nation's "inconvenient" numbers. England appears to have both too many people and not enough. It might be possible to reconcile these perspectives by pointing out that they were voiced several years apart; perhaps Smith changed his mind in the intervening years about the nature of the problem confronting the nation, or perhaps his motives altered as Irish settlement presented itself, as it did to so many people, as a tantalizingly lucrative opportunity. As plausible as they might be, these possibilities would not entirely account for the apparent contradiction, though, since it is one internal to the works of a number of commonwealth writers.[42] This is evident in Smith's analysis of enclosure.

On one hand, Smith argues that converting otherwise arable land to pasture replaces existing agricultural enterprises with less labor-intensive ones and thereby eliminates the means of subsistence for large numbers of people.[43] As the Capper details, land that once sustained one hundred to two hundred people now provides a living for only a few shepherds and the owner (49). The Doctor adds to this sense of urgency by asserting that even as the people become less able to provide for themselves, the size of the populace is growing: "the people still increasing and their livings diminishing it must needs come to pass that a great part of the people shall be idle and lack livings, and hunger is a bitter thing to bear" (49–50). "[E]nclosures and great pastures" (49) have thus created the conditions of crisis (in the terms advanced above, an "inconvenient" distribution of resources) by leaving people with nowhere to live and no way to produce or to afford anything to eat.[44]

On the other hand, in odd contrast to the urgent sense of growing numbers, Smith's account of enclosure implies that it effectively unpeoples the nation—an approach that takes literally the common term for enclosure, "depopulation." Should everyone imitate the actions of enclosers, the Doctor asks, "what should ensue thereof but a mere solitude and utter desolation of the whole realm, furnished only with sheep and shepherds instead of good men" (53). Such a formulation, a kind of reductio ad absurdum of the activities of some landlords, treats enclosure as an activity that *really* eliminates people, "depopulates" the entire nation rather than only a few acres, potentially leaving England dangerously vulnerable to the aggressions of foreign nations (53, 89, 91). It is as if, rather than displacing people, enclosures *replaced* them with sheep.[45]

The contrasting accounts of superfluity and lack of people contradict only if we assume that they refer to the same relatively abstract apprehension of persons. Of course, enclosure does not literally depopulate the nation, at least not immediately and not to the extent that Smith asserts. The implication that it does begins to make sense if we acknowledge that Smith is talking about different kinds of people, incommensurable forms of personhood. Recalling Ian Hacking's formulation, we see that commonwealth discourse may be said to "make up people" to the extent that it provides terms that help organize the apprehension of individuals and their relation to the national community. Enclosure is characterized as dangerous because it eliminates opportunities for people to conduct the kinds of existence that would allow them to be "good men" and thereby contribute to the wellbeing of the whole. The people displaced from livelihoods by enclosure may be said to disappear insofar as they fall outside of commonwealth discourse's definition of what it means to lead a useful life, outside of the modes of intelligibility through which people come to be recognized as such.

A primary way in which the descriptive project of making up—or in the above instance, unmaking—people seeks to structure action is by defining proper forms for conducting existence. To suggest that the development of interpretive matrices for thinking about persons attempts to govern individuals' behavior is to acknowledge the connections between the dynamic Hacking identifies and the emphasis upon ethos advanced in the latter two volumes of Foucault's *History of Sexuality*.[46] For Foucault, ethos represents the manner in which people relate to themselves, the forms through which they are able to scrutinize, understand, and reflect upon themselves, to govern their existence, and to modify their actions and capacities. This understanding of ethical self-relation helps render legible key aspects of the governmental effects that commonwealth discourse seeks to produce, effects that hinge on the institution of specific forms of personhood.

Numerous studies have documented the considerable ethical intensification that takes place during the sixteenth and seventeenth centuries across national, confessional, and institutional boundaries in Western Europe.[47] One crucial means through which this heightened emphasis takes place—of considerable relevance to Smith, to commonwealth discourse more generally, and to the argument of this book as a whole—is humanist philological and pedagogical practice, the "critical adaptation and transformation" of classical ethical models within an array of educational sites.[48] Following the lead of scholars such as (but not only) Erasmus and, later, Justus Lipsius, English humanists forged an ideal of what it meant to be a good member of the commonwealth: "a pious, self-controlled, industrious lay-person, active in civic and ecclesiastical affairs, seeking always the common good."[49] This ethos invites people to understand themselves as subjects of the commonweal, oriented toward its security, health, and vitality, possessing certain kinds of agency and imbricated within networks of interdependence and obligation.

The communal orientation of this ethos, the "sense of strict responsibility"[50] toward the larger community that animates it, is evidenced throughout *A Discourse.* Just as ruling authorities are obligated to coordinate their actions with the demands of the whole, each member of the collective body is responsible for conducting life with constant awareness of the effects of his or her actions on the commonwealth. "[W]e be not born only to ourselves," Pandotheus asserts, alluding to Cicero's widely quoted *De Officiis,* "but partly to the use of our country, of our parents, of our kinfolk, and partly of our friends and neighbors." The "image of God in man" prompts people "ever to do good to others and to distribute his goodness abroad, like no niggard nor envious thing" (16). Although people inevitably desire to "seek where most advantage is" (54), they are constrained ethically by the fact that they exist in relation to others and that their self-motivated behavior may have negative effects on the whole. The Doctor argues that "men may not abuse their own things to the damage of the Commonweal" (53); likewise, "they may not purchase themselves profit by that that may be hurtful to others" (51). Smith holds up, as a standard, persons who govern themselves "honestly" (29) and who constantly reflect upon the ways their actions impact others, individually and collectively.

In contrast, those who did not conduct themselves in this fashion—for example, the idle or criminals, as well as certain kinds of enclosers, rack-renters, or people who sold goods to maximize profit rather than to meet the needs of others—were understood to be harmful to the collectivity. The invective heaped upon those who refused to work is well-known; less emphasized is the criticism leveled against those whose behavior under a different dispensation would come to look like perfectly rational economic activity. Understood to be completely indifferent to the impact of their search for what were perceived to be inordinate profits, these persons were figured as lacking the ability to govern themselves; this aspect of their being was read as manifesting a predatory and voracious appetite. They were "unsatiable" in their pursuit of "their owne priuate welthes"[51]; they were "[c]ormerauntes" and "gredye gulles" devouring "menne, women, & chyldren"[52]; they were "caterpillars of the Commonwealth."[53] Possessing no sense of obligation to others or to the collective health and strength of the polity, focused only on gratifying their own desires without concern for the effects of their ravenous consumption, such individuals lacked that which Smith's Doctor argued defined humanity, since animals "study no common utility" (16). Richard Morison spelled out the implications of this logic by refusing national identity to those who behaved with indifference to the national well-being. "What is he that can say he is an Englishman and that he careth not, though the wealth of England be trodden under the foot?" Morison asked rhetorically. "A beast he is, a man he can never be judged, that passeth but on his own wealth and pleasure."[54]

The forms of personhood sketched above are not, or not solely, juridical in nature. Certainly good commonwealth men and women are to be obedient to the law and to the monarch, but they are not exclusively defined by this obedience. The emphasis of commonwealth discourse is less upon laws and quasi-legal restrictions that attempt to differentiate allowed and forbidden acts, and more upon the kinds of attention people are asked to give themselves, the intensity and techniques of their self-relation, the objectives of the work that they perform on themselves. Commonwealth discourse underscores a sense of individual obligation to a larger totality, a sense of responsibility for ensuring the well-being of the whole, a commitment to prosperity and stability that certainly can include obedience and deference to all manner of authorities but is not reducible to such juridical subordination.

A crucial instance of ethical responsibility vis-à-vis the commonweal, one that enables reproductive effects, is the imperative to conduct one's existence within a vocation. One's calling (the daily endeavor to which God has called each person) provides a means for organizing activity into a life of sobriety, discipline, rational effort, and constraint. Max Weber's well-known account of the "Protestant ethic" and the "worldly asceticism" it entails traces the considerable emphasis placed on vocation as a mode of self-relation, an ethical form through which people are asked to comprehend their obligation to work.[55] The emphasis of Weber's study is on the role Protestant doctrines of election and predestination played in increasing the sense of importance granted to one's calling. (I will return to this argument in greater detail in my discussion of Milton's proposal for educational reform in this book's fourth chapter.) The privilege Weber and others grant to Protestant theology as the site in which calling receives its most forceful articulation has been called into question; Margo Todd, for example, points out that non-Protestants also placed great emphasis upon vocation during the sixteenth century.[56] For the purposes of this argument, however, the question of origin is less important than the widespread nature of the appeal to this ethical paradigm. The imperative to work diligently within a vocation forms a key mode of "subjectification" within commonwealth discourse, that is, the "means by which individuals subject themselves to [the] demands" of the commonwealth ethos, "the means by which they come to relate to themselves" as members of the commonweal.[57] It is through vocational activity that persons may have an impact on the life of the collectivity. As one writer put it, each person should "use his calling to profit all, & to damnifie none," with the ultimate focus on the effort "to enlarge the common weale."[58] William Perkins confirmed this sentiment in asserting that "callings" should "be profitable, not onely to the doers, but to the Common - wealth."[59]

Precisely this sense of the impact of vocation on England's collective well-being motivates John Hales's 1548 legislative effort to address the decay of tillage resulting from enclosure. Hales asserts in an early draft of this bill that England's nobility abusively "haue somoche neglected ther vocations" as "shepardes" of the people by engaging in large-scale sheep farming and agriculture. This vocational abdication damages the commonwealth to the extent that it prevents "poor labourers" from making a living, and because it furthermore "constrayne[s] . . . artificers to forsake ther occupacions and . . . leave the cities and townes desolat which by them shulde be mayntayned and inhabited."[60] Enclosure, along with other market and land-use practices, prevents people from engaging in their vocations, places them in a situation in which they cannot be useful to the commonweal.

A Discourse of the Common Weal's analysis of the crises besetting England affirms the import of vocation as a site of ethical responsibility towards the national community. In addition to commenting on enclosure, as noted at the outset of this section, Smith's text addresses the relevance of vocational activity to questions of international commerce and immigration policy. According to Doctor Pandotheus, there is a functional interrelationship between individual vocational activity and international trade. This is evident in the taxonomy of vocations he produces. There are three types of occupations, he argues—those that send treasure abroad (trades that sell imported goods), those that have no impact on the flow of treasure (businesses that manufacture goods consumed domestically), and those that bring treasure into the nation (occupations that make things for export or that replace imports) (90–91; 122–24). By adopting this frame of reference, the Doctor is able to assert not only that vocation is the form in which people become useful to the commonwealth, but also that some kinds of persons are more valuable than others on the basis of their ability to increase the flow of wealth into the realm. Those who make things that would otherwise have to be purchased abroad, or who make things for export, effectively increase the amount of treasure in England and thus are the more beneficial to the commonwealth.

Smith's account of the relative value of different vocations provides a degree of clarity about appropriate policy options. Everything should be done not only to create the conditions for vocational activity, but also to make certain that treasure-increasing vocations are favored at the expense of those that send England's wealth abroad, or that merely circulate it at home. The Doctor suggests that one way to accomplish this objective is to encourage the manufacture of goods that English people currently purchase from other nations by supporting tradesmen and tradeswomen who have not hitherto flourished in England: "cappers, glovers, papermakers, glaziers, pointers, goldsmiths, blacksmiths of all sorts, coverlet makers, needlemakers, pinners, and such other" (91). Through these means, Smith argues, people will be occupied, their tumults brought to an end, and the nation enriched by retaining money that would otherwise go to its international trading partners. This focus likewise underwrites Smith's comments on immigration policy. In response to the Capper's xenophobic anxiety about the possible privileges granted "stranger[s]" in place of apprentices, the Doctor argues that the well-being enjoyed by any given "mystery" should not take precedence over the well-being of a city or the nation as a whole. Consequently, it is in the best interest of a town to allow the free movement of those with special skills in any given "craft" and whose efforts can aid in the production of commodities that augment the treasure of the nation. When a "town lacks inhabitants of artificers it were no policy of the restoration of the town to keep off any strange artificers. For the most part of all towns are maintained by craftsmen of all sorts but specially by those that make any wares to sell out of the country and bring therefore treasure into the same" (125).

In the previous section we noted briefly how reproductive activity could become the object of administrative analysis and, at least potentially, of administrative intervention. These examples illustrate how policy itself could be understood to be capable of creating more of the right kind of people, "convenyent" numbers whose agencies were salutary to the polity.

I draw this section to a close by addressing a possible objection to the argument of the last few pages. Does not my analysis of Smith's (and others') reliance upon the concept of "vocation" or "calling" misleadingly foist religious terms onto an essentially economic discussion? Is this not a kind of category mistake? Such an objection would reinscribe what at the outset I identified as the dominant critical approach to Smith and his contemporaries, the habit of reading them through the lenses of political economy or scientific economics. Rather than project modern categories of analysis back onto Smith's text, I have been suggesting the value of detailing the conceptual vocabularies and practices through which efforts to describe and reform governance sought to know and impact the world. Although I question our ability to separate out the "theological" from the "economic" in early modern texts—and again, moral philosophy constitutes these disciplines as part of the same intellectual enterprise—what we can state is that Smith's text contributes to the eventual consolidation of economics as a discipline and the economic realm as a discrete level of reality. Although it is wrong to read Pandotheus's analysis as a strictly economic argument, the uses made of the theological concept of vocation do open up a certain dislocation from a purely theological perspective. Where presumably it would not matter to God what vocation one pursues, as long as one took up the vocation to which one is called, commonwealth discourse, as we have seen, provides a standpoint from which it is possible to hierarchize vocational choices. This is not to suggest that commonwealth writers participate in a thoroughly secular discourse—far from it. The conceptual vocabulary organized around an understanding of the commonwealth enables a potential displacement of theology's dominance as an authorizing discourse. Smith's analysis of the relative value of different callings represents an early instance of what, during the seventeenth century, will become a highly volatile contest surrounding the prominence that questions of trade should occupy in the governance of the nation, which in turn involves an implicit struggle over the status of work as a sacred or secular activity.[61]

Expertise and Political Agency

Thus far I have endeavored to outline the conceptual vocabularies that commonwealth discourse makes available for thinking about people administratively and ethically. A primary objective has been to determine how dynamics of descriptively “making up people” coordinate with, or enable, efforts to modify human procreative activity or otherwise to produce governed generative effects. In the final two sections of this chapter, the emphasis of the discussion shifts somewhat to an inquiry into the kinds of political agency commonwealth discourse seeks to make available. Smith’s appeal to the oeconomic model helps establish why this is a concern, insofar as this conceptual maneuver implies a foreclosure of agency within the national oeconomy. The Doctor’s analogy begins by talking about people (“whosoever has many persons under his governance”) but closes by talking about “land” and the irrational head of household who would rather sell it than “be troubled with the account of it.” The metonymic slippage from people to land suggests that people are an inert substance, to be utilized and managed effectively but, in the terms of the analogy, possessing no autonomy or capacity for independent action. However, the discussion of the last few pages, and the interdependence, traced there, of administrative and ethical dimensions of commonwealth discourse, counters such a reduction by defining the manner in which the administrative apprehension of persons does not necessarily oppose, ignore, or suppress, but rather is perfectly consistent with, individual or collective agency.

As argued above, the commonwealth at once authorizes and depends upon the agencies of its constituent members for its future health and viability. But how far do such agencies extend? More specifically, what kinds of political implications follow from such a formulation? Although, as Thomas Starkey argued, the “polytyke body” included “the multytude of pepul,” the question of who was authorized to rule this body or to exercise governmental agency upon or within it was a crucial problem for commonwealth writers.[62] In what follows, I argue that Smith’s text negotiates competing accounts of political agency by forging a sense of civic obligation and capacity for political action that is at once expansive and restrictive—imperative for relatively large groups of people, but at the same time highly proscribed in scope and potential impact. In the chapter's final section, I examine the privileged place humanism occupies within such a dispensation.

It is possible to discern within commonwealth discourse two distinct ways of conceptualizing the polity, and these alternatives define sharply differing means of participating in the conduct of collective existence. One way of understanding the commonwealth is as an *objective* to which everyone ideally contributes and from which everyone ideally benefits. To the extent such a formulation implies that each person has a stake in the proper conduct of the realm, it authorizes people to evaluate national and local governments, offers a set of terms through which the well-being of the polity may be gauged, and produces a sense of obligation to exercise certain forms of political agency. Republican models of political organization provide an important source for what we might call a civic ethos, one based on the valorization of the *vita activa*. As Markku Peltonen has argued, the humanist endorsement of republican ideas, forms of social organization, and modes of action rested upon the notion that:

> the common good could not materialize unless everyone was fully committed to promote this aim by exercising the full range of civic virtues. . . . The public good was, therefore, not totally dependent on the qualities and abilities of the prince, but also, and perhaps in particular, on the virtuous civic participation of the people as a whole. What was needed in order to accomplish this end was not so much any specific skill as a more general inclination to serve the commonwealth and a readiness to commit oneself to the advancement of its well-being.[63]

As we have seen, this commitment to the health of the polity did not need to take political forms; simply working in one's vocation advanced the "well-being" of the commonwealth. But, as Peltonen demonstrates, there was lively and highly visible discussion about the nature of civic obligation and a well-developed sense of the need for individuals to intervene in the political life of the commonwealth. We may think here of Lupset's defense of the active over the contemplative life, to Cardinal Pole, in Starkey's *Dialogue;*[64] Smith's Knight likewise asserts the importance of "service" (16) to the commonwealth (I shall have more to say on this below). Such sense of obligation could take even more critical forms. Frequently cited in this regard is the Marian exile John Ponet's assertion that a political body, if necessary, can cut off its own head and replace it with another. Such a view is justified by a sense of the superior responsibility to the commonwealth: "men ought to have more respecte to their countrey, than to their prince: to the common wealthe, than to any one persone. For the countrey and common wealthe is a degree aboue the king."[65] It was possible, as well, for a conceptual apparatus centered on an understanding of the commonwealth to be utilized outside of educational institutions and of the conventions of learned argumentation, and for authorizing agencies not necessarily approved by those who would claim a monopoly on the right to determine political legitimacy. For example, Mervyn James has noted, a number of persons involved in the Lincolnshire uprisings of 1536, as well as the Pilgrimage of Grace and Kett's rebellion, justified their actions as efforts to protect the commonwealth.[66] At the risk of imposing a false teleology on the development and effects of this conceptual vocabulary, it bears remarking that the English Commonwealth of the next century was instituted for similar reasons, justified as a course of action necessary to protect the common weal.

A second way of perceiving the commonwealth, one possibly in tension with the first, is as a *structure*. From the perspective of this point of view, modes of governmental action within the commonwealth are highly proscribed and differentially constituted. In its most extreme versions, the commonwealth represents a quasi-medieval ideal of stasis and order, one that affirms hegemonic relations of dominance and subordination in the polity.[67] Such an understanding potentially conflicts with the objective of commonwealth to the extent that the health of the polity, understood as a common possession or source of political obligation, could serve as a rallying point for people of any station, or as a means of accommodating a wide array of claims and agendas. Indeed, many in authority were suspicious of the political and social implications of appeal to the commonwealth. In the face of what Pocock has called an "obstinate adherence to the vision of England as a hierarchy of degree," advancing claims or authorizing actions as necessary for the well-being of the national community could sound to some like a call for the leveling of all hierarchies and for a radical redistribution of all wealth.[68] When faced with the task of choosing to translate the Latin term *res publica*, Sir Thomas Elyot explicitly avoided the logical equivalent "commonwealth" as too suggestive of democracy.[69]

Such antidemocratic sentiments suggest a need to qualify the expansiveness of Peltonen's formulation above. The ability and authority to participate in the government of the nation was not available to everyone, and for some the possibility that it might be, represented the horrifying specter of the dissolution of government—the triumph precisely of the "many-headed monster." In the terms advanced in the previous section, everyone has a calling but only a relative few are called to govern the nation. In *De Republica Anglorum,* for instance, Smith differentiates the English people in terms of who legitimately may exercise functions of national government (gentlemen, yeoman, and, in some cases and some ways, merchants and artificers) and who may not (women, children, and the "rascabilitie" or lowest classes).[70] Other commonwealth writers were aware of this perception and were careful to specify that their formulations would not lead to apocalyptic ends. Even Ponet, who justified the overthrow of tyrants, distanced himself from those "that will haue to little obedience, as the Anabaptistes" (C8r).

Like Ponet and others, Smith, in *A Discourse,* straddles and works to reconcile these competing emphases of commonwealth discourse—commonwealth's status as a structure and as an objective—and the implications of these alternatives on the constitution of political agency. The key to Smith's efforts is the idea of service upon which the dialogue opens, the Knight having just returned from performing "service . . . abroad among our neighbors" (16) on an enclosure commission. It is the burden of *A Discourse* to extend, at least hypothetically, this imperative to public service to everyone in the realm. Smith does so by advancing an account of human intelligence, what he calls "wit," and its central role in the practice of government. The crucial function of intellectual capacity is evident in the connection he forges between "wisdom and policy." According to Smith, the best rule is that based on intelligence, and as a result leadership generally falls to smarter people: "in all kind of government," he asserts, "for the most part, the wiser sort have the sovereignty over the rude and unlearned as in every house the most expert, in every city the wisest and most sage, and in every Commonweal the most learned are most commonly placed to govern the rest" (24–25). As a good humanist, Smith insists on the value of education to the optimal administration of any given domain of government. Again the oeconomic sphere is central to Smith's understanding of governmental activity, and, as before, he construes an essential continuity between the conduct of the household and that of the city and commonwealth. Just as in a house one would not put someone in charge of a specific function because of lineage or social status, but because the person knew what he or she was doing, national government should be conducted by those with relevant knowledge and experience. Richard Morison made a similar case in his 1536 *Remedy for Sedition:* "But give the government of commonwealths into their hands that cannot skill thereof, how many must needs go to wrack?"[71] Effective policy relies and places a premium upon "expert"-ise, a specialized knowledge of a specific field, a working grasp of how to govern the conduct of others within a given domain.[72]

Consistent with the apprehension of the commonwealth as an objective, Smith suggests that "wit" is a widely held governmental resource, one that potentially everyone has and may contribute to the project of achieving the common good. In contrast to the view of the people as a hydra-like "many-headed monster," Smith asserts that every head possesses some talent for governmental deliberation: "as many heads, so many wits" (11). Consequently, although the emphasis of Smith's comments about "the wiser sort" is upon the intellectually active few as opposed to the governmentally passive many, it is the burden of Smith's argument to establish an expansive understanding of governmental activity based on these intellectual capacities. As he posits in the preface to *A Discourse,* because "[t]he gifts of wit be so divers" (12), it is better to have more people rather than fewer participate in the formation of policy, "for that that one cannot perceive, another shall" (11). A wide array of people has something useful to add to the governmental conversation, implicitly understood to be a kind of collective activity in which the expertise of the many is harnessed and channeled into the project of achieving the common good. Thus Smith states that, in formulating responses to the various national crises, "I would not only have learned men . . . but also merchantmen, husbandmen, and artificers (which in their calling are taken wise) freely suffered, yea and provoked, to tell their advice in this matter; for some points in their feats they may disclose that the wisest in a realm could not [gainsay]" (12). As a dialogue between several representatives of the commonwealth, the very form of Smith's text instantiates this imperative to draw on the intellectual capacities of a relatively wide array of people. Smith's text represents a diverse range of voices and thus implicitly provides a sense that people other than nobles and academics have something valid, indeed vital, to say about the problems besetting the polity and to add to the effort to formulate effective policy.[73]

This is not to say whether Smith's formulation is unequivocally expansive, nor to argue that his text is simply progressive in its incorporation of persons into the political life of the realm. Consistent with the understanding of the commonwealth as a structure, the modes of governmental action imagined within Smith's account of "wit" as expert knowledge sharply delineate and highly limit the scope of allowed actions. For one, the participants in Smith's *Discourse* have their comments, observations, and arguments routed through pre-existing modes of intellectual practice and governmental agency. The imagined exchange, along with many of the commonwealth writers' texts, takes part in the well-established conventions of royal counsel, although it contributes to the redefinition of appropriate objects of conciliar attention and expands the sense of whose counsel is considered relevant. Although counsel enables, and in some cases requires, criticism of the monarch or relevant authorities, positions, or policies, it usually takes place within a highly structured relation of subordination and deference.[74] Furthermore, a counselor does not exercise rule independently of existing governmental structures, and is not necessarily authorized to implement any given policy. Instead, he contributes to the project of government by offering advice, that is, through the exercise of his intellect in the commonwealth's behalf, and by employing what persuasive abilities he has to convince the relevant persons of the validity of his perspective or of the advisability of the proposed actions.[75]

Moreover, although Smith asserts that every head has a wit, and thus that every person possesses something useful to contribute to the task of governing the polity, such expansive possibilities remain only hypothetical in his text. *A Discourse* actually portrays only a highly limited sample of the populace discussing the problems facing the commonwealth, the causes, and the possible solutions. Even allowing for textual limitations (it would be difficult to imagine a dialogue that attempted to register every view on the range of issues Smith takes up), Smith's choice of representative voices indicates some principle of selection. Certain voices (those of merchants, husbandmen, and artificers) are more important than others (those of, for example, women, servants, or vagabonds) and should be privileged accordingly.[76] This sense of the differential value of kinds of expertise is also evident within the conversation

Smith depicts. Although the mutual respect of the participants is made apparent at the outset, the discussion takes place not among equals but rather among representatives of specific vocations, arrayed in uneven status relations. This vocational specificity itself serves as a means to restrict the scope of each person's intervention. In suggesting that every wit is a potentially useful governmental resource, Smith does not intend to authorize everyone to speak about any and all aspects of the commonwealth or to make any policy recommendations whatsoever. Individuals have the capacity to reflect upon the problems they confront, to speculate upon causes, and to offer ideas about valid and effective responses, but only so long as they stay within the boundary defined by their experience. "[E]very man," Smith asserts, "is to be credited in that art that he is most exercised in" (12). Any "man" who wishes may contribute to the task of policy formation. But one may do so only within the sphere of one's competence as defined by experience and specialized knowledge.

Humanism and Government

Although vocation defines a restricted field of expertise for each member of the commonwealth, one vocational representative in *A Discourse* is clearly privileged over the others: Doctor Pandotheus. Smith lays the groundwork for this move in his preface, in which he asserts that, although he seeks to incorporate a relatively large and diverse number of voices into policy discussions, he nevertheless would have the "judgment" of "learned men . . . to be chiefly esteemed" (12, word order rearranged). Accordingly, as the dialogue progresses, the Doctor assumes greater and greater prominence; his putatively more expansive perspective and supposedly more qualified understanding take priority over the views of all the rest, even over those of the Knight with whom he occasionally sides against the Capper, Merchant, and Husbandman. Where the Knight blames clothiers for their disruptive behavior, for example, or the Husbandman holds enclosing landlords responsible for the disordered state of the realm, the Doctor understands these to be epiphenomena. He perceives that the practice of debasing coinage (what we would understand today as monetary policy) is behind each of these secondary phenomena, that cheapening the value of currency is the ultimate cause driving the other effects.[77] The clarity of perspective the Doctor introduces into the conversation, his knowledge and governmental insight, derives ultimately from his learning, and one of the major projects of this text is to validate humanism as vital to the tasks of government.

Although Smith privileges learning in this way, Doctor Pandotheus's authority does not go unchallenged. Even as *A Discourse* works to define and thereby to reaffirm the role of humanism in securing sound government, it also acknowledges the extent to which humanist practice has contributed to the problems of excess and unstable numbers. This is the burden of the Capper's scathing dismissal of learning as a disruptive force in the commonweal. "[T]he devil the good you do with your studies," the Capper asserts, "but set men together by the ears." This "contention," he argues, "is . . . not the least cause of these wild uproars of the people, some holding of the one learning and some of the other" (23). In response to this effort to link intellectual controversy (and, by association, all lettered educational activity) to uproar, Pandotheus justifies learning and its privilege by asserting that humanism provides the knowledge requisite to proper government. "Tell me," the Doctor asks, "what counsel can be perfect, what Commonweal can be well ordered or saved upright, where none of the rulers or counselors have studied any philosophy, specially the part that teaches of manners?" By "philosophy" the Doctor means moral philosophy; consistent with the expansive definition given to this discipline, "manners" encompasses the government of self, family, city, realm, "or any other Commonweal" (29). Humanist study grounds the expertise required properly to govern the commonwealth; educational activity disseminates the knowledge and capacity for perception, deliberation, and decision-making upon which government depends. Thus the Doctor authorizes humanist intellectual practice as crucial to the common weal—not disruptive, but vitally necessary.

This assertion establishes the disciplinary framework for the Doctor's own position in *A Discourse* and, by extension, for other men like him in the polity, but it does not speak to the precise mechanism through which learning invests one with the skills to govern self and others. To clarify how learning produces such effects, it will be useful to note an etymological link that Smith explores in portraying the Doctor's answer to the Capper's charges, specifically the connection between "expert" and "experience." Experience forms the basis of expertise, and, as Pocock contends, the capacity to formulate effective responses to the contingencies besetting the realm is nothing other than the "prudence" that draws on experience.[78] Such an understanding of the coordination between experience and expertise informs the Doctor's account of the function of humanist education. By the Doctor's definition, experience is "the father of wisdom." As he argues, "the experience of an old man makes him wiser than the young because he saw more things than the other" (26). This fact notwithstanding, the sum of wisdom any one person can accrue is temporally and spatially restricted—travel is relatively difficult and humans live only so long. By recovering, and providing access to, the texts of antiquity, humanism functions as a kind of technology of experience that helps overcome, or at least mitigate, these limitations. Erasmus had insisted that education was a way of avoiding bad experiences; rather than "teach . . . the master mariner the rudiments of navigation by shipwrecks," a proper education could allow one "to learn beforehand how to avoid mischiefs" instead of having "with the pains of experience to remedy them."[79] Smith elaborates and reworks such an account by arguing that learning allows one to experience things that have happened throughout the ages, even back to the beginnings of existence, and that it effectively enables contact with "the right manner and usage of every country in the world" (26). Those who derive their experience textually, who have "experience . . . by letters" (27), effectively have "the commodity of life of a thousand years, yes, two or three thousand years, by reason he sees the events and occurrences of all that time by books" (27). Exposure to the texts of antiquity, and to the models of social organization, customs, and behavior that they make available, provides the experience necessary to form humanist expertise.

This account of humanist education enables the Doctor's perspective to take priority over those of the other participants. Status differentials are rewritten as intellectual differentials, and the perspective even of the Knight is subordinated to the Doctor's greater insight born of greater experience, in turn acquired through greater reading.

The Doctor's account of humanism as a technology of experience enables us to consider the links between humanist pedagogy and the task of governing cultural reproduction. The pedagogic regimen Pandotheus describes attributes to humanist practice a capacity effectively to create people, to reproduce educationally the persons necessary to govern. It is important to acknowledge, however, that the Doctor advances his account of learning's capacity to give experience in the face of an awareness of its actual failure to achieve the effects he posits.

Although the Doctor provides a spirited defense of learning to counter the Capper's pointed criticisms, he nevertheless grants that the humanist program of instituting experience does not seem to be working as he has described. The Doctor admits that, rather than produce the governors needed by the commonwealth, England's educational institutions have been producing imbalance, "inconvenience," by failing to reproduce educationally the right kinds of persons. On one hand, there seems to be a lack of men trained in moral philosophy, hence a paucity of those possessing the governmental expertise necessary for guiding the conduct of the nation: "Of truth, there be too few of them that can skill of these sciences nowadays" (30). On the other hand, shortcomings in university education effectively have created disruptive persons: contemporary students, the Doctor argues, are too willing to skip over the elements of a sound education contained in the *trivium* and *quadrivium,* and instead are in a hurry to get to the far more lucrative fields of law, medicine, and divinity. With respect to the last discipline especially, Pandotheus must admit that such hurry results in unqualified people ("every boy that has not read scripture past half a year") taking it upon themselves "to affirm new and strange interpretations" of the Bible. Such activity, the Doctor argues, is "sufficient to overthrow a whole Commonweal where it is used." Illicit judgment without the requisite expertise represents another version of vocational trespass—one, from the Doctor's perspective, with the most dire of consequences for England. "What ship," the Doctor asks, "can long be safe from wreck where every man will take upon him to be a pilot; what house well governed where every servant will be a master or a teacher?" (31). Where humanism aspires to produce men possessing the relevant knowledge (and hence, by the Doctor's definition, the experience) necessary properly to govern the realm, such learning in fact produces men who cause dissension. Indeed, a version of the imbalance confronting the commonweal as a whole faces the domain of learning to the extent that it is failing to produce enough of the right sort of people, competent governmental experts, and too many of the wrong sort, people who disrupt rather than contribute to the good of the whole.

The Capper's questions, and the Doctor's no less damning admissions, engage concerns voiced in England as early as the dissolution of the monasteries, and take up a polemic that ramifies throughout the rest of the century and into the next.[80] Just as anxieties about multitudes serve, within commonwealth discourse, to authorize governmental intervention, fears of the educational generation of superfluous and potentially disruptive scholars lend urgency to calls for pedagogic reform and underwrite appeals for a more effective dispensation of educational government. It will be helpful here to consider one prominent example of such an appeal, advanced by Richard Mulcaster, longtime headmaster of the Merchant Taylor's school, in his 1581 book of educational advice, *Positions.* Mulcaster both embraces the abilities of humanist education to make persons, and sounds a cautionary note about such culturally reproductive capacities. To his mind, as to those of both the Capper and Pandotheus in Smith's dialogue, the nation's schools have become too productive, have spawned more than the commonwealth could support, and have created an imbalance between resources and needs. "[W]ill ye let the *fry* encrease," Mulcaster asks his countrymen, "where the *feeding* failes? Will ye have the *multitude* waxe, where the *maintenance* waines?"[81] Mulcaster's specific concern is that the excess production of learned men will be of advantage to the Catholic Church. Prior to the English Reformation and the subsequent end of the Roman church's limitless "book-maintenance" of scholars, he argues, the Pope was "supported by multitude" (*Positions,* 148) of educated men. The new men, generated pedagogically but without the security of a living, become potential numbers among the ranks of the army of the expelled religion, "and by apparent defection doth encrease the embush, which lyeth still in waite to intercept our possession" (149). Consistent with the position (elaborated at the opening of this chapter) in which the "multitude" is viewed as the antithesis of government, Mulcaster understands the superabundant pedagogic offspring as a dangerous mass, inherently unstable, threatening to run out of control. Thus Mulcaster advances the specter of the commonwealth "pester[ed]" by an excess number of learned persons, a "flocking multitude" (145), and "needeles superfluitie" (135; cf. also 136). Identifying them as scavengers, "*bussardes*" (163) feeding off unwitting patrons, Mulcaster figuratively associates the excess humanist numbers with the hordes of "barbarous offall of all kinde of people" (159) that overwhelmed Rome, sacking it and claiming Roman wealth for their own. Thus understood as threatening utter devastation, the excessive spawn of humanist education straining the commonwealth's resources, a civic "refuse" (153) overcharging the national body (136), should be purged, Mulcaster suggests, from the nation before they turn rebellious (166).

Smith's solution to the educational crisis, as he understands it, is to increase the prestige of government service, which must be accomplished by a prior increase in government appointments by ruling officials, "preferment" (*A Discourse,* 32) to those who have chosen to undertake the studies necessary to the task of governing. With respect to the disruption caused by theological controversy, the Doctor asserts (again) the privilege of expertise: theological controversy should be handled by those qualified to understand the issues, those properly credentialed and recognized as authorities in matters of biblical interpretation and ecclesiastical doctrine (133–137). In contrast, Mulcaster construes the problem to be less a matter of "preferment" than of properly distributing persons to their optimal place, that most beneficial for the nation. "[W]ittes well sorted be most civill," he contends, and "the same misplaced be most unquiet and seditious" (*Positions,* 135). Such distribution does not occur naturally, either because of the too great affection of parents or of the too great generosity of those who would endow more schools or fellowships than necessary (139). Educational generation therefore requires government, and it is a central project of Mulcaster's text to position the grammar school instructor as a privileged agent of prudential calculation in the commonwealth—that is, as an expert whose specialized knowledge is necessary for the proper coordination of educational activity and common good. By emphasizing the importance for the instructor of "discretion" (132)—the ability to adapt general precepts to particular cases, exceptions, or problems in the classroom—Mulcaster invests him with the capacity to make the difficult decisions necessary for eliminating the superfluity threatening the nation. Such a deliberative subject is needed insofar as God has obscured the future, "reserved, his calling and discovering houres, as all other future events to his own peculiar and private knowledge"; all God has left to judge by are "probabilities," likely developments. The "maisters *discretion*" (141) becomes a rational capacity capable of application in behalf of the commonwealth, a faculty charged with the vital task of determining who should be set to learning.[82]

I close this chapter with this brief look at Mulcaster's text, first, because it indicates the way commonwealth discourse proliferates and comes to encompass a broad array of phenomena, institutions, and practices. The understanding of the commonwealth discussed above provides Mulcaster as much as it does Smith with ways of envisioning the interconnectedness of relatively autonomous domains of action, a means of conceptually articulating one activity, education, to the larger collective. In so doing, it provides him with a working vocabulary within which he is able to gauge the effects of education, to evaluate its impact, and to recommend ways of addressing the imbalances it has putatively caused. But more than this, I utilize Mulcaster as a bridge to the chapters that follow, which focus on humanism as the foundation of a dominant form of literary practice. My next chapter argues that concerns about human aggregates and a sense of the necessity for governed poetic generation condition literary activity in early modern England. Just as Mulcaster acknowledged that the very strengths of humanism, its capacity to produce persons to govern the polity, could through success become its greatest weakness, so poetry comes to be both valued because of its generative capacities, and criticized for the destabilizing potentials of this generativity.

CHAPTER TWO

Defending Poetic Generation

Sir Philip Sidney and the Aesthetics of Educational Reproduction

Although Renaissance England would come to be defined by the efflorescence of poetic activity it witnessed, to many contemporaries this poetic abundance was nothing to celebrate. Indeed, for some, the sheer number of people writing was cause for alarm. To take a prominent example, Sir Philip Sidney asserted that England faced what amounted to a poetic population crisis. Echoing Richard Mulcaster's concerns (broached in the last chapter) about the impact of too many graduates, Sidney implied that the unanticipated successes of England's grammar schools and universities had the secondary effect of saturating the literary field.[1] When, in the *Defence of Poesie,* he surveyed the contemporary literary landscape, Sidney saw about him a nation overrun by a "swarme [of] many versefiers,"[2] hacks, pretenders, "Poet-apes" (45) who gave the literary vocation a bad name. It was, Sidney wrote, "as if all the *Muses* were got with childe, to bring forth bastard Poets" (36). Samuel Daniel, writing two decades later, would argue that many poets were simply a sign of a lively literary scene and of the overall importance granted poetry; over time the dross would melt away and the literature worth lasting would remain.[3] By contrast, Sidney contended that the superabundance of "Poet-apes" by their very presence reduced the value placed on poetry, which in turn prevented many who would qualify as legitimate poets from writing. In his complaints about excessive numbers of poets, Sidney is closer to a writer like Stephen Gosson (whose *Schoole of Abuse* [1579] was dedicated to Sidney, and to whom the *Defence* was thought to respond) than to Daniel. Gosson complained that there were "infinit Poets, and Pipers, and suche peeuishe cattel among us in Englande, that liue by merrie begging, mainteyned by almes, and priuely encroche upon euery mans purse."[4]

In his well-known account of Europe's early humanists, Norbert Elias posits that Erasmus and his coadjutors authorized their actions by asserting the capacity of classical learning to guarantee the governed conduct of England's ruling elites. In turn, such claims and their practical implementation had the reciprocal effect of authorizing the status advancement of the humanists themselves.[5] Clearly, by the latter part of the sixteenth century such a project had run into profound complications; the very success of humanist pedagogy produced unanticipated consequences perceived as a threat to the social order. The urgency surrounding the anxiety about poets' agencies derived in large part from the shared understanding that the numerous writers formed a population that directly contributed to the instability of the commonwealth. Gosson contended that, although poets looked innocent enough, they were in fact quite dangerous. Uncloak a poet, he suggested, and one would find ignominy: "pul of the visard that Poets maske in, you shall disclose their reproch, bewray their vanitie, loth their wantonnesse." Just so, as he elaborated, "if you spoke well to *Epaeus* horse, you shall finde in his bowels the destructio[n] of Troy" (A2v). Poetry became a military threat, a kind of surreptitious delivery mechanism for invading troops, like the Trojan horse; poets harbored "vanities" and "wantonnesse" having the same impact as a foreign army and promising to destroy one's soul, family, city, church, monarch, and nation.[6]

Although in his own defensive pamphlet Daniel was relatively unworried about the multitudes of bad writers, in his dialogue *Musophilus* one of the interlocutors shared Gosson's sense of the risk associated with poetic activity. From Philocosmus's perspective, the flood of "Pamphlets, Libels and Rymes" (446) circulating in England, "strange confused tumults of the minde" (447), were symptoms of a "sicknesse" (448) and "disease" (449) that would disrupt the polity. When those who felt they deserved patronage and employment found none, he claimed,

> discontented Sects and Schismes arise,
> Hence interwounding Controuersies spring,
> That feede the Simple, and offend the Wise,
> Who know the consequence of cauelling
> Disgrace, that these to others doe deuise.
>
> (466–70)

As Musophilus himself argues, "great Nature" (247) has been profoundly fecund in generating scholars: she "hath mutiplyed so fast, / That all she hath, on these times seem'd t'haue spent. / All that which might haue many ages grac'd, / Is borne in one" (251–54). Echoing Mulcaster and the Capper of Smith's *Discourse,* Philocosmus intimates that this superabundant offspring of writers will take advantage of the "Simple" and foment rebellion. The "strange confused tumults of the minde," Philocosmus fears, will yield devastating political tumult.[7]

What follows develops the previous chapter's discussion by taking up the question of how poetry impacts the commonwealth—or, more precisely, how people talked about how poetry impacts the commonwealth. For two reasons, I begin with a brief view of how poetry was understood to be potentially disruptive. First, acknowledging the anxieties about excessive poets helps isolate a set of concerns about the limits and unanticipated consequences of humanist education, a key site of governmental activity that conditions both poetic production and poetry's impact on the world. Second, considering the concerns of Sidney, Gosson, and Daniel helps pinpoint a dominant vocabulary through which poetry's usefulness (or potential harm) to the polity comes to be adjudicated—its frequent characterization of literary production as a kind of reproduction. Scholars have long noted that parthenogenetic claims are central to Sidney's poetics.[8] Recent feminist criticism has drawn renewed attention to this aspect of Sidney's account of poetry by arguing that his metaphors of reproduction claim for male poets what is properly speaking a strictly feminine biological capacity.[9] While this criticism has been useful for shifting the discussion about reproduction in Sidney from the domain of the history of ideas, the feminist critique drastically underdescribes the complexity of Sidney's appeal to this metaphorics, the governmental objectives this metaphorics seeks to articulate and secure, and the difficulties Sidney confronts in making sure that poetic generation is governed.

In its most optimistic formulations, Sidney's *Defence* can be understood as an effort to call poets to a sense of reproductive responsibility. To the extent that it does so, it provides an implicit answer to the ethical appeal to reproductive duty advanced by a character in his *Countess of Pembroke's Arcadia.* In response to an unmarried young man with deep misgivings about the possibilities of felicity in marriage, the elder shepherd Geron argues for marriage by insisting on the necessity of procreation. "Nature above all things requireth this, / That we our kind do labour to maintain." Not only is one indebted to one's father, to whom one should return the favor for giving one life, Geron argues, "Thy Commonwealth may rightly grieved be, / Which must by this immortal be preserved, / If thus thou murder thy posterity."[10] Reproduction here constitutes an ethical imperative, an obligation to self and others, including to the unborn beings who somehow already exist and assume a kind of quasi-legal standing as potential murder victims. The reproductive metaphorics in Sidney's *Defence* serve a similar purpose by insisting on both the obligation of true poets to engage in generative activity and by simultaneously reinforcing the perception of poets' vital national importance because of their capacity for the governed cultural reproduction of men for the polity. However, the concerns voiced by Gosson, Daniel, and Sidney about too many poets begins to suggest the extent to which this vision of poetic parthenogenesis is advanced under conditions of considerable strain. In the face of potential generative excesses, the challenge for Sidney is to specify how literary (pro)creation may be governed, and thereby may produce the right kinds of people who stabilize rather than disrupt the commonwealth. Since the onus of his generative project is upon engendering *noble men*, his defensive effort raises and seeks to manage a corollary set of concerns about precisely what constitutes noble masculinity, what counts as status-appropriate masculine endeavor. Although the *Defence* works to distinguish the governed from the ungoverned effects of poetic genesis, Sidney is keenly aware of the difficulties and tensions inhabiting such a project. His *Arcadia* acknowledges these difficulties, even as it seeks to exploit them for narrative pleasure.

"Vertue Breeding Delightfulnesse"

Sidney's *Defence* hinges on its claim that poets possess the capacity to "make up people" (to borrow again Ian Hacking's phrase). Poetry depicts ethical forms, ways of thinking about and acting upon oneself and others, and seeks to transform readers via these models of personhood. Consider the ethical effects of the precedent set by Aeneas:

> Onely let *Aeneas* bee worne in the Tablet of your memorie, how hee governeth himselfe in the ruine of his Countrey, in the preserving his olde Father, and carrying away his religious Ceremonies, in obeying Gods Commaunment, to leave *Dido,* though not onelie all passionate kindnesse, but even the humane consideration of vertuous gratefulnesse,

> would have craved other of him: how in stormes, howe in sports, howe in warre, howe in peace, how a fugitive, how victorious, how besieged, how besieging, how to straungers, how to Allies, how to enemies, how to his owne. Lastly, how in his inwarde selfe, and howe in his outward government, and I thinke in a minde moste prejudiced with a prejudicating humour, Hee will bee founde in excellencie fruitefull. (25)

Sidney's account of the use to be made of Aeneas's image, as with poetic images more generally, draws on mimetic techniques central to early modern grammar school practice—imitation of classical models of usage, tropes, stylistics, as well as of the instructor himself.[11] As a paragon of government available for mnemonic inscription, Aeneas serves as a pattern of conduct in any situation, through the vagaries of calamity and victory, at play, in battle. He illustrates how to govern one's self, how to relate to others, and (as the Dido episode shows) how to deliberate between competing obligations. Guided by "the divine consideration of what may be and should be" (10), Sidney's poet possesses the capacity to produce "loftie Image[s]" that "enflameth the minde with desire to bee woorthie: and enforme . . . with counsaile how to bee woorthie" (25). Poets therefore possess a kind of fecundity, a generative capacity "not onely to make a *Cyrus,* which had bene but a particular excellency as nature might have done, but to bestow a *Cyrus* upon the world to make many *Cyrusses*" (8).[12] It is true that Sidney's poet "freely raung[es] within the Zodiack of his owne wit" (8), a formulation that implies a striking aesthetic, if not moral, autonomy; it is also the case that through the poet's reproductive potential Sidney would functionalize this autonomy, direct it to the service of the polity by creating well-governed and well-governing subjects.

At least, this is Sidney's objective. However, as recent work on gender performativity has emphasized—and here I think specifically of Judith Butler's account of "citationality" in her *Bodies That Matter*—imitation is an unstable process that provides no guarantee of success.[13] Though citational instability offers Butler a political resource, by enabling the strategic rearticulation of identities and hegemonic relations of dominance and subordination, in the context of early modern poetics an understanding of the incapacity to control the ethical effects of poetic images is understood to be dangerous precisely because of the instability such images promote. To take a prominent instance of the strident critique such a view enabled, Stephen Gosson's account of poetry opposes

Sidney's by insisting that poetry does not form, but deforms, people. Where Sidney argues that the notable images of worthy exemplars effectively propagate well-governed men and women for the commonwealth, Gosson contends that the degenerate stuff of poetry and plays causes a vicious reproduction. While at the popular stage, for example, one could see "Such ticking, such toying, Such smiling, such winking, & such manning [women] home, when the sportes are ended, that it is a right Comedie, to marke their behauiour, to watch their conceates" (C1v). Theatrical productions reproduce themselves through the audience, comedically scripting their behavior in ways that disseminate poetry's illicit fantasies beyond the stage, mimetically sending its degenerating eros out into the city of London and beyond.[14] Poets, according to Gosson, are inherently mendacious, and consequently should (like Satan at John 8:44) "bee accompted . . . the fathers of lyes" (A3r); because of this deformative imitation, they also possess an even more insidious paternity, a capacity to generate dangerous men who, like the troops inside the Trojan horse, will devastate the nation.

Where Sidney claimed that poetry invested one with the capacity for governing oneself in any contingency, Gosson insists that poetry prompts ethical failure. According to Gosson, "Man is enriched . . . with knowledge, to serue his maker and gouerne himselfe" (D1v). Contrary to this ideal, the English demonstrate an incapacity for self-government, and consequently seem always to be tending to excess: "we which haue both sence, reason, wit, and understanding, are ever ouerlashing, passing our bounds, going beyond our limites, neuer keeping our selves within compasse" (D1v–D2r). Laura Levine has observed perceptively the ways Gosson advances an account of persons who are "pure appetite, perpetually insatiable."[15] Gosson imagines people as "voracious"[16] monsters, with appetites out of control, completely lacking in self-government. For example, the figures he lambastes in his tract—poets, players, jesters, dancers, among others—are "Caterpillers of a Com[m]onwelth" (title page) who, like the insect, exercise a destructive consumption, feasting without providing anything in return, surfeiting without use. Just so, theatergoers watch plays until they "burst their guts" (B4v). The new men of England are like a composite of international vices: "Wee haue robbed *Greece* of gluttony, *Italy* of wantonnes, *Spayne* of pride, *France* of deceite, & *Duchland* of quaffing" (C1r). This vicious amalgam represents a decline from an imagined golden era of England's past, an ancient regimen of extreme continence, extraordinary feats of self-abnegation. This is the "olde discipline of Englande":

> English me[n] could suffer watching & labor, hunger & thirst, & beare of al storms w[ith] head & shoulders, they used slender weapons, went naked & wer good Soldiours, they fedde uppon rootes and barkes of trees, they would stande up to the chinne many dayes in marshes without victualles, and they had a kinde of sustenaunce in time of neede, of which if they hadde taken but the quantitie of a beane, or the weight of a pease, they did neither gape after meate, nor long for the cuppe, a great while after. The me[n] in value not yeelding to *Scythia,* the women in Courage passing the *Amazons.* (B8r–B8v)

Gosson answers the threat of complete loss of self-control by advancing an ethic of profound ascetic mastery. The celebration of England's lost martial glory, a military Eden that putatively existed before the fall into present luxury and abuse, outlines an ideal of perfect ethical regulation, a self-government that will in turn secure the church and nation against their enemies. This example of radical continence authorizes, at the national level, Gosson's endorsement of Plato's civic repudiation of poets—as he notes, the philosopher "shut them out of his Schoole, and banished them quite from his commonwealth, as effeminate writers, unprofitable members, and utter enimies to vertue" (A3r)—as well as, at the personal level, Gosson's recommendation of a policy of radical abstention, an absolute withdrawal. "Let us . . . shut uppe our eares to Poets, Pipers, and Players," Gosson argues, "pull our feete backe from resorte to Theaters, and turne away our eyes from beholding of vanitie." Do these things, Gosson asserts, and "the greatest storme of abuse will bee ouerblowne, and a faire path troden to amendment of life" (D3r).

To be sure, Sidney endorses Gosson's emphasis upon martial prowess.[17] However, his understanding of the operations of desire and the function of pleasure counters the specter of ethical failure and licentiousness offered in the *School of Abuse.* Indeed, as Margaret Ferguson has aptly observed, "[t]he defense of poetry necessarily involves a defense of Eros."[18] In vivid contrast to Gosson's ascetic imperatives, which afford little place for pleasure, Sidney emphasizes pleasure's positive impact. As a form of education, poetry is more effective than the ministrations of historians or philosophers insofar as it introduces "delight" into the equation, making what would otherwise be unpalatable to a student—the arid complexities of philosophy, the morally ambivalent minutiae of history—lovely and desirable. Right poets, Sidney argues, "imitate both to delight & teach, and delight to move men to take that goodnesse in hand, which without delight they would flie as from a stranger" (10). Poets strive to produce movement, since "mooving . . . is well nigh both the cause and effect of teaching. For who will be taught, if hee be not mooved with desire to be taught? And what so much good doth that teaching bring foorth . . . as that it mooveth one to do that which it doth teach" (19). Outside of the institutional framework of the school, the promise of pleasure guarantees motion, the movement requisite for learning and thus for the subsequent regulated action that poetic education aspires to create.[19] This is the scope of the poet, his claim to priority over other disciplines—a capacity to produce and manipulate pleasure, to manage desire by presenting what should be done in beautiful images. Invoking the authority of Plato and Cicero, Sidney asserts "that who could see vertue, woulde bee woonderfullie ravished with the love of her bewtie. This man setteth her out to make her more lovely in her holliday apparrell, to the eye of anie that will daine, not to disdaine untill they understand" (25). Sidney understands the ability of the poet to incite pleasure, as in the "fruiteful" example of Aeneas, as a crucial dimension of poetry's fecundity; "ever-praise woorthie *Poesie,*" he asserts, "is full of vertue breeding delightfulnesse" (45). The incitement and management of pleasure, the propagation of desire, enables rather than disables the poet's generative project.

Sidney would distinguish himself from the "Poet-haters" (26) like Gosson by embracing the regulative effects of delight, but he nevertheless acknowledges the destabilizing reproductive potentials that the promise of pleasure enables. Poetic reproduction must be governed to insure that what Sidney calls the "straunge . . . power in Love" does not lead to the degenerative results Gosson feared. The following passage addresses just these concerns. In it, Sidney differentiates delight and laughter by turning to a moment in the career of Hercules that elicits both—a moment in which the hero, cross-dressed, spins at the distaff for the Amazon Omphale:[20]

> *Hercules,* painted with his great beard, and furious countenaunce, in a womans attyre, spinning, at *Omphales* commaundement . . . breedes both delight and laughter: for the representing of so straunge a power in Love, procures delight, and the scornefulnesse of the action, stirreth laughter. (40)

This tableau illuminates a pervasive difficulty with efforts to appeal to classical figures as moral exempla—figures whose textual lives are filled with morally complex episodes or behavior not everyone would consider virtuous.[21] Sidney attempts to manage the ambiguity in the Hercules example by insisting on a clear distinction between what is delightful about the image and what merits scorn, between the "straunge . . . power in Love" and the risible spectacle of a virtuous man submitting to the command of a woman. Hercules's actions in this case allow Sidney to illustrate the extraordinary effects of eros, to underscore the "delight[ful]" ability of desire to spur action. Although this is precisely the "straunge . . . power" that fuels his program for the mimetic generation of ideal men, he attempts to foreclose the possibility of a faulty imitation, of someone moved to do scornful things by this strange power, by implicitly allowing for a kind of mimetic refusal, an inherent ability to recognize that which should not be imitated but rejected. While the love that procures the delight is the very reason for that which produces the ludicrous action, the imagined viewer knows to scorn Hercules, knows how to separate out the delightful from the laughable components of the tableau. We might compare this capacity to Sidney's ability to resist the sophistry of the Italian John Pietro Pugliano's defense of horsemanship and enthusiastic praise for the horse; Sidney asserts that "if I had not bene a peece of a *Logician* before I came to him, I thinke he would have perswaded me to have wished my selfe a horse" (3). Like the poet, who is "reined with learned discretion" (10), and like Sidney himself who is a "peece of a *Logician*," Sidney's ideal reader is educationally preconstituted with a capacity for deliberative reasoning.[22] Without such mimetic discretion (a faculty Gosson seems not to acknowledge), one is susceptible to any argument that comes along, threatened by the possibility of dishonorable metamorphosis or bestial deformation: an imitation that does not make men but, after a fashion, unmakes them.

Such discretion enables Sidney to address a further serious challenge built into his mimetic project. Although he claims for poetry the capacity to make "many Cyrusses" it is not entirely clear that everyone would share Sidney's enthusiasm for this objective. Would it be entirely feasible or even desirable to imagine that everyone who could read would be able to become a modern-day Cyrus? William Barker, who translated Xenophon's *Cyropaedeia* in 1567, seemed aware of the disruptive potential implicit in the prospect of a nation filled with men of this stature and ambition. In his dedication to Philip, Earl of Surrey, the son of his employer, the Duke of Norfolk, Barker counseled the young earl "to think the time will come, when you shall be called of your prince to take such journies as you shall see that Cyrus appointeth to such as you are, and to do such services as your most noble progenitors have done by the commandment of their princes."[23] Barker felt compelled to try to guide the reading experience, and to insist that the education of Cyrus trained one not to be Cyrus, but to be like the people Cyrus commanded. Sidney's approach is similar. Though he never broaches the possibility that having a bunch of Cyruses roaming around England might not be a good thing, he does insist that "the *Poet* nameth *Cyrus* and *Aeneas,* no other way, then to shewe what men of their fames, fortunes, and estates, should doo" (30). For both Barker and Sidney, mimetic discretion conforms to the dictates of status, which thus performs a significant part of the function of sorting and distribution Mulcaster would arrogate to the humanist pedagogue, as discussed in the previous chapter. Although there is no intrinsic reason why "fame," "fortune," and "estate" should all line up and reinforce each other, and in turn guarantee the effects of reading, Sidney simply assumes that they do and thus that literary generation will be governed rather than disruptive.

Generating Masculinities

Although what I have called mimetic discretion provides a kind of local solution to challenges built into Sidney's generative project, this capacity for prudential deliberation has its limits. The difficulty arises out of confusions in the understanding of what counted as status-appropriate masculine endeavor. It is all well and good to be able to choose between positive and negative exemplars, but in Sidney's moment the very notion of what might constitute a positive exemplar was up for grabs. The last chapter emphasized how, within commonwealth writings, domestic economy came to serve as both a privileged model and a site of governmental activity, a condition of possibility for the eventual consolidation of political economy as a dominant governmental discourse; here I wish to examine how the increased emphasis on domestic economy placed pressure on definitions of noble masculinity. Such pressure is hinted at in the account of Aeneas, who is praised as exemplary in part because he "obey[s . . .] Gods Commaunment, to leave *Dido,* though not onelie all passionate kindnesse, but even the humane consideration of vertuous gratefulnesse, would have craved other of him." Sidney magnifies Aeneas's exemplarity by underscoring the competing demands upon him; dwelling on the difficulty of the Trojan's decision has the additional effect of suggesting that, under other circumstances, staying with Dido would have been not simply acceptable but perfectly consistent with the ideals of well-governed masculinity. Sidney's brief aside points to the possibility of alternative definitions of masculinity, in which there might be a compelling case to be made for the importance of relations with women. I turn in what follows to the *Countess of Pembroke's Arcadia.* Although scholars have compellingly read this text as instantiating or illustrating the pedagogic program outlined in the *Defence*,[24] I argue that Sidney uses the *Arcadia* not to confirm the *Defence* but to explore the extent to which the definitions of masculinity are not unified but potentially conflict. Building on the discussion of Sidney's reproductive poetics, I emphasize how these potentially conflicting accounts of masculinity come to be adjudicated through competing accounts of generation.

The conflict between definitions of masculinity is evident in the story of the *Arcadia*'s central male figures, Musidorus and Pyrocles. The latter in fact models his actions on (or at least acknowledges the similarities to) those of Hercules smitten with Omphale. When Pyrocles sees a painting of the lovely princess Philoclea of Arcadia, he immediately falls in love. Because her father, Basilius, fears the ambiguous prophecies of an oracle, he vows to keep his daughters unmarried and has sequestered the entire royal family in a pastoral enclave; consequently, to gain access to Philoclea, Pyrocles disguises himself in the garb of an Amazon, assuming the persona of Zelmane. The prince, in fact, explicitly refers to the classical precedent he follows, wearing an image of the hero on a broach, a "jewel" with "a Hercules made in little form, but set with a distaff in his hand, as he once was by Omphale's commandment, with a word in Greek but thus to be interpreted, 'Never more valiant'" (131). This inscription serves as an ambiguous gloss on the actions of both Hercules and Pyrocles. On one hand, "Never more valiant" suggests that by taking on the garb and demeanor of a woman Pyrocles will never again be valiant, has lost permanently a former state of superior masculinity; on the other hand, the motto indicates that the prince has never displayed more valor than in his current situation.[25] These alternatives figure two competing definitions of masculinity and two corresponding visions of appropriate masculine endeavor in the world: an ideal oriented toward a life of virile heroics and an opposed ideal centered around domestic economy.

When his cousin, Prince Musidorus, discovers Pyrocles dressed as a woman, and hears his explanation of why he is so dressed, he upbraids the younger prince at length. His response takes up the first sense of "Never more valiant," insisting that Pyrocles' transvestism represents a deformative "metamorphosis" (132).[26] Where, in the *Defence*, the love of a woman serves as a paradigm of the love that makes a man heroically virtuous—it is the poet's job to set out "Vertue" in all her ravishing beauty so that a man will be drawn to mime virtue—for Musidorus love of a woman, what he calls "effeminate love" as distinct from "true love" (133) of virtue or heaven, turns one into a woman: "this effeminate love of a woman doth so womanize a man that, if he yield to it, it will not only make him an Amazon, but a launder, a distaff-spinner or whatsoever other vile occupation their idle heads can imagine and their weak heads perform" (134). The prince maps the distinction between "true" and "effeminate love" onto a social terrain starkly divided between the battlefield and the household, and then dismisses the latter as a domain of incapacity, a cultural site more suited to the "weak" and "idle heads" of women. Rather than establish his masculinity through virtuous deeds in battle or spectacular heroics, Pyrocles has become Zelmane, removed himself to the space of a household—understood as a misgoverned location, the site of feminine activity that is as good as inactivity, menial, tedious, ignoble and "vile."

The distinction upon which Musidorus insists privileges a martial vision of masculinity, a definition of masculinity, as noted above, evidenced in both Gosson and Sidney. We may add that this cultural privilege was more than a longing look-back to a regimented past; it was also a motivated nostalgia, an effort to institute a form of personhood considered vital to the future of England as a Protestant nation. The specter of England falling under the sway of Rome—a very real urgency for some, in light of the Spanish successes in the Low Countries, and the Catholic presence in France—necessitated, in the minds of many, including Sidney and Gosson, an active militarization of faith.[27] That the martial ethos associated with this militarized faith conflicted with the demands of domestic economy is evidenced, for example, in Thomas Moffet's posthumous biography of Sidney. Moffet comments on the difficulty the Earl of Leicester, Philip's uncle, had in raising troops for his mission in the Low Countries—the mission, in fact, on which Sidney died. Moffet reports that "one was horrified to observe that many youths sprung from the rank of nobles were—what shall I say?—sons of Mars? Nay, rather nephews of Venus!" In further characterizing these venereal scions, Moffet lumps together those who would rather resort to the "winy brothel" and those who preferred to "pursue peace, to remain with children, wife, and household."[28] It is as if, at least during a time of war, commitment to domestic economy represents an ethical failure equivalent to drunken revelry with prostitutes. Gosson universalizes this view by valorizing an ideal of an austere warring masculinity absolutely opposed to the domain of the household. Gosson praises the Spartans, who "are all steele" (D6v), and the "maintenance of Martial discipline" (D7r) in a host of antique countries—Crete, Scythia, Persia, Thracia—as well as the veneration for soldiers in Carthage and Sparta. Gosson then exhorts his readers to heed the lessons of the past:

> Whe[n] the *Aegyptia[n]s* were moste busy in their husbandrie, the *Scythians* overran them: when the *Assyrians* wer loking to their thrift, the *Persians* were in armes, & ouercam the[m]: when the *Troians* thought themselues safest, the *Greekes* were nearest: when *Rome* was asleepe, the Frenche men gaue a sharpe assault to the *Capitoll:* when the Iewes were idle, their walles were rased & the *Ro[m]mans* entered: when the *Chaldees* were sporting, *Babilon* was sacked. (D7v)

Gosson's point is that a sense of security is dangerous, a delusion lulling the self-satisfied into a vulnerable complacency. In making his point, he aligns husbandry and thrift, the disciplines of "oeconomy," with sleep, idleness, and play. From the perspective of a warring ethos, one instituting and requiring a relentless external vigilance, any activity that takes attention away from the project of defending the polity is a danger no different from the dissolution taught in the abusive schools of poetry. Under such a dispensation, household government looks just like reckless indifference or idleness.

To the extent that he draws on the dichotomy established here, Musidorus lends a vitriolic edge to his account of Pyrocles' deformative cross-dressing. The elder cousin adds a degree of analytical specificity to his critique of his cousin by describing the generative effects of Pyrocles' actions. From Musidorus's perspective, Pyrocles' metamorphosis is the sterile product of an illegitimate fecundity. As he tells his cousin, the latter's love for Philoclea is a "bastard Love," one "engendered betwixt lust and idleness" (133). A love thus generated, Musidorus explains, is barren; it "subverts the course of nature" and is consequently "the basest and fruitlessest of all passions" (133). Rather than love spurring on an imitation that would effectively generate heroes, as Sidney argued in the *Defence,* passion here prompts a degenerate imitation that yields no fruit. Such an assertion carries with it two implications. First, if love for a woman makes a man a woman, then love for a man can make a man a man. Second, if love for a woman is sterile, then love for a man can be generative, can yield reproductive effects.

Although Musidorus does not make this explicit in his screed, Sidney develops this logic elsewhere in the *Arcadia.* Consider the activities of a prior set of friends, the fathers of Pyrocles and Musidorus, Euarchus, king of Macedon, and Dorialus, ruler of Thessalia. The former gives the latter his sister in marriage, "not so much as to make a friendship as to confirm the friendship between their posterity, which between them, by the likeness of virtue, had been long before made" (256). Insofar as the referent of the clause beginning "which between them" is ambiguous, modifying either "friendship" or "posterity," this account of the traffic in women may be read as advancing a parthenogenetic fantasy: the likeness of virtue secures a friendship *and* determines in advance the generation of a posterity, a line that proceeds as if from this similarity and friendship, rather than through affinal alliance. Such genetic capacity between men is elaborated in the description of the defense of Thessalia. Coming to the aid of Dorialus, who is under assault from the king of Phrygia, Euarchus helps his brother-in-law defeat the invader; together, the two "begat of just war the best child, Peace" (257). Consistent with Musidorus's emphasis upon martial prowess, military exploits undertaken by friends represent a means for men to achieve a kind of procreation.[29] A related dynamic informs one account of Pyrocles' activities in Laconia. When Clitophon, the son of Kalander, is taken by the Helots in their battle against the Laconian nobility, Pyrocles intervenes. Saving him from "the furious malice of the Helots" (100), who would supposedly have otherwise killed their prisoner, Pyrocles effectively gives birth to the soldier. Clitophon introduces Pyrocles to Kalander as "he who (as a father) hath new-begotten me and (as a god) hath saved me from many deaths which already laid hold on me" (100).[30] Such formulations seek to authorize and privilege masculine activity in the world outside of the household by figuring such activity as a form of generation. Implied in Musidorus's sharp response to Pyrocles is that, through his metamorphosis, Pyrocles eschews precisely these forms of masculine generation, leaves them aside in favor of the love of a woman, the "fruitlessesest of all passions."

This last sentiment is a point of debate. Even as Sidney's Protestant allegiances committed him to a project of military activism and consequently dedicated him to an ideal of martial virtue, his Protestantism invested him in a countervailing emphasis upon household government. Christopher Hill, among others, has demonstrated that the reconfiguration of, and intensified emphasis upon, religious discipline precipitated by the Reformation in England, an emphasis sharpened under the aegis of an emergent Puritan rigor, positioned the household as "the lowest unit in the hierarchy of discipline," the basic means for ensuring the right government of England's numbers.[31] Domestic economy—defined as a divinely sanctioned form of vocational effort through which a husband and wife sought to maintain, to reinforce, and to guarantee the present and future prosperity of the family estate—assumed during the sixteenth and seventeenth centuries in England a crucial importance as a means for securing the rule of God and the stability of the kingdom. We can gauge the importance of such an emphasis by noting that, even as Gosson insists upon the dangers of domestic economy, he also celebrates it. Gosson praises the government of "honest housholders and Citizens" (C6v), and tells the story of Anacharsis, who was said to have searched Greece for wise men. Finding none in Athens, despite the abundance of "good schollers" (E2v), he proceeded to the country, where he met "one *Miso*," a man

> well gouerning his house, looking to his grounde, instructing his children, teaching his faimly [sic], making of marriages among his acquayntance, exhorting his neighbours to loue, & friendeship, & preaching in life, who[m], the Philosopher for his scarcitie of woordes [and] plenty of workes, accompted the onelye wiseman that euer he saw. (E3r)

Here, Gosson values activity within the domestic economy—as opposed to the "priuate profit" (E2v) seekers of the university, who conduct their life strictly for their own advantage—as the governmental foundation of the community. The conduct of the household is for Gosson the model for useful masculine occupation in the world.

Sidney's emphasis on the value of domestic economy is evident in general in the third eclogue's celebration of marriage, and in particular in the importance placed, there, on the necessity for married generation. As I briefly noted at the outset of this chapter, Geron asserted that procreation in marriage was an urgent imperative for a man, an obligation to his progenitors, to his posterity, to his commonwealth, and to humanity. In the passage to follow, the old shepherd Geron focuses attention on the place of generation in the maintenance and extension of domestic economy. He answers the reservations of the young bachelor Histor:

> O Histor, seek within thyself to flourish:
> Thy house by thee must live or else be gone:
> And then who shall the name of Histor nourish?
> Riches of children pass a prince's throne;
> Which touch the father's heart with secret joy,
> When without shame he saith, 'These be mine own.'
> Marry, therefore, for marriage will destroy
> Those passions which to youthful head do climb,
> Mothers and nurses of all vain annoy.
>
> (712)

Although Geron's formulation subsumes wife into husband—for Histor to reproduce in marriage is to "flourish . . . within" himself—it does not entirely elide motherhood. In fact, the passage defines the function of domestic economy in terms of a contest between forms of maternity. On one hand, Geron constitutes marriage and marital generation in opposition to the lack of self-government belonging to youth. This ethical failure of youth, the elevation of passions to the proper seat of reason, represents a kind of dangerous maternity that generates "vain annoy." Marriage promises to "destroy" these impulses that degenerate. On the other hand, the parthenogenetic account of the male self flourishing through producing offspring, an activity that is the precondition for the extension of the household into the future, puts in play a vital maternal function; children "nourish"—nurse—the family "name of Histor," ensure its temporal continuity and durability, securing the extension and stability of the governmental domain beyond the life of the father. Domestic economy replaces the misgoverned generation of passions with the abundant generation of children, a move which thus defines marriage as a governmental regimen to which the father submits and to which he is obligated. The constitution of children as "riches" not only incorporates generation into the classical objective of "oeconomy"—for example, as Aristotle observes in the *Nichomachean Ethics*, the end of economy is the production of wealth[32]—but also seeks to invest this obligation with "joy," the father's return for submission to the governmental imperatives of the household.

This investment in household government and in the reproductive activity requisite to domestic economy guides Pyrocles' defense of his actions. Resisting his cousin's assertions that his cross-dressing is both base and sterile, Pyrocles insists that taking a "woman's hue" is not degenerative, but a strategy; his clothes do not transform him into something "vile," but allow him to accomplish the "great work" of a "diligent workman" (136). This rationale insists upon women's virtue as well as upon the centrality of women's role in procreation; if a man is virtuous he cannot have come from someone who is not virtuous. Pyrocles, "born of a woman and nursed of a woman," sarcastically answers Musidorus's outburst: "I am not yet come to that degree of wisdom to think light of the sex of whom I have my life" (134). He continues by advancing the argument that "we men and praisers of men should remember that if we have such excellencies, it is reason to think them excellent creatures of whom we are, since a kite never brought forth a good flying hawk" (135).[33] It is but a small step from the synechdoche in which Pyrocles' mother becomes the entire female "sex" to the equivalence of women and reproduction. That is, Pyrocles' defense of his love of Philoclea celebrates women by constituting femininity exclusively in terms of procreation. The reverence owed women follows from their maternal function, and, as the analogy to hawking suggests, women's virtue is manifest through their production of offspring. Because they have brought forth good children, they must themselves be good. Because women possess a capacity for reproduction, the argument implies, the love of women is not only acceptable, but both noble and vital because directed toward the *telos* of reproduction. Musidorus himself makes this point when he eventually falls in love with Pamela. "Can any man resist his creation?" he rhetorically asks. "Certainly by love we are made, and to love we are made" (170). Love—a man's love for a woman—generates, and in such a way as to ensure its future generation.

Although the arguments outlined above have been cited as instances of an egalitarian vision of gender relations,[34] it is also important to note that the emphasis on female reproductive capacity has the effect in the *Arcadia* of reinforcing gender hierarchies. In response to Musidorus's bilious critique, Pyrocles seeks to constitute marriage and reproduction as forms of virtuous masculine endeavor that do not feminize but, instead, provide the opportunity to guarantee virility. We might compare this effort to Hugh Languet's advice to Sidney himself, in an instance of what seems to have been a frequent refrain of the elder friend: "If you marry a wife, and if you beget children like yourself, you will be doing better service to your country than if you cut the throats of a thousand Spaniards or Frenchmen."[35] Although he seems to establish an opposition between love and war, between married procreation and military exploits, Languet emphasizes the former *in terms of* the latter; the effects of the imagined reproduction are measured through an estimated number of enemies Sidney would have to kill to do as much good for England. Marital generation becomes an important obligation, here, as another form of martial valor, and "beget[ting]" little versions of Sidney a kind of heroic "service." Similarly, Pyrocles assures his cousin that his cross-dressing is not the effeminate outcome of love for a woman, but a means to establish his masculinity. "Neither doubt you because I wear a woman's apparel I will be the more womanish," he tells his cousin, "since I assure you, for all my apparel, there is nothing I desire more than fully to prove myself a man in this enterprise" (136). These assertions place the primary emphasis not on Pyrocles' desire for Philoclea, but on his desire to demonstrate his manhood; such a claim provides the inscription on his "jewel," "Never more valiant," with its more optimistic interpretation.

How stable is such an attempted resolution? The short answer to this question: not very. Although Pyrocles attempts to reconcile competing forms of masculinity, and therefore, in the terms I have been following, works to resolve alternative forms of generation (the parthenogenesis associated with Musidorus's valorization of martial prowess as opposed to the procreation associated with marriage), his efforts are tenuous at best. The narrative of the *Arcadia* tilts the balance against such reconciliation, demonstrates the profound difficulties of forging a coherent and workable solution to the discursive tensions between these alternative masculinities, and between the alternative forms of generation associated with them. Questions of status inform the way the *Arcadia* broaches and attempts to manage the conflict between the investment in domestic economy as a vital governmental site and the imperative to secure and maintain a heroic masculinity. We may here briefly note that, although Pyrocles' understanding of the love of women as virtuous action aimed towards generation is generally consistent with Geron's programmatic endorsement of marriage, it is not entirely so; presumably Pyrocles and Philoclea's children, as well as Musidorus and Pamela's, would be rulers or would at least gain cultural prestige through the maintenance of the distinction between the monarch and any other fathers, and in turn would benefit from the the maintenance of the priority of the "prince's throne" over the rule of any household. Geron, by contrast privileges domestic economy as a form of government that, in the abundant filial wealth that accrues to the reproductive father, surpasses royal authority. This ostensible disinvestment of monarchy is advanced not at the expense of monarchy as an institution—at least not at this moment of English history—but to define and cathect a relatively autonomous, status-appropriate domain of governmental activity.

The untenability of this governmental form for a man of higher status is underscored elsewhere in the *Arcadia.* I have in mind here the depiction of the marriage of Argalus (Basilius's nephew) and the "fair" and "excellent" (88) Parthenia. After their marriage in book one, the "happy couple" does not appear again until book three. We find Argalus:

> sitting in a parlour with the fair Parthenia, he reading in a book the stories of Hercules, she by him . . . with some pretty question, not so much to be resolved of the doubt as to give him occasion to look upon her. A happy couple: he joying in her, she joying in herself, but in herself, because she enjoyed him: both increasing their riches by giving to each other; each making one life double, because they made a double life one; where desire never wanted satisfaction, nor satisfaction ever bred satiety: he ruling, because she would obey, or rather because she would obey, she therein ruling. (501)

This description is, in fact, the only direct representation of a married "happy couple" in the entire romance, a rare peek at the life that follows the highly charged rituals of courtship and erotic pursuit.[36] The couple's relation is defined in terms of mutuality and reciprocity, an impossible economic relation in which giving yields a greater return and desire is always satisfied but never sated; this mutuality, however, is structured hierarchically: both rule each other, but Parthenia's rule is founded upon willing submission.

Despite the obvious discursive investment in this emergent ideal of companionate marriage, which embodies Pyrocles' defense of love of women as virtuous action, the passage suggests a hint of antagonism, a constitutive tension that ultimately accounts for the destruction of the marriage.[37] The "stories of Hercules" may be an allusion to Pyrocles' citation of the exemplar, or perhaps to the labors to which Argalus was subjected by Parthenia's mother, "as many dangerous enterprises as ever the evil stepmother Juno recommended to the famous Hercules" (89); either way, the salient point is that the text *competes* with the marital relation. Parthenia feigns interest, but the colloquy she pursues interrupts her husband's reading in order to direct attention away from the heroic text and to herself, "to give him occasion to look upon her." The narrative immediately exacerbates this tension by sending Argalus off to war. He responds to the messenger sent to summon him, "like a man in whom honour could not be rocked asleep by affection" (502). Such a formulation demonstrates that the logic underpinning Musidorus's vitriolic response to Pyrocles—a fear of the putatively debilitating effects of the love of women—operates even in relation to Parthenia and Argalus's idealized marriage. Argalus's honor is gauged by his ability to resist the soporific effect of love.

Unfortunately for the married couple, Argalus's capacity for withstanding the demands of affection does not translate into an ability to triumph in battle. Despite his many virtues, he is slain by Amphialus. Distraught, Parthenia disguises herself in armor of black, and presents herself as the Knight of the Tomb in an attempt to avenge her husband's death. She is easily slaughtered. The ideal she and her husband represent appears in the narrative only to be effaced. While Geron can privilege domestic economy as a fecund governmental site, the case of Argalus and Parthenia illustrates the incompatibility of married love and the imperatives of noble virility; although Argalus fights under the emblem of married fertility—"In his shield (as his own device)," the narrator explains, "he had two palm trees near one another, with a word signifying, 'In that sort of flourishing'" (504)[38]—he and Parthenia do not reproduce, but die. It is as if the two lovers, once married, cannot exist in the discursive universe of the *Arcadia*.[39]

The story of Argalus and Parthenia demonstrates the extent to which the narrative is biased against Pyrocles' efforts to resolve the tensions between martial and marital generation. Indeed, with respect to his own love for Philoclea, he also admits even though he defends the love of women as virtuous action consistent with the imperatives of a heroic masculinity, that his love is like a "pestilent fever," and that it has made him into a prisoner and a slave (138). To be sure, the *Arcadia* closes with Pyrocles' marriage to Philoclea and with Musidorus's to Pamela (if not actually "solemni[zed]" [847] or celebrated) at least agreed upon, as well as with a gesture towards the future adventures of their offspring. However, the arbitrariness of the deus ex machina conclusion of Sidney's narrative—Basilius's ostensibly miraculous recovery from what had appeared to be death, and his pardon of the princes who had been captured and were to be executed for their illicit wooing—may be taken as a gauge of the difficulties involved in harmonizing the opposed forms of masculinity and their associated opposed forms of generation.[40] The provisionality of the book's close underscores the intractability of the cultural opposition between battlefield and household.

This intractability also foregrounds the extent to which the work is equivocal in its investment in reproduction. Consider the *Arcadia*'s final sentence, which tells us that the protagonists' projected marriages bear fruit, progeny that occasion a proposed future narrative: "the son of Pyrocles, named Pyrophilus, and Melidora, the fair daughter of Pamela by Musidorus (who even at their birth entered into admirable fortunes) may awake some other spirit to exercise his pen in that wherewith mine is already dulled" (848). The imagined work to come aligns poetry and birth; the generation of offspring constitutes a condition of possibility for more narrative, for more poetic abundance. Having noted this happy marriage, we should immediately qualify the sanguine conjunction of generational activities, the integral coordination Sidney imagines in the future of affinal procreation and the poetic making of golden worlds. Although Sidney claimed to be too tired to go on with his story, out of sheer fatigue yearning for another to carry forward the narrative, he did go back and substantially rework the first three books of what is now known as the *Old Arcadia*. In this revision, rather than pursue the itinerary towards the future opened up through the married reproduction of the Arcadian scions, he went back to his original story; as the text is, the production of children remains offstage, deferred to another moment, delegated to someone else to narrate.[41] I emphasize what might be termed a certain reluctance, or at least lack of interest, by way of pointing out that the conclusion of the *Arcadia* resists the easy collapse of poetic production and married generation. Despite the many voices in the work committed to reproductive responsibility, the narrative locates pleasure elsewhere—in delay, in the play of "fruitless" passion, in the failure of or conflict between ethical forms, in the myriad diversions from governed generation.

"This child I am loth to father"

Perhaps because of these ungoverned pleasures, which cannot be reconciled completely to the designs or strictures of Sidney's *Defence*, the *Arcadia* opens with a disavowal. I think specifically of Sidney's dedicatory letter to his sister, a kind of apotropaic gesture that anticipates and seeks to defuse in advance inevitable criticism of the work. Deprecating "this idle work of mine," Sidney explains that his is "a young head, not so well stayed as I would it were (and shall be when God will) having many many fancies begotten in it, if it had not been in some way delivered, would have grown a monster; and more sorry might I be that they came in than that they gat out" (57). Even though poetic creativity serves as a healthy outlet for the intellectual generation of "fancies," a superabundant product of a mind not "stayed" (as Evans glosses, "governed") as well as it should be, the formulation here renders the literary offspring somehow suspect, the "fancies" themselves the regrettable outpouring of a hyperfecund imagination in danger of turning monstrous.[42] Such reservations lead Sidney to nostalgia for infanticidal severity. "For my part," he writes,

> in very truth (as the cruel fathers among the Greeks were wont to do to the babes they would not foster) I could well find in my heart to cast out in some desert of forgetfulness this child I am loth to father. But you desired me to do it, and your desire to my heart is an absolute commandment. (57)

While the text closes on an imagined linkage between poetic generation and marital reproduction—the future of the narrative depending in part on the procreative activity of the royal scions—it opens by suggesting a deep antithesis between textual production and paternal obligations; Sidney recalls longingly a past moment in which a father's discretion could override the imperative to generate. But for his sister's intervention, Sidney asserts, he would sacrifice his textual child. Mary Herbert's authority at once overrides the infanticidal inclinations Sidney harbors and substitutes for his own lack of "stayed"-ness, his inability to regulate the "fancies" that come into his head.

Sidney's fear centers on his imagination, though it also gestures toward a larger anxiety that humanism does not necessarily secure social order, but works "to promote eloquence at the cost of dissolving conviction."[43] Certainly Sidney's problem with "bastard Poets" (36) was that they possessed neither eloquence nor conviction precisely because they were improperly educated; nevertheless, Sidney's unwanted and unregulated fancies, given the form of a literary work, threaten to align him with the very poets he sought to abject in his *Defence,* those who "delivered . . . much matter, which never was begotten by knowledge" (37). We need not go so far as the *Defence,* though, to locate corollaries to Sidney's anxieties about humanism and humanist pedagogy. His dedicatory letter sets up faint yet perceptible connections to one of the *Arcadia's* most reviled figures, Clinias. The latter is a minion of the king of Arcadia's sister-in-law, Cecropia, who through her henchman seeks to install her son upon the throne of Arcadia:

> This Clinias in his youth had been a scholar so far as to learn rather words than manners, and of words rather plenty than order; and oft had used to be an actor in tragedies, where he had learned (besides a slidingness of language) acquaintance with many passions and to frame his face to bear the figure of them: long used to the eyes and ears of men, and to reckon no fault but shamefastness: in nature a most notable coward, and yet more strangely than rarely venturous in privy practices. (387)

Recalling Mulcaster's concerns broached in the previous chapter, and Samuel Daniel's touched upon at the outset of the present chapter, the depiction of Clinias suggests ways humanist training not only leads to moral groundlessness, but also disrupts the polity. The extremity of the dangers Sidney associates with Clinias may be gauged by the fact that the latter's primary action in the *Arcadia* is stirring up the Enispian revolt, a rebellion of peasants and artisans who attack and very nearly succeed in overthrowing the royal household of Basilius.[44]

Discouraged from killing his literary offspring as many of the Arcadian rebels and eventually Clinias himself were slaughtered, Sidney seeks to prevent association with Clinias-like disorder by drastically limiting the scope of the book's circulation; "it is done only for you, only to you," he tells his sister.[45] At most, he assures himself that the manuscript will be passed around only among a small coterie predisposed towards its author; "if you keep it to yourself," he writes, "or to such friends who will weigh errors in the balance of goodwill, I hope, for the father's sake, it will be pardoned, perchance made much of, though in itself it have deformities." Again he insists, "for severer eyes it is not." Finally, Sidney asserts that the *Arcadia*'s "chief safety shall be the not walking abroad" (57). The litany of efforts to define the proper audience for his text and to delimit the perimeter within which it should move bring into dramatic relief the fact that we have access to the *Arcadia,* and that it was read widely in the century after its initial publication, going into its fourteenth edition in 1725.[46] Sidney is quite clear about his intentions, and I do not consider his request just before his death that the *Arcadia,* among other works, be destroyed merely false piety or obligatory deathbed formality. Sidney did not publish his poetry.

The Sidney we have, and Sidney as he was retrospectively constituted after his death in 1586, is in a very real sense the product of the Countess of Pembroke. Margaret Hannay has shown us the extent to which Mary Herbert worked not only to memorialize her brother, but also to produce him, exercising considerable editorial control, guiding into print the works by which he has come to be known. "As patron, she encouraged works that glorif[ied] Sidney," Hannay writes.[47] "As an editor, she published the works that have established Sidney's literary reputation," including the *Arcadia, The Defence,* and *Astrophil and Stella.*[48] Although the countess was figured as her brother's "phoenix," rendering her in a way his offspring, or at least the most recent form of her brother,[49] she also may be said to have generated Philip, his wishes notwithstanding.

Justifying publication of Sidney's poetry required an active reorientation of his life and work.[50] In spite of Sidney's wishes that his poetry be consigned to oblivion, Sir Fulke Greville defended the works in his biography of Sidney, and justified their usefulness by construing them as exempla for virtuous behavior. Referring to the adventures of the *Arcadia,* Greville argued that "his end in them was not vanishing pleasures alone, but morall Images, and Examples, (as directing threds) to guide every man through the confused Labyrinth of his own desires and life."[51] Exemplarity authorizes the printing and circulation of what even Greville suggests are the morally uncertain vanities of ephemeral pleasure.[52] The purchase of this logic, its privileged status as a way of authorizing cultural production, may be noted in the way Sidney himself served as an exemplar alongside his works. This is the approach of Thomas Moffet in his posthumous biography, *Nobilis* (mentioned briefly above). Moffet underscores the fact that Sidney produced no male children; on his deathbed, according to Moffet, this was the reason Sidney gave for wanting to stay alive. Such a statement is striking for its consistency with Geron's procreative imperative: "About to die, the sick man cried out that life would be welcome to him for the sake of begetting a son and assisting the commonwealth" ("*Filii gignendi et Reipub. augendae*").[53] ("Assisting the commonwealth" seems a rather muted translation of the Latin "augendae"—to enlarge, to make grow, to enrich.) By Moffet's account, the best reason Sidney could come up with to keep on living was to produce a son; the formulation speaks powerfully to the gender differentials structuring the urgency surrounding procreation. As Moffet notes, Sidney already had a daughter; his considerable affection for her notwithstanding, a daughter implicitly does not augment the commonwealth and a father's obligation is to produce a son. The death of Sidney, "he whom all Englishmen had chosen and expected to father another Theseus or Hercules for us and our country" (85), robs England of both hero and heroic progeny. Moffet's text, by describing the ideal noble man, seeks to repair this loss. *Nobilis* is "sent by way of an example to Sidney's most honorable nephew William Herbert" (67); it is offered as a gift to the Countess of Pembroke's son.[54] Moffet elaborates at the close of his text:

> there cannot be praise enough of him whose pattern of life was so marvelous that the last of his days harmonized with the earliest, the mid-period with the beginning and the end, and all with virtue and lettered learning. Therefore do you embrace, cherish, and imitate him. (95)

A life becomes thinkable only in relation to previous lives, becomes narratable only through the conceptual resources available for describing lived being. The effort to shape a life prospectively, though, to make it accord in advance with the dictates of prior examples, can perhaps only disappoint. So far as we know, William Herbert was no Theseus or Hercules. But who could have matched his uncle's glorified example?

To stop here would be to suggest that Sidney's image fails to produce the desired effects simply because the bar was placed too high, and that the reverential image of Sidney's life set up an ideal it could only be possible asymptotically, if at all, to approach. However, just as appeal to the ethical precedent set by Hercules was a fraught gesture, so could the appeal to the life of Sidney produce unforeseen and morally ambiguous effects. Consider the self-portrait of one Gullio, from the anonymously authored *First Part of the Return from Parnassus.* Fatuously responding to sarcastic praise of his capacity for polished speech, the bombastic soldier and fashion-mongering lover expands upon his style:

> Oh Sr, that was my care, to proue a complet gentleman . . . insomuche that I am pointed at for a poet in Pauls church yarde, and in the tilte yarde for a champion. . . . I had in my dayes not vnfitly bene likned to Sr Phillip Sidney, only with this diference, that I had the better legg, and more amiable face. His *Arcadia* was prittie, soe are my sonnetes; he had bene at Paris, I at Padua; he fought, and so dare I; he dyed in the lowe cuntries, and soe I thinke shall I.[55]

Differences notwithstanding, Sidney is the standard against which Gullio is compared, as well as the model of "complet gentleman," poet, and warrior that Gullio exercises his "care" to embody. Sidney's example prompts the creation not of new heroes for the nation, but of ridiculous posers. And the comparison rebounds upon Sidney, whose life and especially death in the "low cuntries" takes on illicit resonance in its subsequent citation. Sidney had a sense of humor, to be sure; even so, it is difficult to imagine that he would have found this portrait all that amusing. Although he took great pleasure in Pyrocles' imitation of Hercules cross-dressed as an Amazon, the deformative imitation of his own image implicates Sidney in the cultivation of the "bastard Poets" he so scorned. Much has been made of Sidney's ideological function, the role his image and life narrative played in consolidating English national manhood well after the Renaissance.[56] Gullio gives us a glimpse of a different story, a kind of counter-exemplarity that underscores the limits on the ability to manage mimetic practices of ethical formation, even as it reminds us of Sidney's own insistence on the pleasures to be derived from imitation gone awry.

CHAPTER THREE

Staging Government

Shakespearean Theater and the Government of Cultural Reproduction

From the very earliest moments of their emergence in the late 1570s, England's popular stages prompted fears that they were multiplying out of control. This was the case not only insofar as some—including at one point Queen Elizabeth and her privy councilors—worried that the structures were growing too numerous and consequently that most should be torn down;[1] it was also the case that the theater's most vocal opponents understood the institution capable of producing unruly hordes of dissolute persons. The anti-theatricalists argued that the theater did more than simply provide a venue for (ominous) multitudes to gather and "recreate themselves."[2] To their minds, England's stages possessed a monstrous fecundity, and thus were responsible for creating numbers of libertines and rogues, idle, disordered, and hence dangerous persons who would violate England's laws, would treasonously betray their monarch, or would give themselves over to sensual abominations and thereby bring down the wrath of God upon a reprobate nation. Stephen Gosson's account of the reproductive effects of the mimetic dynamic at the popular stage, in which audiences imitated the outrages they saw performed by actors, represented (as briefly noted in the previous chapter) an early intervention in an extended polemic against England's theaters.

As a point of reference and point of departure for readings of several plays by Shakespeare, I shall elaborate the ways the controversy around the stage—the complaints sketched here, and the defensive response to them—took up and developed Gosson's and Sidney's claims about the generative effects of poetry. My objective in this chapter is to detail how Shakespeare acknowledges and responds to the issues raised by this debate about the cultural impact of the popular theater. Shakespeare's works, I argue, are imbricated in processes of distinguishing and generating different kinds of persons, as well as of evaluating and attempting to manage the effects these people produced as they coalesce into either feared or valued aggregates. Both in the subject matter of his plays and in the way he characterizes the effects of playing, Shakespeare foregrounds reflection upon the governance of cultural reproduction.

Anti-theatricalist Henry Crosse's *Vertues Common-wealth* offers a place to begin to gauge the sorts of fears associated with stages and play-going, and to view the manner in which they are understood to be dangerously (de)generative. First, from Crosse's perspective, the most telling and most damning characteristic of playhouses is their unholy clientele. Those who attend plays, he argues—"the very scum, rascallitie, and baggage of the people, theeves, cut-purses, shifters, cousoners"—are the very children of Satan.[3] They are "an uncleane generation, and spaune of vipers," a "broode of hell-bred creatures" (Q1r) and their presence at the stage simply proves this reptilian lineage, transparently registers their satanic descent.[4] But the theater does not come under scrutiny only because it attracts such miscreants. Crosse and others understand plays to be a threat because they possess the capacity to transform people into this kind of person. Retrospectively, as it were, the theater realigns personal origins in a way that numbers playgoers among the multitudinous progeny of Hell. Here is Crosse's account of what he insists is typical conduct at the playhouse: "doth it not daily fall out in common experience," he asks, "that there is either fighting, whereof ensueth murther? robbing and theevering, whereof commeth hanging? or spotting the soule with wickednesse, that he becommeth the very sonne of *Beliall?*" (Q1r–Q1v). The self-evidence of the causal links Crosse posits between brawling and murder and between theft and execution seeks to lend an obvious inevitability to the idea that the "he" who perhaps innocently wandered into the audience will be transformed into the offspring of a demon, "the very sonne of Beliall."

These observations confirm that the anti-theatrical polemic puts into play fears about inherently unstable or groundless selves, expressing the worry that playgoers would mimetically deform into what they saw.[5] Crosse's brief description elaborates such concerns into a generative politics of the stage. The retrospective logic underpinning the assertion that the theater makes its viewers demonic offspring invests the theater with a reproductive capacity, accounts it a source for the unsettling multitudes pestering England.[6] This claim about the theater may be compared to Crosse's account of the effects of alehouses: "the surplusage of Ale-houses, especially those that are kept by vnconscionable and irreligious persons, who make no scruple to open their doores to euerie drunken mate, is no small meanes to multiply a swarme of monsters in the Common-wealth" (T2r). Like alehouses, playhouses offer a site of promiscuous contact with dangerous people, contact that effectively produces more dangerous people. Such an understanding of the impact that theaters have on both people and the polity informs Gosson's assertion that the stage is a kind of demonic mother. Plays are, he argues, milk "suckt from the Devilles teate."[7] Philip Stubbes confirms Gosson's point. Whether or not the plays on stage are sacred or profane, "they are quite contrarie to the word of grace, and [are] sucked out of the Devills teates, to nourish us in ydolatrie hethenrie, and sinne."[8] Thomas White, preaching at Paul's Cross, offered to list the sins carried out at the stage, "the monstrous birds that brede in this nest." At the same time he identified the audience as a "multitude that flocketh" to plays.[9] White's avian metaphorics, consistent with Gosson's, Stubbes's, and Crosse's heated vitriol, implies that the stage reproduces, that it generates both sins and sinners, spawns them and spews them out into the commonwealth to work their satanic designs. As White argues, the consequences of this demonic genesis will be dire; indeed, in allowing the abomination of stage playing, England has equaled already the biblical precedent of a polity destroyed because of the failure of every form of government: "the olde world is matched," he writes, "and Sodome overcome."[10]

The claim that the English theater could produce disruptively violent and wicked multitudes did not go unchallenged. Thomas Heywood, one of the few who bothered to intervene in print in behalf of the stage, answered not by denying the theater's fertility, but rather by insisting upon the salutary effects of stage generation.[11] Indeed, according to Heywood, the public stage at its origin was integrally linked to a project of making up people. Heywood pointed to the tactics of Romulus, founder of Rome, as evidence of the benefits of the theater to the commonweal. Once Romulus had located a suitable place to build "so famous a Citty," he was faced with a dilemma:

> how to people the same, his traine wholly consisting of Souldiers, who without company of women (they not having any in their Army) could not multiply; but so were likely that their immortall fames should dye issueless with their mortall bodies. Thus therefore *Romulus* devised; After a parle and attonement made with the neighbor Nations, hee built a Theater, plaine, according to the time; yet large, fit for the entertainement of so great an Assembly, and these were they whose famous issue peopled the Cittie of *Rome,* which in after ages grew to such a height . . . to which all the discovered kingdomes of the earth after became tributaries.[12]

According to Heywood, the theater solved a major problem for the Romans, how to extend into the future the accomplishments of the warriors who founded the city. Heywood's narrative transforms the rape of the Sabine women into a policy of national generation of "issue," and aligns the stage with a program of biological reproduction. The theater makes up for the incapacities of the "mortall bodies" of the military men, and thereby enables Rome to flourish into an empire.[13]

In his account of the contemporary function of the stage, Heywood develops and modifies this originary association between the theater and procreation. Specifically, Heywood's defense of playing understands the theater's effects in terms that immediately recall Sidney's defense of poetry as a means of pedagogically making men. In contrast to the antitheatricalists who viewed the stage as a site of "diabolical pedagogy,"[14] Heywood invests the contemporary theater with the capacity for properly educating its viewers, an instructive dynamic that generates exemplary subjects for England.[15] Heywood appeals to the precedent of the staged education of Hercules:

> [T]here was in his nonage presented unto him by his Tutor in the fashion of a History, acted by the choyse of the nobility of Greece, the worthy and memorable acts of his father *Iupiter.* Which being personated with lively and well-spirited action, wrought such impression in his noble thoughts, that in meere emulation of his fathers valor (not at the behest of his stepdame *Juno*) he perform'd his twelve labors: him valiant *Theseus* followed, and *Achilles, Theseus.* (B3r)

Rather than account Hercules's labors a punishment by Juno—as was conventional—Heywood recasts them as filial acts of mimetic valor. Like Sidney in his account of poetry as a "speaking picture" capable of transforming representations into regulated behavior, Heywood argues that the stage presented to its audience classical exemplars for emulation. Thomas Lodge explicitly invokes the Aristotelian rationale for this practice, in his defense of playing: "men are greatly delighted with imitation," and thus it is "good to bring those things on stage, that were altogether tending to vertue."[16] Crosse, though among those who lamented the putative effects of stage education as it was practiced (P4v), nonetheless rehearsed the argument of the theater's defenders: "when as the comely deedes of good men are feelingly brought to remembrance, it cannot but move other to imitate the like goodnesse" (P3v). The people enjoy the depiction of virtue, and that very delight to repeat those things they see represented. As Heywood illustrates, those who insisted upon the stage's merits understood plays as enabling just such a formative repetition of ideals in the theater, a presentation of the finest examples of men and women from biblical, classical, and English antiquity that would constitute well-governed members of families, of churches, of cities, and of the realm.

In Heywood's argument, moreover, the imitation of classical exemplars does not simply supplement paternity but acts as an alternative form of paternity, a self-sufficient form of producing ideal men. According to Heywood, Aristotle followed the precedent of Hercules's theatrical education, and staged before Alexander the exploits of Achilles. So moved was the student by the performance, Heywood argues, "that all his succeeding actions were meerly shaped after that patterne, and it may be imagined had *Achilles* never lived, *Alexander* had never conquered the whole world" (B3r). After the fashion of Sidney's contention that by providing ideals for virtuous action poetry could "make many Cyrusses," Heywood argues that Alexander was Alexander only by virtue of his mimetic education, his insertion into a lineage of ideal men through a practice of theatrical imitation.[17] The generational dynamic here, in which Achilles is used theatrically to produce Alexander, pointedly answers the specter of monstrous fecundity advanced by the anti-theatricalists. Heywood at once maintains and reworks the use to which Romulus was said to have put the theater, in that Heywood's ideal accomplishes the objective of producing persons, though it imagines a form of generation that seems to require no women, indeed, that is presented as if entirely removed from biological reproduction.

The discussion thus far has sought to demonstrate how the theatrical polemic hinged on a shared understanding of the stage as generative. On one hand, those who defended the theater insisted on its capacity for making exemplary rulers and for peopling the nation with well-governed persons. On the other, the stage's opponents understood it to be a form of cultural activity that effectively produced unruly numbers, a reptilian spawn of ungoverned multitudes who threatened to destroy the nation. While we might imagine that Shakespeare would simply side with Heywood against those who attacked the popular theater, his work undertakes a more complex engagement than simple endorsement or affirmation of one position within the polemic. I shall argue that in *Love's Labor's Lost,* the plays of the Henriad, and *The Life of King Henry the Eighth,* Shakespeare, rather than take sides in the debate, examines its basic terms. Moreover, in these plays he works both to exploit and to resolve the tensions between the opposed accounts of the stage as producing either a demonic generation of destructive multitudes or the multiplication of ideal persons.

The readings to follow highlight a number of spaces within which or in relation to which generation takes place—schools and academies, battlefields, courts, nations. In line with my approach in this book, rather than suggest that these sites are bound together as commensurable elements within a juridical apparatus of sovereignty, I argue that the plays discussed specify and address the relations between relatively autonomous domains of governmental activity. Of particular interest for Shakespeare is the household—and its relation to the stage, frequently constituted as a kind of domestic space (namely, in the frequent reference to it as a "playhouse"). The anti-theatricalists understand domestic economies as absolutely opposed to the popular stage, as placed at considerable risk by the demonic ministrations of the theaters. Heywood's assertion that theatrical activity offered a technique for making good subjects responded to the argument that playing assaulted households, understood to be the governmental foundation of the community. Gosson, for example, maintained that playhouses propagated "a mischief that may privately breake into every mans house."[18] Thomas White, in the sermon referenced earlier, anticipated Gosson's anxieties; according to White, the assault of the stage went directly to the heart of the household, destabilizing the subjects that constituted it: "[m]any a man hath the leuder wife, and many a wife the shrewder husband by it . . . Wherefore if thou be a father, thou losest thy child: if thou be a maister thou losest thy seruaunt" (197).[19] Shakespeare implicitly answers these assertions in a number of ways, both in his thematic treatment of domestic economies and in the various inductions, epilogues, and choruses, moments in which an actor speaks directly to the audience gathered at the playhouse.[20] During these liminal moments, Shakespeare reflects upon the relation of the stage to its audience and to society at large, and specifies his understanding of the governmental and reproductive impact of theatrical activity.

Love's Labor's Lost: Generating "Oeconomy"

Of Shakespeare's plays, *Love's Labor's Lost* is among the most concerned with the effects and limits of humanist practice. It comes as no surprise, then, that from its opening moments the play engages the issues broached in the polemic surrounding the theater, specifically the claims and concerns about governed and ungoverned generation. The play begins with the King of Navarre founding a "little academe," whose members will agree to undertake a program of austere living for three years.[21] In contrast to the dangerously ungoverned persons putatively generated by and on the stage, Navarre, in his dedication to the study of "living art" (I.1.14), seeks to produce a perfectly regulated form of masculinity. The man he seeks to institute is one to whom desire and affection constitute objects of reflection and targets of a military intervention, one who wages war against the world and against himself through submission to a strictly governed routine of fasting, loss of sleep, and removal from women.[22] Here, Navarre describes the rationale for submitting to his proposed regimen and projects the benefits from such ascesis:

> Let fame, that all hunt after in their lives,
> Live regist'red upon our brazen tombs
> And then grace us in the disgrace of death;
> When, spite of cormorant devouring Time,
> Th' endeavor of this present breath may buy
> That honor which shall bate his scythe's keen edge
> And make us heirs of all eternity.
> Therefore, brave conquerors—for so you are
> That war against your own affections
> And the huge army of the world's desires—
> Our late edict shall strongly stand in force:
> Navarre shall be the wonder of the world.
>
> (I.i.1–12)

At the outset, Navarre describes his three-year program as a morbid inscription, one shoring up "grace" against "disgrace," ensuring that his men's mortal remains will remain legible as "fame"—a kind of estate planning, of working out in advance what will be carved on their headstones. But Navarre's speech, as it continues, reworks this ideal, shifts the focus from a writing that cannot be erased to an active and pedagogically regimented endeavor through which the men can circumvent the necessity of "disgrace" and indefinitely forestall the ravages of time. Rigorous study purchases "honor," enables the king and his men to overcome "cormorant devouring Time" and to extend the austere and learned self into perpetuity. As Longaville notes in affirmation of the king's plan, the program of studious austerity directs appetite into an acceptable, noncorruptible form: "The mind shall banquet though the body pine," he asserts, explaining that "Fat paunches have lean pates, and dainty bits / Make rich the ribs, but bankrout quite the wits" (I.i.25–27). Longaville establishes the opposition between "paunch" and "pate" to render the latter an appropriate site at once of consumption and of savings, and constitutes learning as an allowed form of indulgence, a "banquet" that does not "bankrout."[23] The consumptive expenditure upon learning provides an absolute return, represents an indulgence that allows for no surfeit, or a surfeit that in fact overcomes waste and decay. As the king insists, he and his men, rather than be the food of time, either will be the patrimony of all following generations (all those to come will inherit their example of rigorous ascesis) or will exist outside of time, inheriting all the treasures of eternity in the form of knowledge. Through their proposed ascetic achievements, the men imagine, they effectively will extend themselves into a perpetual future, achieving a kind of immortality.[24]

It would be difficult to imagine a more expansive, or for that matter more aggrandizing, statement of the ambitions of humanist education. Such objectives notwithstanding, much of the humor of the play derives from the speed with which Navarre's plan goes awry and the nobles forsake their oath of radical continence to begin wooing women. The problem, though, is not simply one of failed implementation; the proposed life of study and strenuous self-regulation is fraught in its very design. Navarre's vision contrasts sharply with the emphasis upon humanism as an institution, a specialized knowledge and a set of practices oriented towards the well-being of the commonwealth (as noted in the first chapter), and implicitly informing Heywood's defense of the stage. Rather than active engagement with the world, the regimen of learning that Navarre outlines represents a Prospero-like withdrawal from the world. Rather than make the nobles better able to govern others, their efforts at extreme self-government render them unable to conduct the business of the realm. The play underscores this fact by forcing the men almost immediately to violate the terms of Navarre's "edict" in order to meet the King of France's daughter, who has arrived on a diplomatic mission to negotiate disputed territorial claims. Since Navarre establishes his academy through the violent exclusion of women, who will lose their tongues if they come within a mile of court (I.i.119–23), the arrival of the French embassy places the king and his men in an intractable double bind. At their first meeting, the Princess identifies the impasse confronting the king: "I hear your Grace hath sworn out housekeeping," she informs him, "'Tis deadly sin to keep that oath, my lord, / And sin to break it" (II.i.103–5). Alfred Harbage's editorial gloss on "housekeeping" (with which numerous editors concur) is no doubt correct; Navarre's program rejects "hospitality" (II.i.103n) in ungraciously forbidding the women to approach the court, and thus requiring that they be entertained and lodged in the outlying fields. Such a reading underscores that whatever Navarre does, turn away the women or invite them in, he violates either the demands of "gentility" (I.i.126), as Berowne has it, or the dictates of his own oath.

Although Harbage's reading is no doubt correct, it does not exhaust the potential implications of the Princess's response to the "academe"; "house-keeping" has a more focused contemporary sense of "oeconomy," the government of a household.[25] Read with this definition in mind, the Princess's observation not only draws attention to the governmental implications of Navarre's academy—a rejection of domestic economy in turn associated with political incapacity—but also opens the door to a consideration of the relation between the noblemen's actions and the anxieties raised about the destabilizing effects of the popular stage. A discussion of the household as a privileged locus for governance, especially for governing reproduction, in early modern England will help prepare for a fuller consideration of the generative implications of the men's actions, and will also help clarify how these actions bear upon Shakespeare's response to the theatrical polemic.[26]

While the focus on the family is hardly new in Renaissance scholarship, the point pursued here stands in tension with the dominant critical approach to understanding the place and effects of early modern domestic economy, a criticism marked by scrutiny of the role of the "traffic in women" in the production and reproduction of relations among men. I refer here specifically to the critical opportunities opened up through the groundbreaking work of Gayle Rubin.[27] Her anthropological framework provides a supple approach for reading gender dynamics in many of Shakespeare's works, and underscores the almost pervasive concern in them with the disposition of daughters, or with assaults upon a father's right to marry off daughters as he sees fit. However, Karen Newman has recently voiced reservations about this approach by drawing attention to the dangers of subsuming all gender relations within "'the traffic in women' paradigm," which risks a critical reduction of all gender relations to those of objectification and exchange.[28] In her words, "[w]oman-as-object is only one dimension of the force field that figures a sex/gender system" (49). To be sure, the discursive constitution of "oeconomic" discipline acknowledges a father's responsibility to marry off his daughters well. However, following Newman's lead, we can note that within the discursive specification of household government, the exchange of women does not constitute the exclusive horizon or even a primary focus guiding the imperative to describe and secure the right government of the nation's households. If this form of government instituted various status differentials, or produced and policed a range of invidious hierarchies, primarily ensuring the superior cultural authority of men (which it did), it was not simply "patriarchal" in the biblical sense of a father standing above and outside of his family, disposing of them according to arbitrary whims. "Oeconomy" placed emphasis upon the submission of all members of the household to relations of mutual obligation and a discipline of regulated behavior. Indeed, as a condition of his position of authority in the household, the husband himself was required to provide an ideal of self-regulation for the rest of the family; he subordinated himself to the demands of his estate through a series of carefully defined relationships to his wife, his children, and his servants, stewarding them in conjunction with his spouse, working within a more or less carefully specified division of responsibilities to augment the household's stock.[29] As one R. Cleaver wrote in 1598, "The dutie of a husband, is to get goods: and of the wife, to gather them togither, and save them. The dutie of the husband is, to travell abroad to seeke living, and the wives dutie is to keepe the house. The dutie of the husband is, to get money and provision: and of the wives, not vainely to spend it."[30] A father had an obligation to both past and future generations; "hee is no more Lord of his goods, but only a Tutor," according to the English translation of Peter de la Primaudaye's *French Academie,* "and that if they should be wasted or lost through his negligence, he were no lesse faultie than hee that should steale them."[31] To liken a father to a pedagogue is, within a traditional dispensation, to situate the father as a functional element of the household, as opposed to an authority external to it. Indeed, within the strictures of "oeconomicall science,"[32] all members of the household were, albeit differentially, subject to a regimen of acquisition, savings, and expenditure, a regimen oriented toward preventing waste, ensuring a frugal mode of existence, and extending the family estate into the future.[33]

The array of governmental activities constitutive of a domestic economy included the strict regulation of eros. In part, this was a matter of ensuring the proper reproduction of children, one of the key means through which households were linked to other governmental domains. Consistent with the sense of reproductive obligation advanced by Sidney's Geron, the well-governed household produced more souls for the glorification of the church and God, populated the godly commonwealth with pious numbers, and thus contributed to the strength and future viability of church and nation. However, to fulfill these functions, simply complying with God's first instruction to humans, "Be fruitful, and multiply" (Genesis 1:28), was not enough. According to Cleaver, the marital relationship required a pious vigilance. "[M]arriage is not a madde and dissolute estate," he warned, pointing to the ever-present potential for "immoderate, intemperate, or excessive lust" (155). Consequently:

> Christians therefore must knowe, that when men and women raging with boyling lust, meete togither as bruite beastes, having no other respects, than to satisfie their own carnall concupisence, when they make no conscience to sanctifie the marriage bedde with prayer, when they have no care to increase the church of Christ, and the number of the elect, it is the just judgement of God, to send them eyther monsters, or naturall fooles, or else such as having good gifts of the minde, and wel proportioned bodies, are most wicked, gracelesse, and prophane persons. (302)

Within the domain of "oeconomy," the mere fact of monogamous marriage was no guarantee of the propriety of the relationship. Erotic congress must be the object of solemn reflection, and both partners must contain their desires, orient them strictly to the godly ends of increase.[34]

It is important to keep in mind that this cultural investment in the household does not manifest the operations of a transhistorical heterosexuality. Instead, the point is that domestic economy relied upon and sought to guarantee its capacity for governing desire. On one hand, household bonds of respect and obedience required a propagation and management of an intensely erotic attraction. T. K. (perhaps Thomas Kyd), for example, compares the relation between servant and master to that between Petrarch and Laura.[35] On the other hand, in addition to the regimen of mutual self-government described in the previous paragraph, "good housekeeping" required a constant effort to anticipate and foreclose the libertinage that might break out anywhere in the household and that might disrupt its proper operation. The godly wife, for example, "must have a diligent eye to the behavior of her servants, what meetings and greetings, what tickings and toylings, and what wordes and countenances, there be betweene men and maides, least such matters beeing neglected, there follow wantonnesse."[36] The governmental regime of "house-keeping," the differential subjectivation of men and women through and within an ethical discipline of managing waste, preventing loss, and saving and increasing the family stock countered the pervasive danger of illicit congress with an effort to institute a comprehensive government of eros. This erotic regulation, as one element of a coordinated ensemble of practices within domestic economy, in turn sought to guarantee the proper generation of ethically modulated persons.

We are now prepared to return to Navarre's statement and to qualify somewhat the Princess's assertion that the king "hath sworn out housekeeping." Given the description of household government advanced immediately above, the king's imagined ascetic regimen may be said not so much to displace or to oppose domestic economy (the Princess's critical acumen notwithstanding) as to reconfigure it. Where one primary responsibility of parents within a household was to see to the proper education of the children, and thereby to secure the extension of their estate into the future, Navarre enlists learning as a superior form of governing the royal person and his noble companions so that they need not generate through marriage. Navarre's ideal of austere scholarship defines a non-wasting expenditure of effort, a form of activity that overcomes the absolute wasting consumption of time and death, and yields an absolute return: Navarre and his men, rather than generating heirs, become "heirs of all eternity." As a means of removing himself from the ravages of a voracious temporality, "cormorant devouring Time," Navarre takes literally here an equation of learning with treasure, and conflates it with the "oeconomic" claim that learning will secure the family estate into the future by ensuring the virtue of the children.[37] Instead of generating governed heirs through learning, Navarre posits, he and his men will become heirs of history through their imagined ascetic achievements. Thus they plan to extend themselves into futurity, and aggrandize to themselves an absolute return of allowed wealth, gaining the treasures of knowledge and thereby making themselves immortal.

As I have suggested, this reconfigured "oeconomy" is found wanting insofar as the austere study of "living art" represents a withdrawal from the world, prevents the men from doing the job of running the country—a situation the play exacerbates by making diplomatic negotiations and congress with women the same thing. We can also note that Navarre's ideal of self-sufficient autogeneration does not absolutely exclude women: at least one woman, Jacquenetta, is required for the operation of the royal household. When apprehended for being caught *in flagrante delicto* with Costard and subsequently remanded into the custody of Dull, she is characterized as "allowed for the day-woman" (I.ii.121–22). It may be argued that the king implicitly justifies Jacquenetta's presence at court by simply not accounting her a woman—that is, in his terms, by not even considering her an appropriate object of desire, because of her social status. Even so, the necessity of her presence seems more than simply dramatic convenience (she will later be wooed by the Spanish traveller, Armado); Harbage's clarification—"approved as the dairy-maid" (I.ii.121–122n)—begins to suggest the way Navarre's reconfigured "oeconomy" does not entirely overcome the need for the more mundane type of housekeeping. Furthermore, with respect to the "day-woman," Navarre's ideal fails as a means of governing generation insofar as the noblemen's war against their affections and the world's desires has no effect on Jacquenetta, whose pregnancy at the end of the play disrupts the royal entertainments. Where domestic government ideally sought to anticipate and foreclose the possibility for wantonness, and required a disciplined policing of all members of the household, Jacquenetta moves beyond the studied regimen of self-government instituted at court, constituting both one of its conditions of possibility and one of its limits.

The disruptive effect of the news of Jacquenetta's pregnancy might suggest an opposition between her unlicensed, extramarital procreation, and Navarre's proposed regimen of absolute self-government. This is not entirely the case. In fact, the king allows a certain form of ungoverned generation at court, as seen specifically in the scope afforded Armado, admitted to the otherwise rigorous academy for purposes of entertainment. Navarre describes this knight, known for his ridiculously pretentious use of language, as a "child of fancy" (I.i.167). Taking the genitive in both its objective and subjective senses, this account alternatively infantilizes Armado because of his outrageous speech, and provides a genealogy of the Spaniard, treating him as the offspring of a psychological faculty. Armado, furthermore, is treasured at court for his "high-born words" (I.i.169), a characterization that comprehends the Spaniard's copious effusion of language (delightful to Navarre in spite of, or perhaps because of, the Spaniard's lack of concern with anything like veracity) as a form of masculine generation. These are the very terms with which the pedant, Holofernes, describes his extemporaneous poetry, produced to commemorate the Princess's success at hunting. The ability to turn lines of verse is a "gift," he informs Nathaniel: "These are begot in the ventricle of memory, nourished in the womb of pia mater, and delivered upon the mellowing of occasion" (IV.ii.63; 66–68).

Although Navarre explicitly construes this type of intellectual generation of verbiage as an appropriate recreation for the academy, a licit pastime consistent with a regimen of austerity, the play also gives voice to reservations about this production, suggests that such generation exceeds or undermines the king's objectives of self-government, to say nothing of the governmental parameters of "house-keeping." The Princess, again, points the way. Her reaction to Armado after first hearing him speak is to wonder "Doth this man serve God?" When asked to explain, she replies, "'A speaks not like a man of God his making" (V.ii.522–24), an assertion that reinforces the notion that Armado has a curious lineage, even as it calls the moral valences of this genealogy into question. The play elaborates this concern, the idea that there might be something unsanctified in Armado's origins, in the person of Holofernes, whose cerebral birth is both superabundant and licentious. The poem in question plays on names for deer, transforms a "pricket" into a "sorel" made "sore" by the "prick" of an arrow, and then multiplies this prick into a hundred sores with Roman numerals: "l to sore makes fifty sores—O sore l! / Of one sore I an hundred make by adding but one more l" (IV.ii.58–59), Holofernes boasts. This from "a good member of the commonwealth" (IV.ii.73), as Nathaniel would have it, a prick who multiplies pricks and sores. The pun calls attention to the distance between Holofernes's employment of his learning and the central place occupied by humanist education within commonwealth discourse. Mulcaster (in fact, a prime candidate for the historical figure Shakespeare parodies here) insisted on the vital connection between humanist education and the commonweal's stability and health; Holofernes relates to the polity somewhat differently. Nathaniel, heaping fawning accolades upon Holofernes for his extemporaneous performance, extols the value of an education at the hands of the pedant:

> NATHANIEL: Sir, I praise the Lord for you, and so may my parishoners; for their sons are well tutored by you, and their daughters profit very greatly under you. You are a good member of the commonwealth.
>
> HOLOFERNES: Mehercle, if their sons be ingenious, they shall want no instruction; if their daughters be capable, I will put it to them.
>
> (IV.ii.70–77)

Nathaniel's praise of Holofernes associates the masculine generation of wit with a wantonness inconsistent with either the ideal of ethical restraint to which the king and his men subscribe at the opening of the play or the governmental ideal of domestic economy.[38] That the Princess derisively refers to Navarre and his men as a "breed of wits" at once aligns them with the type of generation represented by Armado and Holofernes, and dismisses them as licentious and incontinent, at the very least unable to keep to the dictates of their "continent canon" (I.i.248). This is, in fact, a critique *internal* to the king's academy. When Longaville characterizes Berowne's studied sophistry against the ethical benefits of study as an unproductive culture ("He weeds the corn, and still lets grow the weeding"), Berowne responds in doggerel, "The spring is near, when green geese are a-breeding" (I.i.96–97). Although the verse is offered as mocking nonsense, it also functions to recast the generational pretensions of the court as an illicit eros. As Patricia Parker points out, "goose" was slang for a prostitute,[39] and insofar as we might assume that the production of bastards transgresses the proprieties and objectives of marital alliance, the comprehension of Navarre's ethical ideal as meretricious congress suggests that the noblemen's studious ascesis constitutes a degenerate form of generation.

Even as he accounts the proposed academic project illicitly fecund, Berowne advances exactly the opposite view, that the planned three years study and regimen of austerity is not fecund at all. Arguing *in utramque partem,* Berowne counters the claim that the regimen of learning will secure the proposed ethically modulated persons against the ravenous exactions of time, will produce men who last eternally, by identifying the imagined program as "barren tasks" (I.i.47), more properly reserved for children. Boyet elaborates such a viewpoint; arriving with news to the French embassy of the new regime at court, he states that the royal household has been either (in the first quarto) "unpeeled" or (in other quartos and the first folio) "unpeopled" (II.i.88).[40] The textual crux here serendipitously underscores Boyet's implicit account of the king's regimen as a household government that lays waste, depopulating where domestic economy has as a primary objective generating numbers. Where Navarre seeks to defend his generational ideal from Berowne's mocking criticism, characterizing him as "an envious sneaping frost / That bites the first-born infants of the spring" (I.i.100–1), Berowne insists that their pedagogic creation produces nothing more than a laughable, vain, and ill-conceived "abortive birth" (I.i.104).

The play seeks to resolve the tensions here—between the commitment academically to generate an ascetic form of personhood that does not need to reproduce via women, and a hyperfecund learning that is nonetheless "barren" or "abortive"—by redefining the proper object of study. In the face of an intractable double bind, when Navarre and his men become infatuated with the Princess and her ladies-in-waiting, despite their oath not to do so, Berowne solves the impasse by realigning the relation between study and love for women. Investing the latter with a natural etiology ("We cannot cross the cause why we were born" [IV.iii.213], he asserts), he shifts study from a means to contain desire and to produce an ethically modulated subject, to a practice that takes women as its object and the generation of heirs as its aim (IV.iii.312–60). Berowne appeals to the force of generation voiced by Benedick in *Much Ado about Nothing,* who, at the moment he buys into the practical joke that would have him fall in love with Beatrice, resigns himself to the fact that "the world must be peopled" (II.iii.221);[41] the generation of offspring takes on the modal force of a moral imperative, unquestioned, axiomatic, self-evident. Men were born to woo and wed women; men woo and wed women to beget children and, in the ideal, to produce male heirs. This is the burden of the punning in Berowne's call to arms:

> Advance your standards, and upon them, lords!
> Pell-mell, down with them! But be first advised,
> In conflict that you get the sun of them.
> (IV.iii.362–364)

Berowne quibbles here on military strategy, and onomastically joins the task of taking women "down" with getting sons.[42] By proposing an erotic military assault on the women, Berowne conceptually recovers the nobles' ideal of military masculinity by reorganizing and shifting the terrain of battle from one's self, one's affects, and the world's desires, to women, and the goal from becoming heirs to generating them.[43]

This reorientation suggests that the men eventually answer the Princess's observation that Navarre has "sworn out house-keeping" by "swearing *in* house-keeping," or at least by attempting to. For our purposes, it is important to note that this provisional solution engages the concerns raised by the anti-theatricalists, to the extent that the men seek to woo the women theatrically. In contrast to the specter of stages destroying domestic economies, Navarre and his men seek to establish stages initially by becoming actors and subsequently by becoming patrons of the stage. Of course, this strategy fails, because the women successfully resist the affinal and reproductive designs of the men. The women do so, moreover, by pursuing an explicitly antigenerational strategy. "Their form confounded," the Princess argues, upon hearing of the impending play commissioned for them by Navarre, "makes most form in mirth / When great things laboring perish in their birth" (V.ii.517–18). "A right description of our sport, my lord," (V.ii.519), is Berowne's response. Although the immediate reference here is to the risible production of "The Nine Worthies" offered by Costard, Nathaniel, Holofernes, Moth, and Armado, the ambiguity of the Princess's "great things" and Berowne's "our sport" acknowledges the applicability of the antigenerational strategy to the designs of the men themselves. Accordingly, the principle outlined here is that of the play framing the spectacle of the worthies, insofar as *Love's Labor's Lost* is without comedic closure, and thus itself represents, with respect to the generic expectations "confounded" by the absence of a wedding, an "abortive birth."[44]

We might take this analysis a step further. That is, the theater that takes place in *Love's Labor's Lost* does not simply fail to secure the nobles' marriages and thereby guarantee the governed generation of heirs and rulers. The theatrical activity in the play, as well as the play itself, resists the association of theater with governed generation. The Nine Worthies as presented by Holofernes, Armado and the rest, hardly can be said to image forth paradigms for emulation; the characters appear ludicrous even before the humiliation they receive from the nobles. For that matter, Navarre and his men attempt a theatrical display that makes no effort to be exemplary. Dressed up as "Muscovites or Russians" (5.2.121) and attended by "Blackamoors" (5.2.157, s.d.), they in fact appear decidedly unexemplary, at least from the perspective of someone like Heywood. The plays within the play seem actively to thwart the project of theatrical generation—do not in their form reinforce social relations but stand removed from such a project, working at cross-purposes to the effort to secure marriage and "house-keeping." The closing lines of *Love's Labor's Lost* confirm and specify the manner in which this is also the case for the play as a whole. The closing debate between Winter and Spring insists upon an implicit disjunction between the theater and domestic economy. The refrain of Spring, the song of the "Cuckoo," "O, word of fear, / Unpleasing to a married ear!" (V.ii.890–91 and 899–900), raises the specter of female marital infidelity, and characterizes domestic government as unable to contain a putatively voracious female desire, a libertinage that thwarts the objectives of household generation.[45] Accordingly, the activities of women in the household are linked to the promiscuous "tread"-ing of birds, as well as a deceptive construction of purity:

> When turtles tread, and rooks, and daws,
>   And maidens bleach their summer smocks,
> The cuckoo then, on every tree,
> Mocks married men.
>
> (V.ii.894–97)

Winter's response answers this picture of a domestic government thwarted by the naturalized infidelities of women by situating the household within a frigid and barren landscape, imagining a house covered with "icicles" (V.ii.901) to which "milk comes frozen home in pail" (V.ii.904). The domestic scene is one presided over by "greasy Joan" who "doth keel the pot" (V.ii.909 and 918), a frozen, anonymous, workaday world of drudgery. My emphasis here qualifies somewhat the idea that "*Love's Labor's Lost* concludes with a song . . . suggesting the alliance among fruitful sexual love, the predictably recurring cycle of the seasons, and the ongoing life of society."[46] Certainly Shakespeare posits a relation between these things, but rather than on "alliance," the emphasis seems to be on antagonism. The closing debate characterizes the household in decidedly unsympathetic terms, and posits an incommensurability between the theater and the governmental domain of the oeconomy. (Such an implication is reinforced by the act of partitioning that ends the first folio version of the play, Armado's "You, that way: we, this way" [V.ii.920], an imperative plausibly addressed to the audience.) The antitheatricalists understood the popular stage to be a cultural site that would destroy England's households. *Love's Labor's Lost* answers this view by deflating the cultural investment in "house-keeping," and, at the same time, by finding both pleasure in the specter of domestic government's failure and a sense of superiority to its chilling monotony.

The Henriad: Governing the Generations of Henry

The distinction of the theater from an ineffective and monotonously harsh domestic economy, attempted at the close of *Love's Labor's Lost,* represents at most a provisional conclusion. As I shall elaborate through a discussion of the Henriad, the debate of Winter and Spring locates the presence of an abiding problematic, rather than final answer, to the questions raised in the play and in the polemic around the stage. The Henriad takes up the tensions considered above, extending and reworking the interrogation of the relationship between the theater and domestic economy, especially in terms of the capacity of these cultural sites to govern generation. To begin to see the way this cluster of plays reorganizes the discursive terrain, we can note that *The Second Part of King Henry the Fourth* explicitly formulates the stage as an "oeconomy," an unregulated *oikos* misgoverned by the figure of Rumor. In the induction, Rumor describes himself as a "pipe" (*2H4* Ind.15) that anyone can play, even "the blunt monster with uncounted heads, / The still-discordant wavering multitude" (18–19). A rhetorical question follows, which shifts figurative registers and at once voices and wryly embraces anti-theatrical bromides; "But what need I thus / My well-known body to anatomize / Among my household" (*2H4* Ind.20–22), Rumor asks. Rumor constitutes the theater as a counter-oeconomy, makes the playhouse a home by casting himself as the misgovernor of a multitudinous domestic space—dissolute, volatile, and monstrous. Consistent with the anti-theatrical fear of the stage's fecundity, the text allusively suggests how Rumor possesses a capacity to produce destabilizing issue. When Henry IV worries that his opposition has mustered as many as fifty thousand troops, Warwick responds skeptically. "It cannot be," he asserts. "Rumor doth double, like voice and echo, / The numbers of the feared" (III.i.96–98). Warwick's confidence notwithstanding, Rumor accomplishes an empty multiplication of numbers, a generation of persons perhaps no more substantial than an "echo," but no less a threat to the epistemological certainty upon which the king seeks to evaluate strategy.

The placement of Rumor in both the playhouse and on the battlefield provides an interesting resonance with the anti-theatrical view of the stage as a dangerously generative entity, but at this point the allusive connection is merely suggestive. The reading of the Henriad that I offer seeks to specify more precisely how this series of plays engages not only the theatrical polemic but also the dynamics of governing cultural reproduction, more generally. The shift in focus from *Love's Labor's Lost*'s thwarted comedic plot (in which geopolitical relations are subordinated to, even as they condition, erotic dalliance) to the genre of the history play and its sometimes more expansive scope of action, enables us to examine how questions of ethical formation, domestic economy, and generativity play out on an international stage. The second tetralogy—*Richard II*, the two *Henry IV* plays, and *Henry V*—displays a preoccupation with the making and unmaking of men, as well as with how such efforts may be, or fail to be, governed, and how these dynamics impact the fate of nations. The primary focus of this section will be upon Henry V as both the product of a dangerous generation and a character who himself possesses a monstrous fecundity. Discussing Henry in these terms makes it possible to detail the Henriad's engagement with England's geopolitical concerns about cultural reproduction, specifically in Ireland, in the moment of this series' composition and performance. Such an approach also helps us gauge how Shakespeare reworks and elaborates the view advanced at the end of *Love's Labor's Lost* with regard to the relation between the popular stage and other sectors of the commonwealth.

For reasons that will become apparent shortly, I wish to draw attention to Falstaff, a figure central to the action and governmental dynamics of the second tetralogy. His relevance follows from not only his status as Hal's surrogate father but also his similarity to Rumor. For starters, we might speculate that, of all the characters in the Henriad, perhaps Falstaff would be most enthused by the vision of group sex hinted at in Rumor's opening speech, the fellatial image of a theater full of people blowing his "pipe." The connections, though, are even more immediate. Not only is Falstaff judged worthy of a position in Rumor's household (the Hostess watching him play Henry IV counts him as good as "one of these harlotry players" [*1H4* II.iv.377–78]), he also embodies Rumor: just as the latter arrives on stage "painted full of tongues" (*2H4* Ind.1 s.d.), Falstaff, commenting on the recognizability of his portly figure, claims to "have a whole school of tongues in this belly of mine" (*2H4* IV.iii.18–19), all speaking his name. Furthermore, like Rumor, Falstaff possesses a disruptive fecundity. Consider his version of the banditry at Gad's Hill, the highway robbery waylaid by Prince Hal and Poins, who, as a prank, disguised themselves and attacked Falstaff, stealing his ill-gotten money. Subsequently accusing Prince Hal of cowardice for not showing up to help in the plot, Falstaff exaggerates the size of the contingent that beset him after taking the money from the travelers. The two persons he fought with, Hal and Poins, increase in the retelling to "a hundred" (*1H4* II.iv.152). Just as Rumor spreads falsehood and generates insubstantial numbers, Falstaff produces insubstantial men. "These lies," the prince asserts, "are like their father that begets them—gross as a mountain, open, palpable" (214–15). This fecundity parallels Rumor's ability to produce nonexistent soldiers. On a search, in *The Second Part of King Henry the Fourth,* for a few good men, or at least "sufficient men" (*2H4* III.ii.90) for the king's defense, Falstaff alludes to the fact that he has filled his troop list with made-up names so that he can collect the extra wages for himself. Presented with one "Shadow," Falstaff determines that he will do for battle, and orders his assistant to "Prick him," adding that "we have a number of shadows to fill up the muster-book" (*2H4* III.ii.130–31). Administrative fictions, the "shadow" numbers are imaginary persons generated by Falstaff as a means to siphon off and batten upon the king's resources.[47] Falstaff's similarity to Rumor also encompasses the latter's position at the head of a riotous domestic economy. As a paternal influence on Hal, Falstaff represents for many in the play an abusive and profoundly destabilizing fatherhood, though of course he sees things quite differently. Where King Henry complains near the close of *Richard the Second* that his son is a "young wanton and effeminate boy" (*R2* V.iii.10) who is dissipating his life among a "dissolute . . . crew" (12), Falstaff asserts that his lifestyle of self-indulgence guarantees that boys become men.[48] This is the tenor of his dismissive critique of Prince John, who instantiates for him an effete restraint that results in what he takes as reproductive failure. "There's never none of these demure boys come to any proof," he asserts, "for thin drink doth so over-cool their blood, and making many fish-meals, that they fall into a kind of male green-sickness, and then, when they marry, they get wenches" (*2H4* IV.iii.87–91).[49] Consistent with the well-known Galenic model of human biology to which he here appeals, Falstaff assumes that a father lacking caloric vigor will beget a child without the requisite somatic heat to prove a man. Such assumptions provide the basis of the knight's argument that a regimen of strict dietary self-regulation results in the generation of daughters, and underwrites the implied corollary defense of an ethics of unregulated self-indulgence. This ethos informs Falstaff's account of his own surrogate paternity of Hal. Where Henry IV feared that Falstaff and his "crew" were turning his son into a girl, Sir John asserts that Falstaff is the reason that the future king has become, from his perspective at least, a proper man. By offering a technique of self-cultivation, Falstaff and his coadjutors have enabled Hal to produce the amount of heat necessary to match the culturally determined standards of masculinity. Falstaff elaborates:

> Hereof comes it that Prince Harry is valiant, for the cold blood he did naturally inherit of his father, he hath, like lean, sterile, and bare land, manured, husbanded, and tilled with excellent endeavor of drinking good and good store of fertile sherris, that he is become very hot and valiant. If I had a thousand sons, the first humane principle I would teach them should be to forswear thin potations and to addict themselves to sack. (*2H4* IV.iii.112–19)

The "tutor and feeder" of the prince's "riots" (*2H4* V.v.63), Falstaff authorizes his government of Hal as a supplement to a failed paternity. His libertinage, at least by his own account, guarantees the generation of "hot and valiant" men even in the face of a thermally deficient bloodline. In *The First Part of King Henry the Fourth,* in the tavern, Falstaff played at being Hal's father. In his defense of his abusive ethos, he imagines himself a more effective father than the king, through an addictive pedagogy able to make a thousand men like Hal.

To be sure, Falstaff's claims do not go uncontested. Indeed, his capacity for generation is understood to possess the most serious of consequences for England. On his deathbed, Hal's father imagines a dystopic future for his country, one in which Falstaff's ideal of self-government has become a principle of state. Considering his son's impending reign, Henry IV makes his last royal act a dismissal of the "sage counsellors" (*2H4* IV.v.120) at court and an invitation to the "apes of idleness" (122) who will inevitably advance after his death. "Now, neighbor confines," he commands,

> purge you of your scum.
> Have you a ruffian that will swear, drink, dance,
> Revel the night, rob, murder, and commit
> The oldest sins the newest kind of ways?
> Be happy, he will trouble you no more.
> England shall double gild his treble guilt,
> England shall give him office, honor, might,
> For the fifth Harry from curbed license plucks
> The muzzle of restraint, and the wild dog
> Shall flesh his tooth on every innocent.

The king concludes his lament by shifting his address to England itself:

> O my poor kingdom, sick with civil blows!
> When that my care could not withhold thy riots,
> What wilt thou do when riot is thy care?
> O, thou wilt be a wilderness again,
> Peopled with wolves, thy old inhabitants.
>
> (123–37)

Henry the Fourth's speech clearly echoes his father's famous deathbed oration (R2 II.i). It also recalls Gadshill's characterization of Falstaff and the "other Troyans" (*1H4* II.i.67) he runs with, who "pray continually to their saint, the commonwealth, or rather, not pray to her, but prey on her" (II.i.77–78). Although Gadshill boasts of the ability of Falstaff, the prince, and the rest to devour the commonweal with impunity, his comments make available a perspective upon which the king critically elaborates. Henry the Fourth's description of the promoted "ruffian[s]" links a series of activities associated with Falstaff—swearing, drinking, carousing, and robbery—to a murderous violence, and thereby insists on the devastation to be caused by the ethical dissolution the knight represents, once it is allowed free reign by the new monarch.

Among Falstaff's most distinctive characteristics is his appetite, and in this dystopic vision this appetite is magnified into a bestial and murderous voracity.[50] "[A]ppetite" is, according to Ulysses in *Troilus and Cressida,* "an universal wolf" (I.iii.121). Consistent with such a characterization, the king transforms Falstaff from what many of the writers examined in the first chapter would call a "caterpillar of the commonwealth" into a lupine invasive force that will "prey" on the polity; the rout of men to be advanced under his son's rule, the king fears, will engage in a feeding-frenzy, devouring "innocent[s]" and thereby depopulating the land. They will also repopulate it; the "ruffian" of line 124, as if under the spell of Circe, has become first "the wild dog" of line 131, and finally the "wolves" who will come to inhabit the land.

Where are these "neighbor confines"? Henry IV's directed imperative is tactfully silent on the matter, although the question of invasion from neighboring countries would have resonated with many in the moment of the play's composition and performance. Although Ireland, a land understood already to be "peopled with wolves," had long been considered "a backdoor to invasion from Spain,"[51] Tyrone's rebellion and the specter of the potential collapse of England's colonial project in Ireland made the possibility of invasion from that country entirely conceivable. As one of the speakers in Edmund Spenser's *A View of the State of Ireland* speculates, perhaps England's failures in Ireland resulted from the fact that "Almighty God . . . reserveth her in this unquiet state still for some secret scourge, which shall by her come unto England."[52] My purpose in observing the relevance of Henry's prophecy is not only to note the considerable emotion Shakespeare elicits through the king's speech by manipulating such anxieties, but also to underscore the way Hal's father poses the question of Henry V's rule. By projecting the ethical precedent embodied by Falstaff outward, and transforming this caricature of the knight into a barbarous rout, he views his son as the leader of a colonial force of invasion that will utterly destroy England. Of course, Hal rejects Falstaff, and considerable narrative effort goes into distinguishing the new king from his past and hence into distancing the son's reign from his father's grim predictions. Nevertheless, Henry IV provides a useful lead for helping us think about Henry V's reign as depicted by Shakespeare, to the extent that the dying monarch approaches it as an exercise in "colonial governmentality." I borrow this term from David Scott, who suggests that, within programs of colonial government, "power comes to be directed at the destruction and reconstruction of colonial spaces so as to produce governing-effects on colonial conduct."[53] This formulation is perfectly consonant with what Henry IV, during his moment of greatest despair, imagines will happen to his kingdom under his son's leadership—at least, up to a point. The difference is that the king believes his son will destroy and reconstitute England not as a space in which "governing-effects" are produced, but as one in which government goes to the dogs, as it were, and incivility reigns. His will be a barbarous rule that seeks not to govern conduct but to remove any limits from individual conduct. Presiding over what might be called a septic colonization, Henry V will subject England to a regressive government that turns back time to a moment before civilization, that will make the nation look like the barbarous country it once was.[54]

Henry V does not so much prove his father wrong as rework the latter's vision; his success on the fields of France, I shall argue, derives not from a rejection of what Henry IV constitutes as a Falstaffian barbarity, but from his capacity successfully to manage that barbarity. A brief discussion of a key aspect of England's colonial policy will help establish how Henry V accomplishes this transformation.[55]

The crisis in Ireland forced a heightened awareness of, and prompted widespread reflection upon, questions of colonial governmentality—not only about the legitimacy of England's efforts, or about the authorization of violence, but also about the nuts and bolts, the day-to-day challenges of conducting the actions of selves and others in a colonial setting. My earlier reference to Spenser's *View* was not unmotivated; Spenser's analysis and set of policy recommendations draw on his experience as a colonial administrator and longtime resident of Ireland to address some of the most basic challenges facing England. In particular, Spenser confronts a state of affairs built into nearly all colonial enterprises, the fact that the colonized populace profoundly outnumbers the colonizers.[56] This is certainly the case in Ireland (as it will be for Henry in France), and, as Irenius' interlocutor Eudoxus reasons, "the greater number will carry away the lesse" (144). This is the fate of the so-called Old English, who have been transformed ("degenerated") into the people they sought to rule, turned into the barbarous *others* it was their mission to civilize and govern. Though Irenius disagrees with the inevitability of this process, he provides an extended analysis of the varied mechanisms through which this "carrying away" takes place, the means whereby the Old English have become "meere Irish." Among the most important ways numerical imbalance produces effects of degeneration are practices of imitation. As the anti-theatricalists complained of the deformative metamorphosis caused by the stage, Irenius attributes the bad behavior of the Old English to the fact that they have been exposed to "ill examples" (67).[57] The dynamic posited is a kind of diffuse imitation of the Irish and their "barbarous rudenes" (54), but Irenius identifies a crucial site within which negative exemplarity takes effect: the home. Among the most debased and degenerate of actions of the Old English, according to both interlocutors, is their use of the Irish language; indeed, this is a primary cause of their transformation, insofar as "the speach being Irish, the heart must needes bee Irish" (71). The mingling of languages is a result of employing Irish nurses to raise children and of miscegenation between English men and Irish women. The former practice is especially noxious because the nurse is the first pedagogue. Irenius asserts that "young children be like apes, which will affect and imitate what they see done before them, especially by their nurses, whom they love so well" (71). Intermarriage operates similarly and produces similar effects. "[C]ommonly," Irenius asserts, "the childe taketh most of his nature of the mother, besides speach, manners, and inclynation" (71; cf. also 143). The dynamic is a mixture of somatic derivation and imitative formation; in addition to the unruly "nature" children receive from their Irish mothers, they mimetically incorporate a barbarous language, ethically abusive customs, and an intractable disposition.[58]

As indicated above, Irenius does not understand this negative imitation to be a necessary result of being in the minority in Ireland; it is, he asserts, only under certain circumstances that imitation results in the spread of barbarous behavior and that the imbalance of numbers produces degenerating effects. Colonial rule rests upon a sense of the human capacity to control and to manipulate the world, to form and to reform environments and people in accord with a set of plans, and to be able to institute stable patterns of domination and subordination among the colonial populace. Consequently, Spenser contends that "where there is no good stay of government, and strong ordinances to hould them, there indeede the fewer follow the more, but where there is due order of discipline and good rule, there the better shall goe foremost, and the worst shall follow" (144). This perspective both constitutes a strong critique of Old English rule and authorizes Spenser's dramatic reformulation of the colonial project, in a plan which includes the creation of a standing army, the application of English administrative units and practices, the fostering of new centers of commerce, and the completion of an array of public works projects. To borrow the words of Talal Asad, Spenser proposes "the reformation of subjectivities and the re-organization of social spaces in which subjects act and are acted upon."[59] He does so, moreover, in hopes of ensuring that the few can have a salutary impact on the many. Put another way, Spenser's proposal for a comprehensive de- and re-organization of the political, administrative, and cultural structure of Ireland attempts to achieve a "multiplier effect." And it does so precisely via imitation. When government is structured and conducted properly, Irenius contends, exemplarity can enable the outnumbered English colonists effectively and efficiently to civilize the putatively barbarous Irish and to reclaim the supposedly degenerate Old English. Where Irish childrearing practices or English-Irish miscegenation relied on what he took to be a deformative imitation of language, bad habits, and customs, in the future an educational program, Irenius imagines, will produce more positive mimetic effects. He counsels a state sponsorship of "liberall sciences" and the propagation of petty and grammar schools for the mandatory education of the children of "the sonnes of lords, gentlemen, and such others as are able to bring them up in learning" (150). As a result of such pedagogy:

> they will in short space grow up to that civill conversation, that both the children will loath their former rudenesse in which they were bred, and also their parents will even by the ensample of their young children perceive the foulenesse of their owne behaviour, compared to theirs. (151)

The institution of children within a civilizing regimen puts in play a kind of reverse mimesis. Where before infants imitated the ill dispositions and behaviors of their mothers and nursemaids, here the sons not only will unlearn the "rudeness" of their infancy but will also provide a pattern of civility for their parents. Within Irenius's plan, the effect of proper governmental examples is felt further down the status ladder. Among the many benefits Irenius imagines for establishing new market towns is their function in propagating proper conduct. When people from outlying regions in the country come to sell their goods, they will, like the parents of the grammar-school children, see what it means to conduct a civilized existence. "[T]here is nothing doth sooner cause civility in any countrie then many market townes," Irenius explains, "by reason that people repairing often thither for their needes, will dayly see and learne civil manners of the better sort" (156–57). Commerce possesses mimetic pedagogic effects that contribute to the effort to reconstitute the Irish and Old English barbarians into civilized Englishmen and Englishwomen. Through these means Irenius seeks to multiply the effects of colonizing subjects. Where the Old English operated within a governmental dispensation that allowed the Irish to overwhelm them and transform them into barbarians, Spenser proposes a regime and regimen within which the actions of a few can impact positively the many, and thereby (he hopes) spread civility, stability, and order.

Of course, a play is not a policy proposal, at least not explicitly and not inherently. I wish to suggest, though, that *Henry the Fifth* engages in a meditation upon the questions Spenser raises and answers in his response to the Irish crisis. Although there are important distinctions between the play and Spenser's text, which I shall discuss further in a moment, it is possible to note parallels between the situation of the English in Ireland and that of Henry's army in France. Just as Spenser understood the relative imbalance of English colonizers to be a crucial fact structuring both the problems the English faced and the policies England needed to undertake to compensate for this imbalance, *Henry the Fifth* foregrounds the extent to which the English troops are outnumbered. The French advantage of "five to one" (*H5* IV.iii.4) at Agincourt is in fact so great that the French pity the English; the Constable wishes for a better fight: "Sorry am I his numbers are so few" (*H5* III.v.56). And just as Spenser imagined redressing the numerical imbalance through, in part, techniques of cultural reproduction, so Henry seeks to overcome his dire situation by employing practices of imitative fashioning that seek to transform his soldiers into an army of men capable of overwhelming destruction. Preparing for battle, the king seeks to reinforce his soldiers through a military pedagogy. He encourages the "noble English" (*H5* III.i.17) by likening their male progenitors to "so many Alexanders" (19), and enjoins them to disseminate their courageous heritage down the status ladder through an educational mimesis; "Be copy now to men of grosser blood," he commands, "And teach them how to war!" (24–25).[60] In a manner that recalls Sidney's vision of creating many Cyruses, Henry V attempts to make an entire army of Alexanders by letting "example / Breed" (*H5* II.ii.45–46) more versions of the classical exemplar. Fluellen's praise of his king, in which he sets up an elaborate analogy between Henry and Alexander the Great, retrospectively casts the project of imitative martial discipline as a form of hyperfecund self-multiplication. At Shrewsbury, Henry IV sought to disseminate versions of himself through a type of liveried generation, sending numbers of his men disguised as kings into the skirmish.[61] Henry V takes this strategy to its limit. Through "copy"-ing many Alexanders, he would make a whole army of himself.

Although Henry's policy of managing and overcoming numerical imbalance resembles key aspects of Spenser's program for securing English colonial rule in Ireland, there are important differences. Spenser's targets are the Irish and the deformed Old English; the subjects of Henry's mimetic pedagogy are his own troops. Further, in Spenser's plan military action (brutal conquest and the efforts of the standing army he would establish) is relatively distinct from the activities of cultural reproduction, although forming their conditions of possibility; Henry V yokes these two together, in instituting a program of educational "copy[ing]" to create troops capable of achieving military victory in the face of impossible odds. We can add a further layer of distinctions. *A View* advances its program for reform in order to prevent the collapse of England's colonial project, and thereby prevent the Irish not only from gaining autonomy but also from participating in an invasion of England. *Henry the Fifth,* by contrast, positions the English as a "barbarous people" (III.v.4) who seek to overwhelm French civilization; this at least is the perspective of the French rulers whose land is under siege. Rather than contest such a representation, Henry V embraces it. Consequently, where Spenser sought to institute civility in his subjects to stave off the barbarizing effects of Old English mingling and imitation, the ethical valences of the model Hal provides are emphatically uncivilized. When Fluellen advances his comparison of his king and Alexander the

Great, he explicitly differentiates Henry and his former boon companion and bad example Falstaff. In addition to noting the similarities between their respective birth places, Monmouth and Macedon, Fluellen establishes the equivalence between Henry and Alexander precisely through Henry's rejection of his former companion. He notes Alexander's fitful loss of self-control, "his rages, and his furies, and his wraths, and his cholers, and his moods, and his displeasures, and his indignations," as well as the fact that he was "a little intoxicates in his prains" (*H5* IV.vii.32–34). Where Alexander in a fit "killed his friend Cleitus, being in his ales and his cups" (41), Henry "being in his right wits and his good judgments, turned away the fat knight with the great pelly doublet" (42–44).[62] Although Fluellen celebrates the king's rejection of Falstaff, this passage in a way represents the persistence of Falstaff; who else but the knight has asserted that intoxication was the same thing as "right wit" and "good judgment"? Such persistence in fact is announced by Fluellen himself, who likens Henry to "Alexander the Pig" (12–13).[63] The playwright's attempt to reproduce the Welsh dialect by having Fluellen pronounce "p" instead of "b" sets up an equivalence between former prince and former companion: "Pig" is another name for Falstaff, the "sow" (*2H4* I.ii.11), the "damned brawn" (*1H4* II.iv.105). By killing Hotspur, Hal assumed as his own the honor Hotspur had "engross[ed]" (*1H4* III.ii.148) to himself; just so, by killing Falstaff, Hal incorporates his erstwhile friend and becomes the greatest of pigs.[64]

The occasion of Fluellen's celebration of his liege, Henry's order to slaughter all French prisoners, suggests that Henry himself has a destructive appetite, one worthy a pig. This is the conclusion to be drawn, at least, if we consider the king's actions in the light of Exeter's threats to the French, in which war figures as a form of devastating consumption: "husbands, fathers, and betrothèd lovers," Exeter promises, "shall be swallowed in this controversy" (*H5* II.iv.108–109). The king's destruction, like the lack of ethical modulation instantiated by Alexander, justifies his adequation to the classical exemplar, and becomes the very sign of Henry's "pig"-ness.[65] Further, Henry's threats delivered before the gates of Harfleur extend this destructive appetite to his soldiers, the army of Alexanders he has pedagogically propagated. The king promises the Governor of the French city to answer any resistance with an unbridled violence against his people—the rape of maidens, the slaughter of children, violent indignities heaped upon the aged, leaving only mothers driven to madness to mourn the devastation. "What is it then to me," Henry asks, "if impious war, / Arrayed in flames to the prince of fiends, / Do with his smirched complexion all fell feats / Enlinked to waste and desolation?" (*H5* III.iii.15–18). Where Henry IV asserted that the "wild dog" of unrestrained "license" will "flesh his tooth on every innocent," his son employs the violent agencies of the "fleshed soldier" (11). These troops represent perhaps nothing less than the perfect embodiment of Henry V's mimetic instruction, the ideal achievement of an army of ethically abusive men, generated versions of "Alexander the Pig."

Henry's imitative pedagogy and direction of his troops achieve a version of what I referred to in my discussion of *A View* as a "multiplier effect." Despite the estimation of the French that they have enough "[t]o smother up the English in our throngs" (*H5* IV.v.21), or that the English "needs must be englutted" (*H5* IV.iii.83), not only do England's outnumbered troops triumph at Agincourt, they do so with unprecedented success—the French lose ten thousand, the English twenty-nine. There are two points to be made here. First, recalling Eudoxus's belief that "the greater number will carry away the lesse," the French predictions about the battle rely on a simple military arithmetic in which strategic advantage is calculated by counting heads, a mode of apprehending the effects of soldiers that pervades the first and second tetralogies. Westmoreland in fact voices this perspective immediately before the climactic battle, drawing attention to the English army's numerical disadvantage, wishing "that we now had here / But one ten thousand of those men in England / That do no work to-day" (*H5* IV.iii.16–18). More bodies, he argues, no matter of what station, would help tilt the balance. To call on men who fall into the category of "those . . . That do no work," a category that could include either masterless men roaming the countryside or nobles without occupation, the dispossessed or the leisured, produces an equivalence between these men and thus instantiates the homogenizing effects involved in such strategic reckoning on the eve of battle. But Henry's troops display a different set of numerical characteristics, traits most frequently associated with noble soldiers, who, because of their putatively superior virtue, courage, and composure in the face of battle, count for many.[66] Henry V, as described by his father, embodies the limit of this hierarchical logic. In response to his son's promise that he will reform his wayward behavior or die "a hundred thousand deaths," the king exclaims "A hundred thousand rebels die in this!" (*1H4*

III.ii.158, 160). Whether or not we take this ambiguous statement to be hostile or friendly, snidely dismissive or celebratory, it implies that Hal is worth one hundred thousand persons. (Bardolph, Pistol, and Nym stand at the other end of the spectrum; as the Boy asserts, "three such antics do not amount to a man" [*H5* III.ii.28].) When, immediately before Agincourt, Henry strategically includes his men in his family and thereby invests them with a provisional nobility ("For he to-day that sheds his blood with me / Shall be my brother" [*H5* IV.iii.61–62]), the troops take on this numerical attribute of the armigerous nobility. It makes perfect sense then that, in response to Westmoreland's hand-wringing, Henry dismisses his view and offers to pay the fare home for the timid (*H5* IV.iii.34–39). The astounding lopsidedness of the victory attests to the success of Henry's efforts to "multiply" his soldiers, to make them each effectively worth many men.

The second point to make about the English success is that the men defeat the French not in spite of their Falstaffian appetite, but precisely because of it. Just as Exeter had promised before the war began, the English are the ones who "glut" themselves on the French. Henry's crowning achievement, the defeat of France, does not represent the outcome of his disavowal of Falstaff; instead, the English king reconfigures and utilizes the capacity to devastate associated with the knight. The French Constable's prescient observation that the English "will eat like wolves" (*H5* III.vii.145) helps bring this discussion back to Henry IV's deathbed vision of a nation overrun by such creatures, ethically abusive "scum" whose outrages would transform England into the uncivilized wilderness it once was. With the benefit of hindsight, it is possible to say that the dying king was both wrong and right. The son does not oppose his father's vision so much as rework it by projecting the ungoverned and wasting generation outward, employing it in his intervention in geopolitical conflict. Henry V does preside over a transformation of Englishmen into what Deborah Shuger perhaps would call "white barbarians," but he does so strategically, not to destroy England but to augment it and extend its dominion.

Although Henry leads an army of barbarians, God approves. This is Henry's claim, at least. When he hears the census of the dead and learns of the lopsided victory, the king's first response is to assert divine intervention: "O God, thy arm was here!" he exclaims, "And not to us, but to thy arm alone, / Ascribe we all!" (*H5* IV.viii.101–03). Irenius tells a similar story, one that bears comparison with Henry V's assertions. Even though Irenius feared the possibility that God would use the barbarous Irish to "scourge" England, on looking back into Europe's ancient history he paints a much rosier picture. In what from a European perspective might look like world-historical cataclysm—the "storme"-like invasion of "the Gothes, the Hunnes, and the Vandals: And lastly all the nations of Scythia" that overwhelms "like a mountaine flood . . . all countryes of Christendome" (50)—Irenius finds the guiding hand of providence. The colonial peopling of these lands by the barbarian races, he argues, represents "a singular providence of God, and a most admirable purpose of his wisedome, to draw those Northerne Heathen Nations downe into those Christian parts, where they might receive Christianity, and to mingle nations so remote miraculously, to make as it were one blood and kindred of all people, and each to have knowledge of him" (51).[67] Irenius's policy proposals and vision of governed mimetic generation do not so much contradict the implied belief that God uses disaster to achieve his goals as they seek to appropriate God's administrative capacity for the English. England's colonial endeavors share God's objective—to transform the barbarians into good Christians, to "mingle" people in such a way as to turn them into a piously unified nation, an English nation. Moreover, if in the meantime England is forced to behave like barbarians, slaughtering or starving tens of thousands, Irenius's account of providence implies that sometimes the Lord works in mysterious ways. Likewise, Henry's appeal to divine agency seeks to authorize his actions by constituting his military campaign as a battle fought beside God, and in his service. The providential narrative to which both he and Irenius appeal enables Henry to reconcile the hellish specter of waste and devastation upon which he relied in his military campaign—the threats to the people of Harfleur, the slaughter of prisoners at Agincourt—with God's nearly inscrutable but overpowering intentions. The appeal retroactively construes the effects of Falstaffian ethos, magnified and multiplied into a barbarous army of wolves, as acts of pious service to the will of God.

Providence notwithstanding, military success presents the triumphant monarch with significant governmental challenges. As the Duke of Burgundy observes, war has transformed France's "houses and ourselves and children" (*H5* V.ii.56) into "savages" who "as soldiers . . . nothing do but meditate on blood" (59–60). Such an account points not only to the task facing Henry in France, the project of governing and reconstituting a nation turned "savage" by war, but also to the problem of how to incorporate back into the English polity his own devastatingly voracious soldiers. By drawing attention to these difficulties, Burgundy points to a crucial—though largely unacknowledged—distinction in the play, the difference between governing war and governing peace.[68]

To be sure, there are voices in the play that assert that there is no difference between these two activities, that conducting soldiers in battle and conducting the affairs of state are perfectly consonant and perfectly integrated elements of the same governmental project. Consider Canterbury's argument for war with France, in which he appeals to the familiar political analogy of the country as a beehive, an example "in nature" that "teach[es] / The act of order to a peopled kingdom" (*H5* I.ii.188–89). Just as a beehive may be said to have "magistrates" (191), "merchants" (192), "masons" (198), "citizens" (199), "porters" (200), and "executors" (203) (to carry out the mandates of the law), it also has "soldiers" who, "armèd in their stings / Make boot upon the summer's velvet buds, / Which pillage they with merry march bring home / To the tent-royal of their emperor" (193–96). Canterbury's model here exceeds the local task of convincing Henry he is justified in undertaking just one war; the characterization of battle as the gathering of sustenance posits that war is constantly necessary as a condition of the nation's survival—not just one conquest, but perpetual military aggression. Although the analogy contributes to the king's decision to go to war, it provides no basis for government once war is completed.

The king's response is similar both for himself and for his men: set up "house-keeping." With respect to the king's governance of France, Shakespeare's play tells us almost nothing of the arrangements for rule under the new dispensation; these details are left offstage to be worked out by Henry's representatives. What Shakespeare stages is Henry's wooing of princess Katherine, in which, as Karen Newman observes, he attempts to turn the princess into an "English wife."[69] The question of national government becomes that of household government, and Henry's focus settles upon the generation of a male heir to the combined thrones of England and France. His designs for his men are similar. As he indicates in the speech before the battle of Agincourt, he imagines a future governmental regime that resituates these men within domestic economies and reorients their devastating appetites towards the perpetual commemoration of the noblemen. Each year on St. Crispin's Day, the anniversary of the battle, every man in the English army at Agincourt will recall the victory:

> Old men forget; yet all shall be forgot,
> But he'll remember, with advantages,
> What feats he did that day. Then shall our names,
> Familiar in his mouth as household words—
> Harry the King, Bedford and Exeter,
> Warwick and Talbot, Salisbury and Gloucester—
> Be in their flowing cups freshly rememb'red.
> This story shall the good man teach his son;
> And Crispin Crispian shall ne'er go by,
> From this day to the ending of the world,
> But we in it shall be rememberèd.
>
> (*H5* IV.iii.49–59)

The "flowing cups" of the former soldiers subtly evokes Fluellen's description of Alexander "in his ales and his cups" and, beyond that, Falstaff's vision of teaching his thousand sons lessons in addiction. Rather than reproduce devastation and waste, a martial subject who destroyed household economies by swallowing up "husbands, fathers, and betrothèd lovers," Henry seeks to situate his military man within a regulated domain of household government. The gentility produced in France becomes here a kind of patrimony pedagogically handed down from father to son, one which, paradoxically, reinscribes status differentials and assures a future existence for the king and his generals; as Katherine Eggert observes, this passage shows the king seeking an "everlasting reanimation in the form of popular remembrance."[70] Where Navarre and his men sought to extend themselves into the future through a regimen of ascetic study that reconfigured the governmental parameters of domestic economy, Henry seeks to be "remembered"—re-embodied—*through* the households of his men, forever to inhabit these domestic economies, as "familiar" as "household words."

This is the king's vision, a future instituted by fathers teaching sons until the end of time. Of course, the objectives of incorporating destructive men into the nation and securing a future existence through "house-keeping" can at best be called provisionally successful, if they can be said to succeed at all. The difficult fit between a military masculinity and the type of governmental ideal envisioned immediately above may be read in the elision of women in the imagined domestic economies; the memory of the king and his noblemen thrives through relations between father and son, who like Banquo's progeny in *Macbeth* extend forward in a line that endlessly reproduces itself, as if "not of woman born." With respect to Henry's marriage, in which the woman is not elided, the difficulties are registered from the outset in Katherine's ambivalent answers to Henry's questions. In their interview, he informs the French princess of their reproductive future and his career plans for their son. "Shall not thou and I," he asks his bride to be, "between Saint Denis and Saint George, compound a boy, half French, half English, that shall go to Constantinople and take the Turk by the beard?" (*H5* V.ii.200–3). Katherine responds in broken English: "I do not know dat" (*H5* V.ii.205). Such an answer registers possible resistance to Henry's designs, and hence signals an implicit violence in the establishment of the new royal household, a complete effacement of female will.[71] It is also prophetic. The dangerousness imputed to the domestic sphere (as voiced in Othello's oath, or Berowne's scourging of his bookmates)[72] is played out in the immediate move from the closing celebration of marriage to the death of Henry and the failure of his son. "Small time," states the Chorus,

> but in that small most greatly lived
> This star of England. Fortune made his sword,
> By which the world's best garden he achieved,
> And of it left his son imperial lord.
> Henry the Sixth, in infant bands crowned King
> Of France and England, did this king succeed;
> Whose state so many had the managing
> That they lost France and made his England bleed.
> (*H5* Epi.5–12)

The Chorus's praise cannot obscure—indeed, underscores—the fact that Henry V marries and dies. In the course of a few lines the Bolingbrokes have lost the throne, as if there was some causal link between marriage and cataclysm, between household government and dynastic failure.[73]

The Chorus's emphasis here upon the failure of domestic and national government brings us back to the characterization of the theater itself as Rumor's household. In fact, the Chorus's formulations revise Rumor's vision of theatrical misgovernment of multitudes, by aligning the stage with the domestic economies imagined by Henry on the eve of Agincourt, the households within which he and his men would be remembered annually and through which the military gentility would be reproduced educationally by fathers teaching their sons. As Henry would have it, at each "Feast of Crispian" (*H5* IV.iii.40), every soldier will "strip his sleeve and show his scars, / And say, 'These wounds I had on Crispin's day'" (47–48). The Chorus similarly points to wounds, those inflicted by the supernumerary governors of Henry VI whose misgovernment lost France and "made . . . England bleed" (Epi.12).

The linkages and associations I've been reading here trace the ways that the Chorus reconfigures Rumor's theater into a household oriented toward the productive recollection of history, a domestic economy that, rather than contribute to waste and loss, justifies itself on its ability to transform loss and destruction into theatrical enjoyment. This ability becomes the very grounds of the theater's viability; referring to the first tetralogy and the national devastation depicted there, "[w]hich oft our stage hath shown," the Chorus implores the audience to "In your fair minds let this acceptance take" (Epi.13–14). The theater seeks to authorize itself (against the claims of the anti-theatricalists) as a domain that can transform the failure of rule into something worthy of "acceptance." The address to the audience's "fair minds" recalls and repeats their frequent invocation as "gentles." The repetition of the past thus not only represents the moment when Henry produced an army of gentlemen, but, like the imagined future education Henry depicts, passes on the gentility conferred to the men in battle to the "gentle" audience. I take this to be the burden of Joel Altman's observation that the king "would seem to have fathered the audience" insofar as "[t]hey are the lineal descendants" of the soldiers Henry generated for battle.[74] The Chorus thus defines, in opposition to Rumor's purposefully misgoverned household, a sphere of cultural activity that turns the failure of other governmental domains into the condition of possibility of its own generative and governmental success. And although the Chorus expresses hope that Essex will return from Ireland triumphant, the theater does not require Essex's victory. As the example of the first tetralogy shows, the theater is capable of recouping loss as pleasurable viewing. This is to argue not that the stage subverts monarchy or any other form of authority (though it certainly may, under certain circumstances) but that the Chorus specifies the relative autonomy of theatrical practice.[75]

This practice, further, requires the audience to take part in theatrical generation. The Chorus draws attention to, and answers the inadequation of, the theater to the chronicle history it seeks to represent by specifying the terms in which the actors may satisfactorily stand for their dramatic subjects. Actors, according to *Henry the Fifth,* are "ciphers to this great accompt" (Pro.17), which, just as "a crooked figure may / Attest in little place a million" (15–16), may stand for multitudes of men who fought upon the "vasty fields of France" (12). This characterization may be termed a "theatrical arithmetic," a multiplication of theatrical persons similar to that accomplished by Henry V at Agincourt; the Chorus, like Henry, seeks to make men who count for thousands. Theatrical multiplication, however, may be distinguished from the king's military generation insofar as it requires the efforts of the audience. The Chorus calls on those in attendance to fill in the gap between historical event and stage representation. In addition to accepting the generic abuses of the unities of time, place, and action, the audience must repair the play's lack of numbers through a collective act of imagination.[76] Thus the Chorus enjoins the audience, "let us . . . [o]n your imaginary forces work" (Pro.17–18). The audience is urged to

Piece out our imperfections with your thoughts:
Into a thousand parts divide one man
And make imaginary puissance.
(Pro.23–25)

The language here alludes to an earlier moment in the second tetralogy, in which Lord Bardolph attempts to explain Hotspur's defeat at Shrewsbury. The young Henry Percy, he asserts,

Flatter[ed] himself in project of a power
Much smaller than the smallest of his thoughts,
And so, with great imagination
Proper to madmen, led his powers to death.
(*2H4* I.iii.29–32)

By this account, the imaginary projection of numbers is a type of insanity. Hotspur fails to the extent that his imagination heightens the inadequation between his "hope" (27) for success and his unlikely prospects, sacrifices his power to the extent that he (like Falstaff or Rumor) in effect multiplies empty or nonexistent men. The stage, by contrast, bases its success precisely upon the gambit that the audience's imaginary generation will repair inadequate numbers. The Chorus asserts that those in attendance can make the necessary "puissance" that will allow the drama to be both convincing and entertaining, can produce numbers that will convert loss and destruction, the stuff of chronicle history, into pleasure. Contrary to the anti-theatricalist's notion that the stage produced ethically dissolute multitudes, set in motion the disruptive spawn of the devil, the Chorus asserts that the audience becomes an agent of theatrical generation capable of overcoming an inherent lack of numbers by transforming a lack into just enough.

Henry the Eighth: Regenerating Governments

That such equilibrium could only be momentary is evidenced by the fact that Shakespeare continued to broach questions of the culturally reproductive capacities of the stage, and to rethink the relation between the stage and other domains of government. In one of his last plays, *The Life of King Henry the Eighth,* he relates the specter of ungoverned multitudes to the elaborate spectacles of monarchy—the highly charged moments of political theater that are this play's trademark. Just as the anti-theatricalists perceived the audiences at the stage as a volatile mass of people, Shakespeare portrayed the coronation of Anne Bullen and the christening of her daughter, Elizabeth Tudor, as drawing overwhelming numbers of unruly spectators. The christening occasions an extraordinary onslaught of people, and, though we might imagine that the fascination with religious and political spectacle would have been encouraged as a necessary condition of royal authority, the household staff's response to this "multitude" (V.iv.64) tells another story. According to the officers and servants of Henry VIII's household, the crowds that descend on the court to celebrate the birth of the royal offspring possess a force as uncontainable as ocean tides (V.iv.16), and assault the court like an enemy army (V.iv.41–44). The coronation of Anne Bullen, is represented as drawing comparable masses. As the Third Gentleman reports, "Great-bellied women / That had not half a week to go, like rams / In the old time of war, would shake the press / And make 'em reel before 'em" (IV.i.76–79). The fecund regiment of women "shak[ing] the press" to get a view of Anne puzzles the Third Gentleman, leaving him astonished by the singularity of the event ("Such joy / I never saw before" [IV.i.75–76], he asserts).

The household staff offers a less generous evaluation of the numbers gathered to see Anne's daughter. The goodwill of the masses notwithstanding, the enthusiasm to get a peek at the child prompts the Porter's Man to speculate that "[t]he devil was amongst 'em" (V.iv.55). Just as Satan has no business at a christening, the royal functionaries assert, the crowd is profoundly out of place at the court. The Chamberlain, concerned by the potential fiasco created by the "rabble" (V.iv.66), chastises his men: "[A]re all these / Your faithful friends o' th' suburbs?" (66–67), he asks. While the Chamberlain worries that the crowds treat the court as a fairground (63–64), the Porter frets that the "rascals" (V.iv.1) who press for a view have mistaken the royal household for the bear-baiting and bull-baiting pit at "Parish Garden" (2). Beleaguered, nearly overrun, the household staff understand the multitudes to be not only confused but potentially confusing, capable of transforming the regal space of the court into a space of popular license, of erasing the cultural distinctions between the seat of royal government and what is perceived to be the ungoverned space of the liberties.

The reactions of the household officials help establish links between their concerns about what they see and the anti-theatricists' anxieties about the effects of England's playhouses. Although the connection between the popular stage and the social sites named (above) by the Chamberlain and the Porter would have been implicit (the popular theaters were located in "the suburbs" and "Parish Garden" was immediately adjacent to the Swan),[77] the Porter makes the association explicit when he speaks of the crowds as the "youths that thunder at a playhouse and fight for bitten apples" (V.iv.57–58). In indicating that court and theater share a common enemy in the unruly "youths" who disrupt the proceedings at each, these lines acknowledge the theatricality of the royal festivities and suggest a structural similarity between the royal household and the popular playhouse. However, the fact that the royal spectacle has attracted the same audience as the theater stands as one measure among many of the magnitude of the crisis the retainers face, and adds descriptive specificity to the pressing anxiety that the multitude will deform the court and vitiate the conceptual distinctions between court and suburbs.

This interesting evocation of the anti-theatrical fear of the stage gains further resonance when we note the ways that Shakespeare links the royal spectacle to an inordinate and illicit capacity for reproduction. Overwhelmed by the numbers at court, the Porter exclaims "Bless me, what a fry of fornication is at door! On my Christian conscience this one christening will beget a thousand" (V.iv.33–35). These comments faintly but perceptibly echo the Third Gentleman's observation that Anne's coronation has attracted a fecund army of women about to give birth, a teeming multitude that presses in to get a view of the new queen. The Porter's lines similarly insist that Elizabeth's christening possesses a threatening fecundity and promises to occasion the spawning of more multitudes.

These passages begin to suggest the ways *Henry the Eighth* broaches and elaborates the issues pursued in the readings I have offered of *Love's Labor's Lost* and the Henriad. As I shall discuss, the disruptive potentials for theatrical generation touched on here trouble a critical tendency to treat this play as a more or less uncomplicated confirmation of monarchy. Consistent with my analysis thus far, I shall not argue that the play is somehow subversive of monarchy; rather, I aim to describe how *Henry the Eighth* represents the conflicting investments in practices of cultural reproduction. This will enable us not only to view Shakespeare's understanding of the complex relations among modes of governing generation, but also to comprehend how this play characterizes the reproductive capacity and impact of the popular stage. To accomplish this objective, it will be helpful to examine further the generative abilities attributed to the future Queen Elizabeth with an eye to the difficult and multivalent reproductive politics informing her representation.

The claims of governed generation are central to the hyperbolic adulation heaped upon Elizabeth during her christening, and to the visionary depiction of the reign to come under the future queen. Often taken to be the play's fullest celebration of monarchy's triumphant reconsolidation and extension into the future, the closing prophecy by Archbishop Cranmer promises abundant goodness during the age of Elizabeth.[78] The future monarch will be, Cranmer asserts:

> A pattern to all princes living with her
> And all that shall succeed. Saba was never
> More covetous of wisdom and fair virtue
> Than this pure soul shall be. All princely graces
> That mould up such a mighty piece as this is,
> With all the virtues that attend the good,
> Shall still be doubled on her. Truth shall nurse her.
>
> (V.v.22–28)

In her important reading of this play, Kim Noling argues that the christening and Cranmer's prophecy participate in a ceremonial displacement of Anne Bullen, perform a kind of discursive caesarian section of the future monarch from a queen beheaded for putative adulteries.[79] Cranmer's account elides reference to Anne and emphasizes the daughter's linkage to her father, suggesting that she is composed of the same virtuous "princely graces" as the king. Queen Anne's attendant, the Old Lady, anticipates this strategy in her announcement to the king and his companions that Anne has given birth to a "lovely boy" (V.i.164)—that is, "a girl" who "Promises boys hereafter" (165–66). She subsequently takes the implication that Elizabeth is a boy in potential a step further, by insisting to Henry that the infant "'Tis as like you / As cherry is to cherry" (V.i.168–69), thus transforming Elizabeth into a mini-version of her father. Noling links the archbishop's visionary celebration of the future queen and the gender transformations to which Elizabeth is subject to the strategic negotiation around Henry VIII's failure to produce a living male heir with either of his first two wives. As she persuasively argues, Cranmer's prophecy, by figuring Queen Elizabeth as a "maiden phoenix" (V.v.40) out of whose "sacred ashes of . . . honor" (45) will rise James I, provides Henry with the boy he always wanted, the sign of divine approval he missed within his previous marriage to Katherine of Aragon.[80] Such a gesture, moreover, renders James, the sitting monarch at the time of the play's production, essentially Queen Elizabeth's progeny—even though his claims to the throne were much less direct, and his own genealogy was stained by treason against the English monarch. Nondirect monarchical succession becomes through these dramatic strategies both legitimate and divine.[81]

Noling's reading of *Henry the Eighth* indicates both the complexity and the import of issues of generation in the play, the stakes invested in these concerns. However, it is possible to qualify her account somewhat by underscoring the limitations imposed by her understanding of government as royal authority. The ultimate and exclusive horizon for her analysis is the question of monarchical succession, and such an approach substantially narrows her reading of the relations between government and generation in Shakespeare's work. The play, according to Noling, stages the "subversion of queens" (306), and does dramatic obeisance to both James I and Henry VIII insofar as it "[a]uthorizes Henry's will by making the tiny Princess Elizabeth . . . a means of producing kings of

England" (292). This account is consistent with a significant line of criticism of *Henry the Eighth,* one that views Shakespeare's play as unequivocally reinforcing the monarchy's pretense to absolute rule by coopting all opposition or instability and enlisting it into the service of the king.[82] Noling indeed expands such a vision of royal authority by extending the implications of Henry VIII's monarchical generation to characterize patriarchal relations as such; just as she envisions the monarchy to be perfectly effective, she understands the patriarchy to be capable of maintaining a stable and seamlessly monolithic gender hierarchy. Such a conclusion implies a totalization of power that Cranmer's prophetic claims do not support. The archbishop asserts that both father and daughter are made up of "all the virtues that attend the good," which suggests a shared relation of subordination to an abstract category of moral value. However, it is also made clear that "good" will flourish under the reign of the daughter: "Good grows with her" (V.v.32), Cranmer promises. Although Henry celebrates the future presented to him, we might read incongruities within Cranmer's prophecy, and displace the unquestioning celebration of monarchy, or of the state that it is taken by critics to represent, by asking if the prelate's version of the generation of Elizabeth is the same as the Old Lady's. Does Cranmer here constitute the queen a perfect copy of her father? (Indeed, might not the Old Lady's account that Elizabeth "'Tis as like you / As cherry is to cherry" work both ways, intimating, perhaps, that Henry is like an infant?) Isn't the insistence that Elizabeth will double the virtues of her father a left-handed compliment? Doesn't the image of unsullied and untroubled harmony in the future implicitly critique the present, a present marked by rebellion and treason?[83]

These questions attempt to trouble the fantasy of monarchical, paternal parthenogenesis, and thus to locate instabilities in the putatively totalized structure of authority that such a reproductive dynamic would seek to secure and project into the future. By rendering legible rifts in the account of government as monolithically singular and perfectly effective, this line of interrogation prompts a closer examination of the play's representation of Elizabeth's generation and, more generally, the governmental implications of such representations. To the extent that the future queen is the product of, and enables, alternative generational dynamics, she interrupts and counters the fantasy of Henry's self-sufficient reproduction of monarchs. For instance, while Cranmer's prophecy asserts that Elizabeth is made up of the same stuff as her father, it also situates her as the product of the pedagogic generation discussed above, as created, like the Alexander described by Heywood, in relation to a model from antiquity. Cranmer's association of Queen Elizabeth with the biblical exemplar of the Queen of Sheba not only alludes to Elizabeth's contemporary reputation as a scholar and exemplary student, but also constitutes the future monarch as a product of a mimetic generation.[84] Cranmer translates Henry VIII's formula for action in governing the commonwealth ("Things done without example, in their issue / Are to be feared" [I.ii.90–91]) into a principle of educational genesis, a well-governed means for producing "issue" derived from the biblical "example," valued all the more for surpassing this example. If the play labors to disassociate Queen Elizabeth from her mother, the account here places Elizabeth within a biblical genealogy of nonpareil women that separates her from her father as well.

This pedagogic form of generation opens onto a larger cultural terrain. Even as Cranmer's prophecy suggests that Elizabeth is generated humanistically, in relation to her biblical precedent, Queen Elizabeth herself is predicted to reproduce pedagogically, turning this form of mimetic subjectivation into a strategy of royal government. Not only is Elizabeth to be a "pattern" to rulers of all nations, she is also transformed into an ethical text that makes men. "God shall be truly known," Cranmer promises, "and those about her / From her shall read the perfect ways of honor, / And by those claim their greatness, not by blood" (V.v.36–38). Queen Elizabeth founds and authorizes a form of humanist generation comparable to the martial pedagogy employed by Shakespeare's Henry V, or to the vision of making many Cyruses through poetry imagined by Sidney. Just as Henry's mimetic education on the fields of France constituted a form of self-multiplication, enabling the creation of a whole army of himself, Elizabeth will, according to Cranmer, during her beatific reign, serve as scripted and scriptive model for those around her. If the archbishop's oration works hard to reinforce prospectively James I's claims to lineal succession to the throne (by rendering him a direct descendent of Henry VIII), it also provides a nonlineal form of generation in which men are made through a status advancement authorized not by blood but by their mimetic merit.

This reading of *Henry the Eighth* has shown how Elizabeth's imbrication within dynamics of imitative pedagogy counter the notions that a unified power structure subsumes the princess's envisioned actions into its overpowering will or that she exists simply to reinforce royal masculine prerogatives. Though the focus, to this point, has been on celebrations of Elizabeth's governed mimetic generation, the play also suggests that the future queen possesses a potentially troubling fecundity. As a way of beginning to detail this aspect of the play's representation of Elizabeth and its treatment of issues of reproduction, it will be useful to consider a prominent example of ungoverned generation—Cardinal Wolsey. The prelate is relevant to this discussion especially to the extent that he embodies—before the fact, as it were—precisely the kind of mimesis authorized during Queen Elizabeth's rule. Cranmer's vatic account of the dispensation under Elizabeth treats imitation of the queen as perfectly allowed, indeed as a sign and mechanism of the godliness of her reign. This celebration of governed humanist generation and the hierarchy it institutes beyond the claims of lineage, however, stands in tension with the play's elaborate vilification of Wolsey, who "claims . . . greatness, not by blood." As if foregrounding this figure's imitation of the monarch, the "king-cardinal" (II.ii.18) arrives on stage miming in his very first line Henry VIII's signature exclamation, "Ha!" (I.i.115). Rather than a guarantee of peaceful stability and virtuous government, Wolsey's mimetic stance toward the king, and all that this stance entails—namely, Wolsey's extraordinary rise through the avenues of learning from humble origins to the highest levels of royal service—is taken by others in the play to be an indication of his unprincipled ambition and insatiable appetite for power.

Cataloguing a number of the charges leveled against Wolsey provides a way to gauge just how disruptive his imitation of the king is perceived to be. Buckingham provides some of the most scornful responses to the Cardinal, as is evident in his supercilious complaint that "A beggar's book / Outworths a noble's blood" (I.i.122–23).[85] Wolsey "outworths" the nobility not only insofar as his privileged access to the king circumvents a traditional hierarchy of lineage, but also insofar as his administrative presence in the nation drains the material resources on which status hierarchies in part depend. Although his allies praise him for possessing "A hand as fruitful as the land that feeds us" (I.iii.56), a "liberal[ity]" (61) that simulates the abundance of the king, his detractors consider him a "fox, / Or wolf, or both (for he is equal rav'nous / As he is subtile)" (I.i.158–60), and attribute to him an overwhelming voracity that promises to devastate all. The prelate's very presence at court at once obscures and siphons off the king's boundless generosity; "I wonder," Buckingham asks, "That such a keech can with his very bulk / Take up the ray o' th' beneficial sun / And keep it from the earth" (I.i.54–57). Wolsey's extraordinary hoarding of "wealth" (III.ii.107) and astonishing "expense" (108) amount to an annihilating consumption that promises to unmake men and undermine all government. Norfolk worries that the Cardinal, through his burdenous taxations and sequestration of noble property, will transform nobles into "pages" (II.ii.46); Surrey projects this fear into the future with his complaint that "our issues . . . if [Wolsey] live, will scarce be gentlemen" (III.ii.291–92). Wolsey's contemporary, the poet John Skelton, had gone so far as to liken him to a resident of the biblical city of Sodom,[86] a sodomite, insofar as he had fallen into a "wylfull blyndnesse" (l.468) of the heart, an occlusion of spiritual vision evidenced in his luxurious self-indulgence and his indiscriminate sexual escapades (ll.215–26) as well as in the necromancy Skelton hints that Wolsey practices (ll.686–707).[87] Although Shakespeare does not go so far as Skelton and explicitly name Wolsey a sodomite, the ethical dissolution and universal ruin associated with the prelate—his libertinage (IV.ii.43; III.ii.294–96), his treasonous allegiance to the pope and Roman Catholic Spain (I.i.156), his misprision in office that effectively produces "loud rebellion" (I.ii.29)—recalls and recapitulates the apocalyptic vision of destruction advanced by the anti-theatricalists, the vision that Thomas White encompassed under the monitory typology of "Sodome overcome."

This invocation of the anti-theatrical polemic begs the question of the relation between the strident critique of Wolsey and the assault on the stage. The connection is more than resemblance. In fact, an important aspect of the extended abjection of the prelate is a critique of his role in staging the elaborate spectacles of diplomacy in France, the theater of state concluded immediately prior to the opening of the play. *Henry the Eighth* begins with an acerbic account of Wolsey's hand in the production of the lavish celebration of accord between France and England at the Field of Cloth of Gold. Evocative of the way the anti-theatricalists considered the popular stage the site of a dangerous generation, and imagined those who attended to be a satanic spawn that would overrun England, the nobles criticize Wolsey's management of the "fierce vanities" (I.i.54) in France as a dangerous animation. The Cardinal, they report, "set the body and the limbs / Of this great sport together" (I.i.46–47), a spectacular display that in its extravagance "swallowed so much treasure" (I.i.166).[88] Commenting on the impact on those forced to feed Wolsey's creation, Buckingham observes that some in attendance were compelled to sell all they had merely to dress for the occasion: "many / Have broke their backs with laying manors on' em / For this great journey" (I.i.83–85).[89] After the prelate's death, Griffith apologetically reminds the dying Princess Dowager of Wolsey's role in founding two universities, institutions identified as children begot upon Katherine, "Those twins of learning he raised in you, / Ipswich and Oxford" (IV.ii.58–59). This account of Wolsey's governed cultural reproduction through largesse memorializes as pious benevolence that which, while the Cardinal lived, was construed as an ungoverned and prodigal *de*generation. The nobles treat the Field of Cloth of Gold as an insatiable person made by Wolsey—indeed, an image of Wolsey himself—insofar as it unmakes titled families by devouring their estates.

Certainly, the play maintains an investment in clearly distinguishing the future Queen Elizabeth from the cardinal. Wolsey's behavior and his management of the kingdom are starkly antithetical to the ideal of economic and social harmony Cranmer projects into the reign of the queen-to-be. And, where the nonlineal generation of men through imitation of the future queen founds a just hierarchy of merit, Wolsey's imitation of the king represents an unlicensed and degenerate status advancement, a sign of and means for his dangerous agency. These distinctions notwithstanding, the accusations of abuse and ungoverned generation targeted at the cardinal are leveled at the princess herself at the very site of the archbishop's privileged glimpse into the future, the scene of Elizabeth's christening. At that event, as noted above, the young princess occasions an onslaught of people out of control, a "multitude" (V.iv.64) so unruly that the Porter's Man speculates that "[t]he devil was amongst 'em" (V.iv.55). Especially in light of the Porter's complaint that the crowds treat the regal space of the court as, among other things, a "playhouse," such an assertion (like the account of Wolsey's staging of the Field of Cloth of Gold) recalls the terms of the anti-theatricalist attack that the stage was demonically fecund. Much as Wolsey's critics reviled him as one who generated a destructively voracious person, the staff of the royal household attribute to Princess Elizabeth on the occasion of her christening the capacity for producing unruly numbers. Wondering what all the fuss is about as the crowds press to get a view of

Elizabeth, the Porter asks, "have we some strange Indian with the great tool come to court, the women so besiege us?" (V.iv.31–32). Foakes, in his note to this line, directs us to *The Tempest* and Trinculo's observation that, if he could get Caliban to England, he could make a fortune charging to see his "strange beast" (*Tempest* II.ii.30). The connection may be developed in the direction of the questions of generation I have been pursuing. In *The Tempest,* Caliban claims that, but for Prospero's intervention, he would have with Miranda "peopled . . . This isle with Calibans" (I.ii.350–51). This fantasy attributes to the indigenous populations of the new world, in the person of Caliban, a violent and predatory eros, in turn associated with a superabundant fecundity.[90] Picking up on the Old Lady's characterization of the infant as "this stranger" (*Henry the Eighth* V.i.168), the Porter suggestively constitutes Elizabeth herself as the "strange" agent of an ungoverned reproduction, hyperbolically masculine, outlandishly potent.

The implication that Elizabeth possesses a disruptive fecundity receives further elaboration in the lines immediately following the Porter's question, (in his exclamation noted at this section's outset). Exasperated by the crowds muscling in to view the queen-to-be, the Porter exclaims, "Bless me, what a fry of fornication is at door! On my Christian conscience this one christening will beget a thousand" (V.iv.33–35). The Porter's analysis advances the idea that the people struggling to view Elizabeth are of an illicit descent, that they are spawned of sin. It also suggests that they themselves will reproduce: the sanctification of the birth of Elizabeth will put in play actions that will generate a thousand more births. Finally, and most relevant to the understanding advanced in the anti-theatrical polemic, the Porter's locution formulates the christening *itself* as the agent of generation. Such an account figures this piece of royal theater as capable of producing numbers of people—more births to be celebrated or more "fry" to augment the disordered "rabble." Presented as a theatrical spectacle, Elizabeth stands not only as a "girl [who] Promises boys hereafter," but also one whose christening "will beget a thousand," an excessively fertile generator of unstable multitudes that threaten to overrun the royal household.

In the face of the unregulated reproduction of Elizabeth's christening, as well as of the similarity of Wolsey's monarchical imitation to the ideal located in the reign to come, Cranmer's prophecy works to distinguish the "virgin" queen, the "most unspotted lily" (V.v.60–61), from the Cardinal and his ethically dissolute presence in the nation by directly opposing Elizabeth's rule to the effects supposedly produced by Wolsey. As if answering the litany of complaints against Wolsey's destructive appetite, his exacting taxation, and his hoarding of the nation's wealth—a self-interest that wastes—Cranmer offers a vision of economic plenitude during the future rule of Elizabeth: "In her days every man shall eat in safety / Under his own vine what he plants, and sing / The merry songs of peace to all his neighbors" (V.v.33–35). In immediate contrast to the specter of Wolsey's degenerative "ill husband[ry]" (III.ii.142) that defies "thrift" (III.ii.109), this is a vision of masculine self-sufficiency, of a nation made up of perfectly functioning domestic economies, households with neither lack nor excess.

Such an ideal, further, opposes the scene of the coronation of Elizabeth's mother. Recall that Anne Bullen attracted an army of pregnant women who did battle to get a view of the newly crowned queen. The mingling in the crowd was so indiscriminate, as the Third Gentleman reports, that "No man living / Could say 'This is my wife' there, all were woven / So strangely in one piece" (IV.i.79–81). By this account, the procession marking the reconstitution of the royal family deconstituted the families in attendance. Cranmer, by contrast, envisions a nation of men, each constituting a closed economy, each under his own vine, eating what he needs, needing no more than the abundance generated with and through Elizabeth, secure and happy in "merry" England.

Of course, this vision of the future is, in the moment of its staging, a future past, and it is not the least of this passage's creative licenses with this past actively to rewrite the social instabilities that marked Queen Elizabeth's reign—vagabondage, hunger riots, political dissidence, open insurrection.[91] Such glaring historical erasures underscore the fact that Cranmer's prophecy has the status of one account among many, a limited effort that seeks to manage the effects of potentially destabilizing cultural reproduction. Although Cranmer celebrates a dispensation in which the merit derived from imitating Elizabeth's virtues underwrites a new hierarchical order, his prophecy arrives only at the last minute, only after the dangers associated with Wolsey have been voiced and linked to pedagogical mobility of the sort Elizabeth will foster, and in opposition to the specter of multitudes out of control at her christening.

By noting the belatedness of Cranmer's prophecy, I do not mean to suggest that Shakespeare subversively embraces the possibilities for deformative generation associated with the pedagogic mimesis enabling and surrounding Wolsey's ministrations and Elizabeth's christening. However, he does offer an alternative effort to manage the disruptive potentials put in play through educational imitation, an effort that seeks to establish the theater's credibility and sphere of reproductive impact. The epilogue to the play addresses these issues by bringing attention to bear upon the activity of theatrical "construction." Such an emphasis broaches simultaneously questions of, on one hand, the relation of the stage to household government, and on the other, the issue of dramatic reproduction. *Henry the Eighth* will not please, the Epilogue asserts, those who came to "sleep an act or two" (Epi.3) or those who came to hear insults hurled at the city. The Epilogue "fear[s]" that, perhaps,

> All the expected good w' are like to hear
> For this play at this time, is only in
> The merciful construction of good women,
> For such a one we showed 'em.
>
> (Epi.7–11)

The Epilogue combines the generative function imagined for the theater by both pro- and anti-theatricalists, with Cranmer's vision of Elizabeth as an epitome of all virtues imitated by those around her; that is, *The Life of King Henry the Eighth* is a play that both "construct[s]" women by presenting them on stage and, through the stage's generational capacity, "construct[s] . . . good women" by offering ideals for imitation.[92] However, the dynamic imagined here clashes with Archbishop Cranmer's vision. Although the Epilogue implicitly counters the anti-theatrical fears of a nation overrun by an ungoverned theatrical spawn, as well as the Porter's account of the riotous "beget"-ing at the royal spectacle of Elizabeth's christening, it cannot be said to endorse the ideal of perfectly regulated reproduction that Cranmer offers. The resistance here can be located in the vagueness of the Epilogue's "one." Precisely who is the "one" good woman mercifully "construct[ed]"? Is it Queen Elizabeth? The claims of the Epilogue might then be read as an elaboration of Cranmer's prophecy. But could the "one" not also be Queen Katherine? The play earlier has endorsed Katherine insofar as she is presented with a masque of fairies to comfort her on her deathbed, a vision of divine sanction that, from the perspective of the Epilogue, would seem to conflict with Cranmer's celebration of Elizabeth.[93] What about Anne Bullen?

The Lord Chamberlain asserts that "Beauty and honor in her are... mingled" (II.iii.76), and the Second Gentleman proclaims that she is "an angel" (IV.i.44). Which of these women should be held up as the "one" exemplar? And what would be the implication if the "one" were the Old Lady? If the Epilogue's "one" conceivably does refer to the Old Lady, a carnivalesque figure who gives voice to "fornication," we might take the dynamic of the "merciful construction of good women" to be a revision of Heywood's ideal, a revision that defines the theater's role in terms of its capacity for festive generation.

Such an alternative is consistent with a second sense of the activity of "construction," understood as an act of interpretation. Following this sense of the word, the Epilogue deferentially and self-effacingly suggests that the women of the audience will be the only ones to approve of the play just presented.[94] The Epilogue thus relies on these women to provide the most "merciful" and generous reading of the play because they were shown "one" good woman. "If they smile," the Epilogue states,

> And say 'twill do, I know within a while
> All the best men are ours; for 'tis ill hap,
> If they hold when their ladies bid 'em clap.
> (Epi.11–14)

As I have argued, Cranmer's celebration of the self-sufficient, male "oeconomies" that will flourish under Elizabeth answered the indiscriminate dissolution of domestic relations at Queen Anne's coronation, and Wolsey's unlicensed hoarding and expenditure. The Epilogue responds by linking the success of the stage to a domain of household government in which women are constituted as agents of aesthetic judgment. That is, if Cranmer's prophecy projected a nation of men subsisting within the abundant equilibrium of perfectly regulated domestic economies, and if the play itself might have been staged to celebrate the marriage of Princess Elizabeth—an arranged marriage in which a woman served as a marker in dynastic diplomacy, an international alliance secured through the traffic in women—the Epilogue counters these alternatives by appealing to women, implicitly insisting on a domestic relation that would not simply subsume women into the husband.[95] My point here is not that this is a feminist gesture.[96] Nor do I see the Epilogue describing the popular theater as a space of radical freedom in which women are afforded a space unmarked by the repression operative elsewhere in the society. My point is rather that the Epilogue's speech describes, and thus seeks discursively to constitute, a specific vision of domestic relations—that it implicitly values and privileges an understanding of household government distinct from a monolithically patriarchal dispensation endorsed elsewhere in the play. This effort to privilege an alternative account of domestic economy underwrites the Epilogue's effort to define, and thus to secure, the viability and cultural effectiveness of the popular stage. Contrary to the anti-theatrical account of the stage as the hyperfecund antithesis of government, the Epilogue invests the theater's success in a governmental relation that hinges on the two senses of the dynamic of "construction." Plays both construct and are constructed by the women in the audience, who in turn are able to "conduct the conduct" of their men (or at least of the "best" ones) and direct that conduct into approval of the theater's efforts.

Just how governed is this conduct intended to be? Certainly the Epilogue's linkage of the success of the popular theater to the redefined ideal of household government counters the anti-theatrical polemic's allegations that the stage constitutes a dangerous threat to the household and hence to the commonwealth as a whole. It does not, however, necessarily imply the imposition of a perfectly governed eros. The bawdy pun, "'tis ill hap, / If they hold when their ladies bid 'em clap," playing on the sense of "clap" as amorous "embrace"[97] or as syphilis, suggests that an ideal of self-control, of ethical containment of desires, presents a risk to the domestic relationship. This, no doubt, is not what Heywood had in mind in his claims in behalf of theatrical generation. Indeed, the Epilogue makes a case for the public stage as a site for governing cultural reproduction not by opposing the specter of "fornication" against which the Porter railed, but by playing off of it; not by denying the anti-theatrical account of the stage's dissolute production of numbers, but by incorporating it. That is, Shakespeare works to define the stage as a relatively autonomous sphere of governmental practice in which a limited form of unruly conduct and generation does not devastate but reinforces the theater's cultural authority and insures its continued viability.

CHAPTER FOUR

The Educational Genesis of Men

Puritan Reform and John Milton's Of Education

Surveying the state of American education in 1962, the well-known Milton scholar William Riley Parker found it in profound disarray. Inefficient, ineffective, and disordered, schooling took place without any clear purpose; whatever motives or objectives informed the activities of educators, contemporary institutional structures and practices promoted an ungoverned generation of what Parker considered useless persons. Especially riling to Parker was the use of electives in university education, a practice that had gained prominence with the increase in scale of American schools over the previous decades. With respect to the "proliferation of new subjects and courses," which either caused or was the result of inviting students to study whatever they wanted, Parker argued:

> Both in the colleges and in the high schools it has compelled us to spawn an entirely new breed of educator, the counselling and guidance expert. Since the youngster is uninformed, he must now talk to an uninformed adult, who can explain to him that only three years of English are required for graduation from high school, and that, if he is going into business, he will never have need of a foreign language. The Government spends millions of dollars annually on counselling and guidance institutes, and many efforts are being made to multiply these academic middlemen, who are in great demand.[1]

Somewhat paradoxically, Parker asserted that secondary and tertiary education failed by being both too responsive to the imperatives of capitalism and not responsive enough. The paradigmatic student for Parker was the young man or woman (though he never explicitly referred to the latter) unprepared for the demands of a global economy; this failure of academic "responsibility" (12) was seen as both enabled and exacerbated by the fact that America's academic institutions had become too much like corporations, complete with a whole strata of midlevel managers catering to the demands of uninformed consumers.[2] Parker sneeringly insisted that the specialized knowledge of the counselling and guidance experts was pointless and served only to rationalize the failures of the system. Their existence was both a symptom of and response to academic incompetence, a situation exacerbated by the "Government['s]" policy of making more such men and women.

Perhaps not surprisingly, Parker argued that the remedy for this crisis in schooling was outlined in John Milton's 1644 plan for improving the instruction of England's youth. Such an assertion actively answered those critics who dismissed Milton's *Of Education* as so indebted to humanist views and practices as to render it unoriginal and hence uninteresting, nothing more than a summary of received wisdom or synopsis of the training Milton received at St. Paul's grammar school.[3] From Parker's perspective, although the tract might have recapitulated existing institutional practice or the stuff of Renaissance conduct manuals, it was nonetheless inspired by erudite greatness, fired by the solemn heat of Milton's synthetic genius.[4] *Of Education,* Parker asserted, thus offered a model of careful, logical, well-ordered and efficient instruction to which America's colleges and universities could aspire. However, the brief pamphlet's relevance to the contemporary moment was a function not only of Milton's intellectual stature, but also of similarities in historical circumstance: "Teaching was almost exclusively in the hands of the clergy," Parker observed, "who taught with the lay objective of multiplying themselves" (2). The verbal connection between the "multiplication" of clergy and that of guidance counselors signaled the extent to which the problems Milton faced coincided with those Parker saw in twentieth-century America—a suspect generation of persons who had a vested interest in perpetuating educational incompetence. Of course, this is self-serving on Parker's behalf; the parallel fuels the moral fervor driving his jeremiad. It is not, however, entirely off the mark; that is, without acknowledging it as such, he picks up on an anxiety pervading Milton's prose works of the 1640s—a fear of a multiplication of persons that threatened to destroy the nation.

This chapter advances a reading of these concerns in Milton's work, and examines how they structure his vision of a reformed educational regimen. Although I take Parker's observations as a point of departure, what follows works against the grain of his appeal to *Of Education.* In spite of his sense of the necessity of briefly describing the educational landscape upon which Milton intervened, Parker's insistence on the timeless value of Milton's program explicitly resists a historicist approach to the pamphlet, a protocol of reading that would take away from the luster of the "great writer" by "bury[ing] him in his milieu" (1). In what follows, I shall, at the risk of burying Milton in his milieu, situate *Of Education* in a series of contests that elaborate and extend the questions pursued in the first three chapters, questions centering on the creation and government of different kinds of persons.

By locating Milton's tract in two related but distinct discursive arenas, this chapter details the specific governmental problems—dynamics of coordination and conflict between different forms of governance, and anxieties about the reproductive effects associated with governmental forms—that Milton acknowledges and seeks to resolve. First, following Parker's suggestive lead, I shall explore the relation between Milton's reflections upon English pedagogic practice and his more extended polemic against the Church of England's miseducation of England's youth. Second, developing insights offered by Christopher Hill and Charles Webster, I shall emphasize the links between Milton's proposal and the work of the Puritan educational reformers, a circle organized by and around the individual to whom Milton addressed his pamphlet, Samuel Hartlib.[5] Hartlib, along with Polish exile Jan Amos Comenius and cleric John Dury, helped raise the cultural stakes placed on educational practice prior to and during the Commonwealth by soliciting and producing an avalanche of proposals for educational reform—plans for universal education, for improving the instruction of language, and for facilitating scholarship and easing the flow of the exchange of knowledge. *Of Education* participates, albeit in a complex way, in this valorization of the education of children as a privileged technique for reforming the nation.

Taken together, the controversy over the prelates and the urgency surrounding educational reform map out the primary terrain upon which *Of Education* intervenes. Milton's program for improving the instruction of England's youth, I shall argue, addresses a failure of government at the levels of church, schoolroom, and family. In response to this governmental crisis, a crisis manifested in the unregulated generation of dangerous persons, the proposed "institution of breeding," an all-male enclave invested with generative capacities, offers a pedagogic regimen capable of producing a new generation of men who, by Milton's account, promise a more securely governed future for England.[6]

Generating Ethos

The previous two chapters examined, in part, the ways a theological perspective enabled a critique of poetry and the theater as dangerously fecund. I wish at the outset of this chapter to modify my approach somewhat and, following Parker's lead, examine how the church itself could come under scrutiny for its own reproductive effects. "Except a man be born again," Jesus tells the Pharisee Nicodemus, "he cannot see the kingdom of God" (John 3:3). This vision of a spiritually transformed life, of a personal "regeneration," served to authorize, and provided an objective for, the ministrations of the church. Although being "created anew" could be accomplished "by no other power, but by the divine and heavenly, by which we were first created," it is precisely through the church that "we come to be citizens and to have anything to do in the city of God."[7] In keeping with such an understanding of the necessary rebirth that must affect the life of each believer, the language of parthenogenesis powerfully describes the desired impact of what ministers do. As John Preston wrote in the early seventeenth century, "a preacher in the University doth *generare patres*, beget begetters."[8]

Although a fecund ministry was certainly the objective, there were those sharply critical of the Anglican Church's reproductive efficacy. According to the Root and Branch petition, signed by approximately fifteen thousand people and presented to Parliament in December 1640, the Church of England was not *making* good Christians but *destroying* them. The petition presented a catalogue of grievances with the Anglican hierarchy and sharply criticized prelatical incompetence, aggrandizement, idolatry, and juridical misprision.[9] A "dangerous consequence" of these and numerous other abuses was the

> discouragement and destruction of all good subjects, of whom are multitudes, both clothiers, merchants and others, who being deprived of their ministers, and overburdened with these pressures, have departed the kingdom to Holland, and other parts.[10]

Milton supported the petition (*Animadversions,* 1: 676–77, 1: 702–3) and likewise indicted episcopacy for its "depopulation" of England, lamenting the fact that "numbers of faithfull, and freeborn Englishmen, and good Christians have bin constrain'd to foresake their dearest home, their friends, and kindred, whom nothing but the wide Ocean, and the savage deserts of *America* could hide and shelter from the fury of the Bishops" (*Of Reformation,* 1: 585).[11]

Among the many "pressures" hydraulically pushing good Christians abroad were concerns about how the Anglican Church mishandled its pedagogic responsibilities.[12] Puritan ministers conceptualized their preaching functions in explicitly educational terms; as Foster Watson observes, the word "minister," at least during the middle decades of the seventeenth century, signified both "preacher" and "schoolmaster."[13] As William Haller attests, the activities of Puritan divines had significant pedagogic effects in the form of expanded literacy and religious discussion; the laity "learned to read, to use a book, to exchange ideas and experiences, to confer intellectually after their own fashion upon common problems."[14] Consequently, the Anglican practice of maintaining pluralities (in which one person held several church offices and collected remuneration for all of them) was perceived to be not only a sign of the greed the church fostered, but also an indication of the church's failure to fulfill one of its central functions.[15] Laud's opposition to the largely Puritan, quasi-independent "lecturers" hired by individual congregations simply confirmed for the church's critics its audacious disregard for its mission.[16] For the petitioners, this disregard was a matter both of not doing enough to provide sufficient ministers and of not taking the needed steps to insure that what education took place under its ministerial aegis stabilized rather than disrupted the polity. In addition to highlighting "the want of preaching ministers in very many places both of England and Wales," the petitioners charged prelates with:

> The discouragement of many from bringing up their children in learning; the many schisms, errors, and strange opinions which are in the Church; great corruptions which are in the Universities; the gross and lamentable ignorance almost everywhere among the people; . . . the loathing of the ministry, and the general defection to all manner of profaneness. (139)

The clergy prevented people from learning by depriving them of educational opportunities, but also actively promoted ecumenical dissension and "strange[ness]." Subsequent complaints about the printing and circulation of licentious works by Ovid and other censured poets (139) reinforced this sense that the Church of England was not simply failing to prevent a "general defection to all manner of profaneness," but was dangerously encouraging such degeneracy.

Milton shared the Root and Branch petitioners' concerns about the contemporary educational dispensation. Indeed, his critique of the Anglican Church elaborated their sense that the prelates were causing degeneracy, characterizing their pedagogic activities as dangerously generative. Rather than "begetting begetters," the church was explosively fecund in the worst imaginable ways. Prelates, Milton asserted, propagate "schisme and combustion" ("the very issue of your bodies, your first born" [*Reason*, 1: 793]). At the very institutional origin of hierarchy in the church he identified a fertility out of control, multiplying heresy as soon and as fast as the hierarchical structure was put in place: "Heresie begat heresie with a certain monstrous haste of pregnancy in her birth, at once borne and bringing forth" (*Reason*, 1: 781). Milton argued that the educational activities underwritten and policed by the Anglican Church resulted in the unbounded production of dangerous persons—a specter of an ungovernable, conceivably infinite generation of prelates who sought learning only out of greed. From the admixture of "low pitch't desires" for financial reward and the "heavenly intentions that draw a man to this study," Milton contended,

> it is justly expected that they should bring forth a baseborn issue of Divinity like that of those imperfect, and putrid creatures that receive a crawling life from two most unlike procreants the Sun, and mudde. (*Animadversions*, 1: 720)

Compare with Milton's formulation from earlier the same year in which the system of clerical rewards functioned as a mechanism of papal genesis:

> The soure levin of humane Traditions mixt in one putrifi'd Masse with the poisonous dregs of hypocrisie in the hearts of *Prelates* that lye basking in the Sunny warmth of Wealth, and Promotion, is the Serpents Egge that will hatch an *Antichrist* wheresoever, and ingender the same Monster as big, or little as the Lump is which breeds him. (*Of Reformation*, 1: 590)

In his response to the Root and Branch petition, Lord George Digby claimed that the assault on the church hierarchy would lead to a kind of demonic papal genesis; although the petition argued against what it saw as Catholic tendencies in the English church, Digby held that the assault on order the activists suggested would fragment religious authority and thereby "set up a Pope in every Parish."[17] From Digby's perspective, religious dissidence would enable a kind of papal assault on England; instead of one Pope in the Vatican, there effectively would be multitudes dispersed across England. Milton, by contrast, took prelatical pursuit of reward in the ministry through learning to be a vile, demonic autogenesis. Ignoble, alien, and "putrid," the church spread instability throughout the commonwealth by spawning antichrists.

The seriousness of the threat that Milton perceives this ungoverned generation to hold for England may be gauged in his invocation of the biblical city of Sodom. By mapping prelatical ministrations onto this highly charged landscape, Milton suggests the ways that what he took to be a crisis in church government ramifies across other governmental spheres. Here is the sardonic appeal for mercy for the Anglican hierarchy with which Milton closes *The Reason of Church-government Urg'd Against Prelaty:*

> Though God for lesse than ten just persons would not spare *Sodom,* yet if you can finde after due search but only one good thing in prelaty either to religion, or civil government, to King or Parlament, to Prince or people, to law, liberty, wealth or learning, spare her, let her live, let her spread among ye, till with her shadow, all your dignities and honours, and all the glory of the land be darken'd and obscurd. (1: 861)

No appeal for mercy, really, since Milton ultimately insists that any quarter would make England a second Sodom, indeed, that prelacy's ministrations already have exceeded Sodom's abominations ten-fold. Milton's dis-identification—a differentiation that nonetheless secures the connection between the Anglican Church hierarchy and the residents of Sodom—implicitly invokes the highly charged, complexly overdetermined, legal discourse of sodomy. Sodomy, as emphasized in the previous chapter in relation to the anti-theatrical polemic and the characterization of Cardinal Wolsey, does not translate the contemporary term "homosexual," its residual medico-juridical connotations of pathology, or its assumption of a stable identity coherently and diametrically opposed to a presumptively stable, presumptively normal heterosexuality. Indeed, Milton organizes within the civic borders of Sodom a whole series of abuses grouped together not as transgressions of heterosexual norms, but as signs of degeneracy. This gesture may be illuminated by examining the Puritan John White's accusations against prelacy. Defending Parliament's disestablishment of numerous ministers in 1643, White invited those readers who wanted "the Land yet more defiled with cursing, swearing, drunkennesse, whoredome, Sodomie," to "put thy shoulders still to the support of the said Church-Government and Governours."[18] Sodomy figures the limit of White's accusations and metonymically stands in for the rest, encompassing episcopal crimes within a rubric of an absolute failure of government over themselves and others. Just so, Milton's situation of the Nile-istic "reptilian spawn" of prelacy within the city limits of Sodom condenses a whole array of abuses. The degenerate and ungoverned prelates threatened the commonwealth through a dangerous miseducation of the king, a pedagogy marked by a treasonous complicity with Roman Catholic Spain: the episcopacy's "*Spanioliz'd Bishops,*" Milton writes, "dandle the *Royal Ball* with unskilfull and *Pedantick palmes*" (*Of Reformation,* 1: 587). By such means, Milton argues, prelates, dressed in the "whorish attire" of a Catholic mass, seek through "their spirituall fornications" to make Englishmen the Pope's "Bastards" (*Animadversions,* 1: 728); their intentions toward England, he insists, are no better than were the incestuous rapist Amnon's toward his sister Tamar (hating her more after his crime than he loved her before) (*Reason,* 1: 851). Their ungoverned appetite fueled an unrestricted consumption of England's stores of money and goods. Like a "Wen" (*Of Reformation,* 1: 583) or a leech (1: 589) this conspicuous consumption returned nothing to the commonwealth. "[W]hat an excessive wast of Treasury," Milton exclaimed, when he considered the Church of England's "Idolatrous" (*Of Reformation,* 1: 589–90) architectural, decorative, and sartorial luxuriance. Their budgetary license constituted a destructive fury comparable to "that huge dragon of Egypt breathing out wast, and desolation to the land, unlesse he were daily fatn'd with virgins blood" (*Reason,* 1: 857).

Though Milton immediately specifies the political implications of his simile—the king and nobles should be like St. George and save the virginal church from the bestial episcopacy—this allegorical decoding does not exhaust the suggestiveness of this comparison. If it figures the subhuman prelates as a threat to a victimized woman, it also opposes them to an ideal of absolute bodily restraint. Milton's argument advances (in the terms detailed in this book's first chapter) an ideal ethos, a vision of perfectly governed desires and regulated behavior. As is evident in his polemic, this ethos is crucial to his definition of English masculinity. Contrary to the licentious behavior countenanced by the prelates, Milton asserts:

> Liberty consists in manly and honest labours, in sobriety and rigorous honour to the Marriage Bed, which in both Sexes should be bred up from chast hopes to loyall Enjoyments; and when the people slacken, and fall to loosenes, and riot, then doe they as much as if they laid downe their necks for some wily Tyrant to get up and ride. Thus learnt *Cyrus* to tame the *Lydians,* whom by Armes he could not, whilst they kept themselves from Luxury; with one easy Proclamation to set up *Stews,* dancing, feasting, & dicing he made them soone his slaves.

"[S]o," Milton argues, "have they hamstrung the valour of the Subject by seeking to effeminate us all at home" (*Of Reformation,* 1: 588). Consistent with my previous discussions of the rhetoric of effeminization, when Milton voices despair at the effeminacy of his contemporaries, the transformation he laments amounts to a falling away from a socially instituted ideal of masculinity, a loss of self-mastery signaled by a susceptibility to "Luxury," to festive excess, to gambling, to erotic riot. Thus Milton etiologically locates prelacy's outrages in a voracious hunger, an unlicensed "avarice, & ambition" (*Animadversions,* 1: 720), an "insatiate desire" (*Of Reformation,* 1: 590) out of control. Accordingly, episcopacy is an institution given "to a mercenary whordome" (*Reason,* 1: 849);[19] the prelates teach each other masturbatory tricks (*Animadversions,* 1: 696); those complacent with the Anglican Church hierarchy are dissolute "Libertines" who brook no discipline whatsoever (*Of Reformation,* 1: 570).

This book has emphasized the ways humanist philological and pedagogical practice works to locate and reshape ethical models from classical antiquity to functionalize them for contemporary purposes. Certainly Milton is no exception, as evidenced in the reference to Cyrus above, just one example of his nearly ubiquitous appeal to classical exempla. However, it is important to underscore the extent to which the ethical ideal Milton projects—sobriety, diligence, chastity—delineates the contours of a specifically Puritan vision, an early modern ethos most fully accounted for by Max Weber.[20] According to Weber, the Calvinist solution to the epistemological uncertainty implicit in the doctrine of predestination—the idea that God determined whether or not one was elect or reprobate, and that no human action could modify or influence that decision—required a life of rational activity, restraint, and sobriety, a governed existence or, in his phrase, a "worldly asceticism."[21] Such a life would not effect one's status as elect or not, but would produce signs of election. The notion that the state of one's soul could be read in one's thoughts and the outcomes of one's actions encouraged intense self-scrutiny, a minute and perpetual attention to even the most negligible of life's details. Weber insisted that "the valuation of the fulfillment of duty in worldly affairs as the highest form which the moral activity of the individual could assume . . . inevitably gave every-day worldly activity a religious significance."[22] This significance granted to, in Haller's words, "the most trivial circumstances of the most commonplace existence,"[23] not only furnished an index for estimating the status of one's soul, but also instituted a projection to an unknown future day of account taking; this rationalizing calculus through which one sought to maximize the return on investment of the talents given by God instituted a sober discipline upon daily life, "a regulation of the whole of conduct which, penetrating to all departments of private and public life, was infinitely burdensome and earnestly enforced."[24]

Milton's polemic against prelacy advances such an ethos of sober discipline as the linchpin holding together the godly polity. The life of regulated conduct, a life exemplified in the ideals of Greco-Roman antiquity but put into play within a Puritan conceptual framework, forms both the standard that the prelates miserably fail to maintain and the foundation for right government of church and nation. Just as, by Milton's account, lack of self-government is a form of slavery, an ethical abandon that leaves open the door for a "wily Tyrant" to seize rule, the life of "manly and honest labours . . . sobriety and rigorous honor to the Marriage Bed" enables a proper government of "Liberty." This is the hard work of freedom, a "Liberty" that is not the ability simply to do as one likes, but the result of constant vigilance and careful effort. It is the business of government, in all its forms, not to repress people, but to institute the ethical self-regulation necessary to avoid a slavish subjection to licentiousness and, so, to repel the possibility of tyrannical rule, a government proper only to those who cannot rule themselves.

Thus discrediting prelacy, Milton joined the Root and Branch petitioners in working to disarticulate the church hierarchy from the monarchy, to break the alliance envisioned in the lapidary formula "no bishop, no king." The church's supervision of education and its system of educating people to enter the ministry by offering "rewards" was failing abjectly in the minds of many, and did nothing to encourage ethical self-regulation, inviting instead ethical dissolution. Consequently, Milton favored disestablishing the church hierarchy, eliminating prelacy "root and branch." The church's pedagogic functions could be handled more effectively, and Milton presented a couple of policy options. For example, he voiced approval of the Root and Branch petition's proposal to set up schools with dean and chapter funds (*Of Reformation,* 1: 590). With respect to the clergy in particular, Milton imagined God educationally reproducing enough ministers to generate, in turn, a race of saints.[25] God could, he asserted, "stirre up rich Fathers to bestow exquisite education upon their Children, and so dedicate them to the service of the Gospell"; and through their labor, "by the faithfull worke of holy doctrine," these could "procreate a number of faithfull men, making a kind of creation like to Gods, by infusing his spirit and likenesse into them, to their salvation, as God did into him" (*Animadversions,* 1: 721). Milton's parthenogenetic program echoed the likes of Preston in conflating the regeneration of souls with the creation of persons. However, where the Church of England either ran people off or dangerously spawned "putrid" and destructive subjects, Milton imagined a pedagogic dynamic that would "make up" people and thereby bolster the strength of king and country.

Vocational Education

The comments just above begin to render legible the connections between Milton's *Of Education* and the anti-prelatical polemic. What follows argues that *Of Education* constitutes another version of Milton's ideal of a pedagogy to "procreate a number of faithfull men"; his "institution of breeding" (*Of Education,* 2: 408) sought to make up people able "to perform justly, skilfully and magnanimously all the offices both private and publike of peace and war" (2: 378–9). To flesh out this argument, though, it is necessary to give further attention to Weber's account of the Protestant ethic, which will help clarify the points of overlap with the programs of pedagogic reform advanced by Samuel Hartlib and his circle of correspondents.

In the first chapter, I noted the importance granted to the category of vocation by commonwealth writers of the sixteenth century; I argued that vocation constituted a crucial ethical form through which people structured their lives and conceptualized their relationship to the common weal. It is helpful here to elaborate upon Weber's account of vocation as a privileged form through which Protestants sought to rationalize their existence. Weber argues that one's calling, the vocation assigned by God through which one carried out his plans and glorified him with one's talents, offers a primary site within which one, in Foucault's phrase, "intensifi[ed] . . . the relation to oneself." A vocation, Weber notes, provided a means for organizing one's activity into a life of sobriety, discipline, rational effort, and constraint: "The God of Calvinism," Weber writes, "demanded of his believers not single good works, but a life of good works combined into a unified system."[26] This is, in John Guillory's phrase, the "slippage from 'works' to 'work'"—not penitential labor that could affect God's disposition towards the sinner, but an entire life of effort in a calling, systematically organized and disposed through reference to an ultimate day of account-taking.[27]

Milton's extended attack on episcopacy relies upon two specific governmental effects of the form of vocational activity, effects immediately relevant to his proposal for educational reform. First, insofar as he insisted that the office of prelate was not a vocation—"we doe not count Prelatry a Calling," Milton informed Bishop Hall (*Animadversions*, 1: 673)—and that Anglican education spawned men unfit for the ministry, Milton demonstrates how the vocational structure could be enlisted to specify appropriate and inappropriate forms of social activity, could underwrite the policing and vilification of those perceived not to have a vocation. As Michael Walzer details, William Perkins's discussion of callings excluded four groups (standard objects of Puritan scorn) from his vocational framework: "1) rogues, beggars and vagabonds; 2) monks and friars; 3) gentlemen who 'spend their days in eating and drinking'; and 4) servants—'for only to wait . . . is not a sufficient calling.'"[28] Not to be living in a calling was to live contrary to the disposition God intended; from a Puritan perspective, this was to risk perdition. Even from a less orthodox point of view, a life outside a vocation was a life wasted, and the vocational structure authorized social intervention against those not included within the catalogue of callings. William Petty, another of Hartlib's correspondents, and future member of the Royal Society, in his 1648 *Advice of W. P. to Mr. Samuel Hartlib, for the Advancement of some particular Parts of Learning* refined and intensified the Protestant emphasis on vocation with his proposed encyclopedic "history of trades." This planned text was to specify in elaborate and minute detail all professions, inventions, and industrial processes "wherein all the practised ways of getting a subsistence, and whereby men raise their fortunes, may be at large declared."[29] The rational deliberation over all available vocational choices, Petty believed, would enable anyone to choose the most appropriate career, the "one that best suits with his own genius and abilities" (13). New jobs created by this "history" would put to work "beggars, feeding upon the labours of other men, and even thieves and robbers (made for want of better employment)" (13), as well as those formerly considered unable to labor. Indeed, he would have set people to work identifying "how all impotents, whether only blind, or only lame; and all children of above seven years old might earn their bread, and not be so long burthensome to their parents and others" (11–12).

Petty's efforts to bring more people into employment illustrate a second governmental effect of the vocational structure, one following from the instrumental logic that dictated that one's labors in a calling be *useful.* The standard of usefulness provided a means of evaluating both the endeavors of each person and the total effect of the collective godly vocational effort. Petty's outline for educational reform exemplifies this preoccupation with usefulness, and participates in the efforts of Hartlib and his network of correspondents to institute schemes for rationalizing social life. Awareness of each trade—of the mechanical processes, the tools and materials employed, the temporal rhythms of production and distribution of goods—would reduce opportunities for fraudulent tradespersons by making consumers less gullible, would enable an increase in experimentation and consequently the development of new inventions and industrial methods, and would allow tradespersons to increase the efficiency of their manufacturing practices. The reduction of superfluity achieved through efficient vocational distribution would multiply the productive force of each person: "one man, or horse," Petty asserts, "shall do as much as three, and every thing be improved to strange advantages" (13). (Hartlib similarly claimed, with respect to his Office of Public Address, that facilitating the movement of information could make any person "more useful to the publick a hundred-fold."[30]) Consistent with the way Milton and the Root and Branch petitioners participate (as discussed above) in the "making up" of certain kinds of persons, Hartlib and Petty describe and help to consolidate the "useful person," a specific form of individuality made available through the concept of vocation. Petty's intensified attention to vocation, moreover, his elaboration of it as an object of knowledge, his proposal for an exacted description of every trade and of the instruments, procedures, and "oeconomy" (11) proper to each, addresses an implied concern about a dearth of population by tripling the capacities of each individual. And while an emphasis on thrift, on the rational use of resources, eliminating waste and improving talents, informs Petty's scheme at every point, the metonymic equivalence between human and horse in the passage above registers and attempts to capitalize upon the instrumental logic underwriting the Protestant conception of vocation. By suggesting an equivalence between animal and human, Petty undermines his earlier emphasis on the rational estimation of talents and inclinations by a volitional agent. Like horsepower, subject to disposition by a farmer or driver, the human energies of the useful person were to be administered for maximum productivity.

Milton's studied excoriation of prelates, an elaborated description of vocational failure, implicitly traced the outline of a vocational ideal—the true minister—and marshalled disciplinary effects (outlined above) against episcopacy. Not only did prelacy not count as a calling, but education under prelatical rule spawned, in the Calvinist sense, vocationally unfit men, namely, the "learned foole" and the "learned Hypocrite." The former, Milton argued, "is ever coopt up at his empty speculations, a sot, an ideot for any use that mankind can make of him, or else sowing the World with nice, and idle questions." The latter,

> is still using his sophisticated arts and bending all his studies how to make his insatiate avarice, & ambition seem pious, and orthodoxall by painting his lewd and deceitfull principles with a smooth, and glossy varnish in a doctrinall way to bring about his wickedest purposes. (*Animadversions,* 1: 720)

"Empty" and "idle"; a passive "sot," or an active agent of dissimulation; "insatiate," duplicitous, "wicked"—these were, by Milton's account, the fruits of a prelatical educational policy that relied on, and thus reinforced, the most base tendencies of a desire always in danger of spinning out of control, desire that promised to ruin the commonwealth. These specific types of persons ("learned foole" and "learned Hypocrite") were, within the parameters embraced by Petty and Hartlib, useless.

Hartlib and his associates extended this polemic against the universities and the useless persons there. The circle of reformers did so by detailing the universities' abusive effect on the education of children in terms identical to Milton's anti-prelatical invective and concerns about ethical dissolution, voracious appetites, and waste. Comenius, in a text Hartlib translated and published in 1642, asserted that contemporary schooling, ineffective, inefficient, worthy of the contempt of all, wasted the time of children, "consumed their years," imprisoned them in the study of "unnecessary, and unprofitable things."[31] Thus he imagined an education to counter "ambition, drunkennesse, and other like vaine courses" in which people "mispend, and lose both their parts, and lives" (59). John Dury, writing a few years later, similarly produced the specter of "time . . . lost," and emphasized that each moment of the child's day be utilized for learning something.[32] Coincident with Petty's vision of multiplying each person's usefulness, Dury argued that the end of the instruction of children was "to train them up to know God in Christ, that they may walk worthy of him in the Gospel and become profitable instruments of the Commonwealth in their generations." Children took on this instrumental value, moreover, through activity in their vocation, "lawful callings for profitable uses," a means for them to avoid "becom[ing] a burden to their generation by living in idleness and disorderliness."[33]

Such formulations lead critics like Ernest Sirluck and Oliver Morley Ainsworth to characterize the Hartlib circle as motivated by a narrowly circumscribed agenda; according to the former critic, their interests are "so immediate and so predominantly economic that their educational purpose must be described as vocational."[34] The equivalence between "economic" and "vocational" points out that Sirluck does not have in mind the early modern sense of calling as analyzed by Weber—as briefly sketched above, a problematic of government, a concern for ethical self-management, and a framework within which the demand for more prudent investment of time and the specter of excess takes on a specific and pointed urgency.[35] Thus defining—thus dismissing—the Hartlibians, Sirluck, Ainsworth, and others read Milton's proposal as "fundamentally opposed" to the reformers' concerns,[36] viewing him as the proponent of a "liberal education"[37] that transcends the Hartlibians's somehow less exalted set of objectives.

Contrary to these Miltonolatric accounts, *Of Education* engages the concerns of Hartlib and his associates not by rising above vocation, conceived of as a sphere putatively sullied by basely utilitarian and financial interests, but by intensifying attention to vocation, by elaborating and extending the catalogue of abusive, nonfunctional persons begun in his anti-prelatical pamphlets. According to Milton, the schoolmen's curriculum fails the commonwealth through inadequately preparing students for their several callings, yielding ethically ungrounded and self-serving public officials. Upon graduation, Milton argues (in language immediately recalling the specter of prelatical surfeit), students were led:

> either to an ambitious and mercenary, or ignorantly zealous Divinity; Some allur'd to the trade of Law, grounding their purposes not on the prudent, and heavenly contemplation of justice and equity which was never taught them, but on the promising and pleasing thoughts of litigious terms, fat contentions, and flowing fees; others betake them to State affairs, with souls so unprincipl'd in vertue, and true generous breeding, that flattery, and court shifts and tyrranous aphorismes appear to them the highest points of wisdom; instilling their barren hearts with a conscientious slavery, if, as I rather think, it be not fain'd. Others lastly of a more delicious and airie spirit, retire themselves knowing no better, to the enjoyments of ease and luxury, living out their daies in feast and jollity. (*Of Education*, 2: 375–76)

Milton peoples his tract with, in addition to these "mercenary" divines and lawyers, "flatter[ers]" at court, uninspired and uninspiring ministers in the pulpit, or men living lives of private dissipation, a host of empty, putrescent, wasteful, and wasting individuals. These are, for Milton, not only the "poor, shaken, uncertain reeds, of such a tottering conscience, as many of our great counsellers have lately shewn themselves" (*Of Education*, 2: 398). They are also the rotting bodies of young soldiers (2: 393), and the "empty" (2: 372) and "unballasted wits" (2: 375) of children set afloat amid the waters of a scholastic syllabus. At the very limit of this insubstantial cultural reproduction are situated a host of imaginary persons allowed to flourish by the contemporary schools. These are specifically the nonexistent soldiers listed on the falsified rosters of "empty & unrecrutible Colonells of twenty men in a company," invented to defraud the commonwealth and to batten the officers with "the wages of a delusive list" (2: 412). This, we may recall, was Falstaff's scam, and just as the knight multiplied "shadows to fill up the muster book" to line his pockets, these virtual persons, administrative fictions existing only on paper, would sap parliamentary resources and channel them into self-aggrandizing officers' purses.

Milton's plan for educational reform answered this account of superfluous numbers of useless nonpersons by detailing a program that sought—as did those of Comenius, Dury, and Petty—to eliminate waste.[38] For example, Milton reasoned that the Latin works on agriculture that he included on his syllabus would provide an occasion to encourage his pupils "to improve the tillage of their country, to recover the bad soil, and to remedy the wast that is made of good: for this was one of Hercules praises" (*Of Education,* 2: 389). Milton's claim recalls and literalizes his complaint in his third "Prolusion," his bridling at the schoolmen's "inane arguments" and the useless wasteland of their scholarship, "thick and bristling with thornbushes and brambles, and covered with thistles and stinging nettles." "[H]ow often have I wished," Milton writes, "that I had been set to shovel out the Augean ox-stalls rather than struggle with such absurd assignments."[39] Thus, in *Of Education,* Milton not only enlists education in the project of efficient utilization of the nation's arable resources, but aligns that rational cultivation of talents with reform of an education that provided students only with "that asinine feast of sowthistles and brambles which is commonly set before them" (2: 377), a childhood wasted "either in learning meere words or such things chiefly, as were better unlearnt" (2: 376). The grammar schools and universities, he argues, preside over a barren intellectual landscape, their pedagogic cultivation of which yields nothing more than wasted time. In response, Milton relentlessly insists on the need for speed. The very brevity of his pamphlet—a characteristic to which he explicitly drew attention (2: 364, 415)—aspires to save time even in the act of outlining an educational regimen premised upon the necessity of saving time. He laments the "time lost" in "too oft idle vacancies" (2: 371) granted school children and university students. To utilize more effectively the time that "we do amisse to spend" (2: 370) through contemporary instructional methods, Milton's pedagogic alternative claimed to transform the schoolmen's seven- or eight-year project of teaching languages into the work of one.[40] Milton's plan, like those of Hartlib's correspondents, is "vocational" through and through. It founds and justifies its effectiveness on a temporal projection to a future day of

Calvinist reckoning, where expenditure of time will be measured against accomplishment; it offers a means "whereby we may best hope to give account to God of our youth spent herein" (2: 374).

In this last quotation, "youth" designates a number of years for which England's pedagogues are responsible. However, the insistence that instructors are "account[able]" to God for their disposition of this time recalls the parable of talents, which in turn suggests that the time of youth also represents a kind of financial resource. When writing against prelacy, Milton reminded his readers that among the factors that reinforced a monarch's rule were "the multitude, and valor of the people, and store of treasure" (*Of Reformation,* 1: 585);[41] the passage I am reading here effectively combines these two factors by treating people *as* treasure. Capable of being "spent," youth in this sense must be invested optimally by being rationally channeled into its most productive, efficient, and profitable uses for the commonwealth. We may recall that Sir Thomas Smith's *Discourse* posited a hierarchy of vocations based on which callings brought more treasure into the realm, thereby privileging certain people based on their net impact on the nation's hypothetical balance sheet. Milton does not advance exactly this argument—though he does take its premises a step further, for to create concern about the proper expenditure of youth treats them as a kind of wealth, what we might today call "human capital."[42] This is not to suggest that Milton's tract, or William Petty's *Political Arithmetic,* which (as we shall see) puts a dollar value on people, evidences the ruptural emergence of capitalism. However, it does help identify an important genealogical component of the conceptual framework organized by the discipline of political economy, in which analysis centers on the coordination of individual action and the "wealth of nations."

Abundance and Waste

My focus in the last few pages has worked to establish the conjunction of Milton's project with that of the Puritan educational reformers. However, it is important that, although Milton operates on the same terrain as the Hartlib circle, there are significant distinctions between Milton's tract and the proposals of the Comenians. Consider Comenius's own proposal for cutting in half the time an education could take, or alternatively for doubling the work an instructor could accomplish. He suggests, as a preliminary step to any reform, removing the following subjects from the contemporary pedagogic regimen:

> First, whatsoever is not of the essence of learning, of which sort are the most part of the vanities of the Gentiles, the name of their petty Deities, together with their lying histories, and fables. Next, such things as weary out mens braines to little benefit, of which sort are most of the rules of Grammar, which overburden childrens minds, and consume their yeares, and other things of like nature, which have no use but onely in Schooles. Lastly, all circumlocutions, and windings, and turnings of expressions, which fetch not out the kernell, but onely make a few assayes upon the shell. (*Reformation of Schooles,* 12)

Despite Comenius's dismissive rhetoric, and the fact that he treats humane learning like a poison, "infected with serpentine venom" (10), or a woman in meretricious clothing who "should be utterly stripped of all her inticing dresses, and allurements" lest she should "subvert" any whom Christ might save (33), neither he nor any of his coadjutors proposed completely scrapping classical subjects, the study of foreign languages, rhetoric, grammar, and logic. As Brian Vickers details, the criterion of usefulness enabled Puritan reformers to maintain these subjects on their syllabi.[43] The judgment about whether something was useful or abusively useless, furthermore, takes place through a Baconian critique of university and grammar school education. Such a critique, typical of Hartlib and his associates, including Milton, assails what is perceived to be a pervasive confusion between the essential and inessential, rule and substance, word and thing: where instruction should only impart the truth, it has become preoccupied with falsehoods and vanity; where grammar rules should be a helpful guide for language learning, they have obscured, indeed eclipsed, such study with their tiresome strictures; where words should stand in an indexical relation to the world they seek to represent, should enable a pure and transparent grasp of things, they no more than meander along the vain husk of reality.[44]

Because Comenius's account of scholastic failure focuses so intently on stylistic concerns, it should come as no surprise that his proposals for redressing the problems of contemporary schooling emphasize stylistic reform. By addressing stylistic abuse, Comenius seeks to render classical study usefully disinfected, stripped of dangerous raiment. These proposals for stylistic reform help locate a point of disjunction between

Milton and Hartlib's associates. A brief look at the parameters of Comenius's critique and an assessment of the cultural stakes involved will help clarify this distinction.

Comenius elaborates upon his opposition to "circumlocutions, and windings, and turnings of expressions," by taking a principled stand against what he calls the "luxuriating stile." By his definition, this kind of writing is present:

> when in the explication of things, improper, tropicall, hyperbolicall, and allusive words or sentences, and expressions are used: especially when Poets, or Oratours (and sometimes Philosophers and Divines acting their parts) falling upon any subject, which they would amplifie, or extenuate according to their manner, use with their figures, and colours so to alter things, that for the most part they appeare not in their native, but in a borrowed, and adventitious forme. (19)

Comenius assails an abundance of language and copiousness of expression that constituted an ideal embraced by humanist education. We may recall here Richard Halpern's argument that grammar schools in the sixteenth and seventeenth centuries, primarily through the influence of Erasmus (for example, through his widely read *De Copia*), emphasized not adherence to one standard but the mimetic incorporation of many styles, the study and imitation of several authors, methods of argument, genres of exposition, and figures of speech.[45] In the above passage, Comenius attributes to this abundant language the capacity to deform "things," "alter" them in ways beyond recognition. So too, by his account, does stylistic luxuriance blur appropriate vocational boundaries, tempt learned men into a theatrical imitation of the florid and extravagant—and thus suspect—language of poets and orators, lures them into "acting their parts." The instabilities Comenius anxiously details here provide instances of the way, as Halpern argues, the grammar schools' propagation of abundance was thought to generate effects outside of the classroom; the luxuriant autonomy encouraged by copious anti-Ciceronian style was often treated as a threat to existing forms of order.[46] Lord George Digby's response to the Root and Branch petition, mentioned above in passing, conveniently exemplifies this suspicion. Digby scornfully dismissed the text of the petition as a copiously unruly and disordered multiplication of assertions, a jumbled list of claims that failed to conform to his definition of the strictures and paradigms of learned discourse: "what have wee here a multitude of Allegations, a multitude of Instances, of abuses, and depravations of Church government" (B1v).[47] Much in the way that Sidney's *Arcadia* depicts the minion Clinias, who "had been a scholar so far as to learn rather words than manners, and of words rather plenty than order," Digby takes the stylistic excess of the petitioners' prose to be evidence of a politically destabilizing force. According to Digby, discussion in Parliament should conform to the demands of logic, but the petitioners' list of grievances lacked anything that looked like a clearly defined argument: "There is no Logick, no reasoning in their demands" (B1r). "A Petition," he elaborated, "ought in this to be a kind of Silogisme, that the Conclusion, the prayer ought to hold proportion with the premisses, that is with the Allegations, and Complaints, and to bee reasonably deduc't from them" (B1r–B1v). Lacking intellectual refinement, the uneducated multitude of petitioners assaulted reason itself, and in so doing assaulted the proprieties of civic order. Thus the Root and Branch bill, and what Digby considered its audacious list of demands, was not only "irrational," but also "contemptible . . . and presumptuous" (A4v), its nonsyllogistic argument an affront to the claims of traditional forms of political and cultural deference.

In his assessment, Digby opposes the ideal form of scholastic logic to the destabilizing autonomy of abundant prose—an implicit opposition between a people governed under a traditional regime of learning and the unlearned and ungoverned mob. Comenius, by contrast, links the two forms by suggesting that stylistic excess—prose or verse that obfuscates "things" with a deformative veil of "words"—enables scholastic multiplication of redundant jargon, the mechanism and tool of disputation over abstract and obscure points. Indistinct language in the schools ("homonymies, and ambiguous expressions") serves only to "breed . . . dissensions" (42). Rather than ground "serious knowledge," their "vulgar Canons in Logick are so farre from being exact rules of truth, or usefull in demonstrations, that they serve onely for disputation . . . and indeed appears to be nothing else but learned brangling" (43). Where Digby imagines a space for legislative discourse ruled by the imperatives of Aristotelian logic, and constructs a public domain through criteria established, maintained, and disseminated by the schoolmen, Comenius construes the universities and their promotion of pointless quibbling to be disruptive. Thus collapsing scholastic and humanist modes of excess, and echoing Milton's critique of the "learned foole" and the "learned Hypocrite" characterizing Anglican rule, Comenius excoriates:

> The prophaneness, the luxury, the pride, and revelling, the quarrelling and impudencie of our Universities.... And alasse! even the learning it selfe, which is there obtained, proves unto many but a whetstone of mischiefe, and an helpe to do evill all their days. (10)

"Luxuriating stile" both signifies and is promoted by the ungoverned and profane excesses of the schools, their pseudological methods and their pagan inspired knowledge. Extravagantly wasteful, contentious, and dissolute, the schoolmen pursued an ethically abusive existence. From the reformers' perspective, the universities, as noted above, both failed to keep Christian souls from frittering away their lives in drunken idleness, and ramified their unlicensed and uncontained profanity by propagating stylistic luxuriance via exposure to the learning of pagan antiquity. "Hence arose that scoffing proverb," Comenius asserts, "*Bonus Scholasticus, malus Politicus,* A good scholler, and a bad Commonwealths-man: whereas indeed the Schoole ought to prepare us for things incident to our lives" (9).

Despite the stylistic and ethical abusiveness pagan learning putatively signified and generated in schoolmen's instruction and lives, Comenius grants that "the Gentiles, and Arabians ... cannot but have observed profitable things" (33). Against the earlier stigma placed on classical learning, associated with a deformative and luxurious style, Comenius transforms the wasteful, unlicensed, and destabilizing efforts of the schoolmen to useful ends, indeed into "profit," through a process of extraction. Thus Comenius argues that "[t]he gold and silver which was gotten away from those impure Egyptians, did not at all defile the Israelites, or the Tabernacle" (86). The Mosaic narrative of escape allows Comenius to figure reformation as liberation, and the fugitive appropriation of the captor's treasure reconfigures the luxuriantly wasteful expenditure of the schoolmen into a divinely sanctioned source of wealth. Its nonabusive content abstracted, the pagan treasure of classical learning can be made available for the right use of all:

> it hath beene the custome of former ages, not to suffer the mysteries of wisdome to be published in vulgar languages, for every ones understanding, but in strange and forraine languages (as the Latine and

> Greeke) which must be of purpose learned for them: by which meanes wisedome it selfe was esteemed the peculiar treasure of such onely, as had access unto those fountaines: But wee claime it as the publique possession granted unto all mankind, which ought to be recovered to their common use and behoofe. (74)

Although this formulation explains the popularity of the Hartlib circle's work among England's radical sectarians, who critiqued the "engross-[ing]" of learning in almost identical terms,[48] the governmental vision implicit in such statements, James Holstun reminds us, does not imagine a leveling of hierarchies into a radically democratic dispensation, but instead outlines the dream of a more extensively disciplined existence.[49] Comenius envisions a Christian regime in which universal education would not precipitate anarchy but would secure instead the foundations of an order in which "All will know how the actions and endeavors of life should be regulated, within what limits we must progress, and how each man can protect his own position."[50]

Comenius's ideal of appropriating and redistributing the treasures of classical antiquity does not completely escape the humanist ideal of stylistic abundance that he would disavow. That is, in his trenchant critique of copia he both engages and reworks a familiar trope for copia; Erasmus himself, as Halpern notes, equates stylistic abundance with "material wealth."[51] Comenius rewrites this figure in terms that attempt to shift the wealth from style to "wisdom"—from "vanity" to "essence," from "shell" to "kernel" (12). Milton's critique of the schoolmen draws upon this same rhetoric of substance, upbraids the schoolmen's educational program as more interested in language than in the bedrock of matter: thus his dismissal, in *Of Education*, of an education in "meere words" as opposed to an education in "solid things . . . as well as . . . words and lexicons" (2: 369). However, when he further details his resistance to the schoolmen's pedagogy and begins to suggest his own alternative procedure, Milton argues not that copious language is the immaterial husk obfuscating the kernel of useful truth, but that copia is the substance with which to fill the emptiness of youthful heads. Milton dismissed the schoolmen's "preposterous exaction" as a program that got last things first and "forc[ed] the empty wits of children to compose Theams, verses, and Orations, which are the acts of ripest judgement and the finall work of a head fillèd by long reading, and observing, with elegant maxims, and copious invention" (2: 372). Milton would cultivate linguistic abundance and "elegan[ce]" over ten years, and not only maintain Erasmian treasure as the substance of an appropriate education, but also institute copia as, rather than a form of wasteful luxury, a culturally appropriate and ethically useful form of wealth. Where Comenius sought to extract profitable wisdom from Latin and Greek, an antidote to the dangerous luxury promoted by the schools, Milton constituted this luxuriance as useful—reconfigured wasteful expenditure as a productive investment, capable of generating solid men in the future to replace the ephemeral men failing England in its moment of crisis.

Household Government

This account of abundant language informs Milton's efforts to conceptualize and to justify his own literary endeavors. Consider his inscription to *The Doctrine and Discipline of Divorce* (published immediately before and after *Of Education*), Matthew 8. 52: "Every Scribe instructed to the Kingdome of Heav'n, is like the Maister of a house which bringeth out of his treasury things new and old" (2: 221). Education provides access to grace, this verse implies, and such pedagogic election situates the divinely instructed subject in a position of domestic mastery over a storehouse of language. In Milton's case, the treasures scribally dispensed were nothing less than the copious productions of his left hand, his massive textual output during the 1640s and 1650s, a spending spree encompassing his defenses of himself and the English people, his interventions in the divorce controversy, his effort to resist licensing of printing, his plan for educational reform, his polemic against the prelates.[52]

Against the vision of abusively learned prelates, or of the ethically insubstantial spawn of the schoolmen—situations in which linguistic abundance threatened the commonwealth—Milton constitutes his extraordinarily prolific linguistic abundance as licensed expenditure of copia by linking it with the governmental domain of the household, the primary classical locus of education. Traditionally the training of children was a function of domestic "oeconomy," a division of cultural labor reinscribed by Milton himself when in his *Second Defense* he characterized *Of Education* as a matter of "domestic liberty" (*Second,* 4: 624). In *The Doctrine and Discipline of Divorce* Milton insisted that the education of children, an activity located in a "private" (*Doctrine,* 2: 223) sphere, was absolutely necessary to mend the "tyranny" of "houshold unhappines on the family" (2: 229). Michael Walzer argues that Protestants considered fatherhood an "office," a calling instituted by and instrumentally subordinated to God.[53] Fathers were vocationally responsible for the right managing of their household, and thus for the education of their children, as duties to their maker.[54]

Of Education prepares future fathers for their administrative responsibilities by offering "Economics" as a distinct object of instruction (*Of Education,* 2: 397); Milton's letter of educational advice also construes the actions of the instructor in terms of fatherhood. As he sketched the contours of the most proper allocation of England's youthful resources—an ideal curriculum, a suggested regimen of exercise, a set of dietary recommendations—Milton also implicitly produced a job description, an account of the vocation of instructor who would oversee the expenditure of youth in behalf of the nation. In establishing his standards, Milton appealed to the stringent precedent of a classical father: "I believe," he argued, "that this is not a bow for every man to shoot in that counts himselfe a teacher; but will require sinews almost equall to those which Homer gave Ulysses" (2: 415). Milton's emphasis upon the strength of Ulysses's sinews recalled synechdochically the Protestant discipline instituted in Milton's academy, the regimental care of the body through exercise and diet.[55] In Homer's poem, the heroic musculature distinguished Ulysses's body from the bodies of the luxuriantly indulgent suitors, and etiologically accounted for his victory over them, foreclosing their voracious surfeit and resecuring his place as husband and father. That is, where Plutarch, in a work Milton included in his syllabus (2: 384 and n72), underscored the value of education as a means for a father to secure his estate into future generations by ensuring the virtue of his children—an investment as important as any other element of the household economy[56]—Milton's pedagogue was himself a father, governing the next generation, providing a governed form of cultural reproduction through the institution of a Weberian Protestant ethic, a rationally ordered distribution of time.[57] Thus positioning the instructor in the place of the father, Milton tactically authorizes the pedagogue's labors for the nation.

Just as the instructed scribe of Matthew was only "like" the master of a house, though, Milton's attribution to his ideal teacher of the governmental authority traditionally granted fathers implies a critical distance from the household domain. The tension between the father's disposition of the household and the instructor's supervision of the schoolroom, moreover, has a specifically Protestant cast. Calvinism both bolstered patriarchal authority and acted as a solvent upon its claims to authority.[58] Protestants in the early seventeenth century insisted that "even paternal authority must be tested by the Word of God. Indeed, the Puritan critique of custom often led the ministers to question radically the authority of fathers."[59] Keith Thomas and Christopher Hill provide us with abundant evidence of resistance to a traditional dispensation of fatherly rule especially, but not only, among the Puritan sects.[60] Hezekiah Woodward's 1640 *A Childes Patrimony* demonstrates the ways that education offered both a site and a means for such resistance. Indeed, as a way of securing the cultural status of the pedagogue, Woodward both registers and exploits the conflicting Puritan dispositions toward paternal authority. While William Gouge, writing in 1622 in a popular manual on household management, argued that "a family . . . is a school wherein the first principles and grounds of government and subjection are learned,"[61] Woodward figured the *parent* as a student, a pupil in the discipline of appropriate childrearing practices. His experience as both parent and instructor authorized his advice and lent his text pedagogic credibility and agency: "Therefore have I penned mine own Duty, with mine own hands; which may serve for a parent at large, to direct and teach him, his."[62] Despite Woodward's delineation of appropriate "jurisdiction[s]"[63] for master and parent, his reconfiguration of parenting as pedagogy, and pedagogy as reparenting, blurred the distinction between the two functions. Constructing parents as students, moreover, Woodward subordinated parental claims on cultural authority to the privileged knowledge of the schoolmaster.

His stated and implicit allegiances to a traditional regime of domestic rule notwithstanding, Milton's plan in *Of Education* similarly resisted the dictates of fathers. Milton's program, in fact, assumed parental incompetence in the instruction of children. Although Milton reflects at the end of his letter to Hartlib that his method did not begin "from the cradle, which yet might be worth many considerations" (*Of Education,* 2: 414–45), the pedagogical subject he envisions is one already formed through inappropriate instruction. For example, Milton requires that his pupils not only develop the patriotic feelings his education will instill, but also "despise and scorn all their childish, and ill taught qualities, to delight in manly, and liberall exercises" (2: 385). Miltonic education is re-education, an effort to repair the pedagogic mistakes of a child's parents or to redress their incompetent disposition of youth. Further, insofar as "[t]he end then of learning is to repair the ruins of our first parents" (2: 366–67), Milton considers the misjudgment of Adam and Eve to have made it necessary to provide children with orthopaedic instruction to correct the misprision of the Edenic couple.[64] Milton justifies his educational plan against the incapacities of various parents, offering pedagogy as a more secure technique for gaining access to divine perfection and for governing the nation's youthful resources.

Another way of describing these moves is to note that, although Milton's efforts would supercede a failed household government not by rejecting domestic economy but by embracing "oeconomics," the logic and imperatives structuring domestic economy, his proposal demonstrates the way "oeconomy" as a mode of governmental action could serve a compelling organizing and legitimizing function. Thus his work participates in a crucial reconfiguration central to a genealogy of modern forms of governance. To speak of a totality as an "economy" requires an abstraction of the "oeconomic" framework out of its initial formulation in the household, and a dispersal of its explanatory and regulative force to other arenas of existence.[65] Petty's imagined "History of Trades" evidences this proliferation, as well, insofar as this "History" was to have specified the "oeconomy" of each area of productive activity, to have provided an elaborated account of:

> What seasons of the year are most proper to each work, which the best places and times to buy materials, and to put off the commodities when finished; how most thriftily to hire, entertain, and oversee servants and workmen; how to dispose of every excrement and refuse of materials, or of broken, worn, or otherwise unserviceable tools and utensils; with all cauteles, impostures and other sleights good or bad, whereby men use to over-reach one another. (11)

Petty's attempt to organize conceptually the respective activities of each trade into a regularized flow of purchasing and selling so as to bolster against the vagaries of fraud and the contingencies besetting the enterprising tradesman, extends "oeconomy" in applicability and scope to domains outside the household—relatively autonomous sites not necessarily devoted to household maintenance or prosperity, possessing their own specificity and objectives. This extension does not yet represent the formation of "the economy," an autonomous, self-regulating sphere of reality only conceptually organized in the eighteenth century (within the discourse of political economy). It does however gesture toward an intensification around questions of commerce and trade in the seventeenth century, an intensification to which contributed, as an unforeseen and unintended effect, the religious practice of vocation.

This is not to suggest that the proliferation of domestic economy as a governmental logic happened seamlessly or uniformly. Indeed, aspects of Milton's program of pedagogic reform run counter to the "economization" of governance to which he and others contribute. To see how this is the case, I wish to note briefly the opening of Petty's letter of advice to Hartlib, which begins with an advertisement that makes further explicit Petty's commitment to commercial efficiency and forms an interesting corollary to Milton's ideal of paternal scribal expenditure. Petty solicited interest in a machine for double writing designed mechanically to augment scribal labor. It was, Petty claimed, "an instrument of small bulk and price, easily made, and very durable, whereby any man, even at the first sight and handling, may write two resembling copies of the same thing at once, as serviceably and as fast . . . as by the ordinary way" (1). The dream of a perfectly reproduced hand, a boon to "lawyers and scriveners . . . to merchants, intelligencers, registers, secretaries, clerks," as well as "to scholars" (1), strives for a pure, unimpeded multiplication of effort. Just as he sought to triple the effects of any man or horse, Petty imagined, in theory at least (his machine, because too heavy, was feasible ultimately only for draughting [*Advice of W. P.*, 1, n2]), a perfectly disciplined hand as a means of doubling the useful effects of any person.[66]

To be sure, Milton's ideal of scribal disbursement of knowledge for the country coordinates (as does his educational plan to generate more men capable of just such copious expenditure) with Petty's vision of effortlessly multiplying any writer's usefulness. Milton's work also shares Petty's implicit valuation of trade, evident in the latter's objective of facilitating the transactions of lawyers and scriveners and in his claim to be able to detect forgeries and thus to guarantee the integrity of a form of individuality able to enter into commercial arrangements. For example, Milton suggests that God's plenty encompasses commerce: when in *Of Education* he recommends taking students on field trips to view nature's "riches," the students' attention is to be directed to "all commodities of building and of soil, for towns and tillage, harbours and Ports for trade" (2: 412–13). Trade stands as a component of the abundance God has given the nation, a means for utilizing the talents given the country. Similarly, in Sonnet XII, Milton laments the "waste of wealth and loss of blood" (l.14) affecting the commonwealth during the Civil War, invoking the connections made in the anti-prelatical polemic between the treasures frittered away by episcopacy and the numbers banished abroad.[67] Framed in this way, *Of Education* may be said to coordinate an imagined pedagogic oeconomy with the larger oeconomy of the English commonwealth.

It will be helpful to recall William Riley Parker's twentieth-century effort to functionalize for our own times Milton's program of pedagogic reform. This effort seems, based on the reading advanced here, consistent with the dominant tendencies of Milton's letter to Hartlib. As suggested, Parker picks up on and, without explicitly acknowledging it, repeats some of Milton's polemic against the latter's contemporaries. Where Milton excoriated the churchmen for their incompetence, Parker lambasted the horde of incompetent educational "experts" who ineptly tried to provide guidance to befuddled students faced with designing their own education from a "cafeteria-style" menu of electives. Milton, Parker argued, by contrast offered a solidly grounded and rationally integrated educational experience, surpassing the essentially irrational program available in the early nineteen-sixties. In Parker's argument, that is, Milton not only obviated the need for experts, but displaced the experts by providing a more compelling form of expertise that would help America develop a national system of schooling appropriate to the needs of the times.

As I have indicated, Parker's understanding of Milton's integration of pedagogy to the polity's needs is indeed faithful to the letter of advice, although it stands in contrast to an alternative trajectory embedded in Milton's text. *Of Education* advances a pedagogic regimen dedicated not only to improving and reforming the commonwealth, but also to a countervailing withdrawal from the polity, a rejection of the demands of the national domestic economy in favor of an alternative realm of value. Consider the invitation Milton extends to Hartlib, an offer to lead him to an educational landscape more enticing than the classical locus presided over by Orpheus. Milton offers, in *Of Education,* to lead Hartlib:

> to a hill side, where I will point ye out the right path of a vertuous and noble Education; laborious indeed at the first ascent, but else so smooth, so green, so full of goodly prospect, and melodious sounds on every side, that the harp of *Orpheus* was not more charming. (2: 376)

The appeal to Orpheus, the classical exemplar Milton would match or excel, recalls the standard connotations of the ancient poet as a civilizing force, transforming and pacifying his auditors with song. The "charm" of Orpheus's instrument, moreover, also suggests his role as founder of pederasty, at least to the extent that Milton's enticing plan relies upon and seeks to manage an uncontrollable yearning on behalf of England's youth for this putatively appealing educational regimen, an "infinite desire of such a happy nurture" (2: 377). Certainly it is possible to read this view of the pedagogic experience as Orphic retreat, as imagining a temporary, necessary withdrawal that will be followed by a subsequent rejoining of the world, at which time the vocational education received will begin paying dividends to the nation. Be this as it may, I would like to juxtapose this view of Milton's invocation of pedagogy as Orphic withdrawal into a privileged community with his sense of anger at and anxiety about the intellectual incapacities of the English people. We may recollect Sonnet XII and note that Milton responds to the audience that his prose writings of the early 1640s, especially his divorce pamphlets, found. His scribal expenditure of treasure was answered by the "barbarous noise" (l.3) of a rout "Of Owls and Cuckoos, Assess, Apes and Dogs" (l.4). Their cries against his prose interventions represent the failure of his learned "oeconomy," insofar as they debase the copious "things new and old" paternally dispensed from his "treasury" by refusing to recognize these things as wealth at all.

The vision of the people as a bestial rout confirms the apt characterization of Milton as a "revolutionary who distrusted the masses."[68] It also prompts him to comprehend learning as a means of retreating from the multitudes, a sphere of activity that allows one to rise above what he took to be the anti-intellectual mob. A poem written not long after *Of Education* elaborates this view. Written on the occasion of the loss of the 1645 volume of poetry sent to the librarian of Oxford for inclusion in the university's collection, "Ad Ioannem Rousium" figures the Bodleian as a "blessed retreat . . . where the insolent noise of the crowd never shall enter and the vulgar mob of readers shall forever be excluded" (ll.79–80, Hughes's translation).[69] Rouse, according to Milton, serves as a Delphic priest, "a faithful warden of immortal works and a custodian of wealth" (ll.54–55). Milton hoped for his book, in opposition to the fate of being "scraped by the dirty, calloused hand of an illiterate dealer" (ll.42–43), that it might "be carried on oaring wing to the courts of Jupiter on high" (ll.45–46). Milton contrasted here a diverted itinerary into the marketplace to an ideal Ganymedean trajectory to "blessed retreats" (l.76) of learning, "*studia sanctus*" (l.30)—pure, blameless, sacred studies, removed from the "accursed tumults among the citizens" (ll.29).[70] This is a strategy not of reform but of disengagement. *Of Education* attempted to link the governed reproduction of youth to the project of governing the nation, answered the specter of reptilian prelates spawning multitudes (or of the schoolmen abusively propagating ethically hollow persons) with a vision of making up "renowned and matchless men." By contrast, this poem refused such a linkage and the implicit equivalence between populousness, national treasure, and national strength underwriting the promise of generating governed saints. And such withdrawal, as I have suggested, is written into *Of Education* itself, in the very choice of Orpheus as the classical ideal that Milton would surpass. Milton's account of his educational program as an orphically charming landscape, even as it figures the eros that would reform the commonwealth, traces the limit of his governmental designs. Such a characterization constitutes educational practice as a means not of creating serviceable persons but of, in the Latin sense of the word, distinguishing them, separating them from an ungoverned and ungovernable multitude.

CHAPTER FIVE

Paradisal Arithmetic

Paradise Lost *and the Genesis of Populations*

Do numbers matter to Milton's God? While one might expect the divine monarch not to be concerned with how many faithful subjects he has—he is, after all, omnipotent—in his post-rebellion survey of heaven he evaluates the effects of Satan's revolt specifically with an eye to numbers. God asserts that although Satan took many angels with him,

> Yet far the greater part have kept, I see,
> Thir station, Heav'n yet populous retains
> Number sufficient to possess her Realms
> Though wide, and this high Temple to frequent
> With Ministeries due and solemn Rites.[1]

Despite God's sanguine insistence that enough functionaries remain to keep the empire intact and to keep up worship and praise, the notion of "number sufficient" presupposes the possibility of there being number *insufficient.* The Creator's arithmetical interest in the populousness of his realm suggests that had Satan incited more to rebel he might have impaired the business of heaven.

The implications here raise difficult questions about one of the poem's central conceits, the representation of God as a monarch. The devil himself takes these implications to their logical conclusion with his assertion that the new creation seeks "to repair that loss" of angels incurred by the "Rebel Foes" (*Paradise Lost,* 3.678, 677). What renders such a statement so difficult (and so devilishly interesting) is the underlying assumption that there is a functional relationship between the divine monarch's position and his management of his subjects, that he has to be concerned about the size of his populace, and that he won the war simply because he had the bigger army. God broaches the premise of Satan's claim—that God would need to compensate for anything in his creation—in order to defuse it. His "generation" of earth and mankind (7.102), God insists, is not an effort to recover from an assault on his numerical wealth and security:

> But lest his heart exalt him in the harm
> Already done, to have dispeopl'd Heav'n,
> My damage fondly deem'd, I can repair
> That detriment, if such it be to lose
> Self-lost, and in a moment will create
> Another World, out of one man a Race
> Of men innumerable.
>
> (7.150–56)

As William Empson acerbically notes, "God is struggling to make the necessary excuses without admitting that there is anything to excuse."[2] We can elaborate on Empson's insight: God operates within a conceptual framework in which numbers matter insofar as they are related to the security of his rule, so for God to insist on the indifference of numbers produces a point of discursive incoherence, a tension so exacerbated that it has God tripping over his own words. Although God contends that he occupies a position of "inaccessible high strength, the seat / Of Deity supreme" (7.141–42) and asserts that his genesis "out of one man a Race" answers Satan's potential celebration (rather than makes up for any putative loss), numbers constitute a significant object of knowledge and a relevant, even urgent, domain of strategic intervention. While Adam insists, in his colloquy with God, that his Maker need not "propagate, already infinite" (8.420), God and Christ both rejoice at the proposed reunion of heaven and earth (7.160–61) and at the restored plenitude of numbers (3.260–65). Somehow, then, the numbers do not quite add up.

The notion that God created Adam and Eve to replenish heaven's lost numbers had been a doctrinal commonplace since at least Augustine.[3] What needs to be accounted for is why such a commonplace becomes so hard to articulate. Under what conditions does the representation of God's relationship to the numbers of people and angels become so vexed? I argue that the conceptual dilemma in these lines of *Paradise Lost* corresponds to contemporary problems of government. The latter decades of the seventeenth century witnessed a general effort to rethink forms of national and personal government and to redefine the relationship between individual conduct and the security and well-being of England. To the extent that this rethinking raised anxieties about the size of the nation's populace, it placed considerable burdens on reproductive behavior, much as God's acknowledgement (and concurrent denial) that fruitfulness and multiplying carry universal implications has significant theo-political effects. Precisely what these are, and what objectives render generation both necessary and urgent, is a topic of much speculation in *Paradise Lost.* Outlining the competing accounts of the importance of procreation will help us determine how Milton's poem both responds to and participates in a genealogical reconfiguration of the ways persons counted in the aggregate.

During the Civil War and the Restoration, scrutiny of national government and the effort to rethink it was intense. Not simply the best form of political organization for England but the very objectives of national government were under review. What were its aims? How was it authorized? By what criteria might it be judged? "National prosperity," for example, became a rallying cry for government reform in the late seventeenth century; it was a privileged object of knowledge, a subject of polemic, and a target of intervention.[4] Wealth came to be a national goal and the basic standard for evaluating the administrative effectiveness of national government; indeed, anxieties about trade and prosperity significantly underwrote the restoration of Charles II.[5] These redefined objectives of national government prompted an intensified focus upon human aggregates. The work of two of Milton's contemporaries, William Petty and John Graunt, represents one of the more important efforts to formulate numbers of people and their reproductive activity as objects for governmental reflection and potential manipulation. The title of Petty's *Political Arithmetic,* written about 1671 but not published until 1690, may be used to encompass a diverse collection of analyses linked by the commitment to describe England and its inhabitants quantitatively.[6] Petty's surveys of Ireland and of England and its trading partners, along with Graunt's measurement of the "health of the nation," are "a form of the state's secular knowledge of itself and of rival states. [Political arithmetic] objectifies individuals and their activities as calculable component elements and forces contributing to the state's wealth and strength."[7] Building on the framework developed by

Thomas Smith and others in the sixteenth century, Graunt's and Petty's demographic efforts and policy recommendations treat people, international trade, and national wealth as functionally coordinated and bureaucratically manipulable elements of English security. In a manner that develops the understanding of family management as a model of government (discussed earlier in this book), Graunt and Petty understand the nation to be an "oeconomy," a household, the resources of which were to be wisely stewarded, disposed, and improved.[8]

Under the aegis of political arithmetic, Petty formulated reproduction as a crucial object of knowledge and therefore of governmental intervention, oriented toward an array of cultural aims and thereby rendered an urgent responsibility for individuals. The link between numbers and wealth, which allowed Petty to treat persons as a measure of national prosperity and in some instances to put a monetary value on them, justified the imperative not only to count mankind but also to ensure its "multiplication."[9] Petty estimated the numbers of "teeming women" and "breeders," and formulated policy recommendations for utilizing such resources effectively to increase the number of English people and hence the nation's prosperity (*Petty Papers*, 2: 49).[10] He sought to remove the stigma of illegitimate births ("Let it be no sin or shame") (2: 49; see also 2: 54) and suggested programs for accommodating the needs of unwed or poor mothers, including hospitals for pre- and post-natal care (2: 49–51). Unwanted children could profitably be raised at the nation's expense, "the woman leaving her Child to be a servant to the Government for 25 yeares" (1: 267); schooling in trades would guarantee the usefulness of wards of the state; orphanages would be financed by a tax levied against those who did not produce the requisite number of children.[11] Petty imagined the procreative benefits of what he called (presumably acknowledging the source of his ideal in reports from the far western regions of the New World [2: 48]) a "California marriage," a conjugal arrangement between twelve persons. Two women would live with, and try to reproduce by having intercourse with, five men and one man would live with and attempt to impregnate four women (2: 52–54). He considered schemes for penalizing women who did not have a child every three years, a target he later revised to every two-and-a-half years (2: 51, 1: 267).

Petty's formulations were but one contribution to the rethinking and reauthorizing of government in the late seventeenth century. Although such ideas circulated, they did not immediately achieve dominance as accounts of the functions and ends of national government. Indeed, the governmental technology Petty advances did not come into its own in England until the nineteenth century, when statistics became a privileged mode of producing knowledge about the world.[12] His understanding of political arithmetic not as a representation of the state's actual power but as one view of how national rule might be redefined, reoriented, and relegitimized counters the way in which a number of Milton critics read Petty's and Graunt's works and their relation to Milton's. David Quint, for example, takes Christ's disparaging reference to King David's census (2 Sam. 24; 1 Chron. 21) in *Paradise Regained* as Milton's rejection of Petty's demographic project. According to Quint, Milton reacts to the failure of the Commonwealth by cathecting and seeking refuge in the "individual conscience," a realm of "inwardness" opposed to monarchy and demography alike. Such a response ushers in "a modern conflict between individual and state" in which the latter makes ever more intrusive demands on the former in an inexorable arrogation of repressive power.[13] Nancy Armstrong and Leonard Tennenhouse argue that Milton is writing at the moment of modernity's emergence on the heels of the fire-like or plague-like cataclysm of civil war. For them, the image of London rebuilt after the fire of 1666, as described in Thomas Sprat's *History of the Royal Society*, figures the supersession of an aristocratic, monarchical world order by one recognizably our own;[14] whatever Milton's and Petty's differences, they share "much the same vision of the world" and contribute to the ideological framework of a "protocapitalist economy" (102, 108).[15]

Although Quint, Armstrong, and Tennenhouse usefully foreground the fact that the concept of population has a history, the historical narrative of systemic rupture upon which they rely oversimplifies the complex overlap and disjunction between Milton and Petty. Rather than view these writers in terms of either equivalence or opposition, I wish to examine how *Paradise Lost* engages the kinds of questions and problems that political arithmetic sets out to address, but does so in a way that cannot be viewed in terms of an unequivocal endorsement or condemnation. A key point of overlap is on the issue of national wealth, which political arithmetic takes as an objective measure of national security and a goal of national government. By contrast, Milton's *Ready and Easy Way to Establish a Free Commonwealth*, written on the eve of the restoration of Charles II, displays deep ambivalence about the standard of national prosperity. In this text, Milton takes up the cudgels on behalf of a form of government that "aims most to make the people flourishing, vertuous, noble and high spirited" (7: 460), and that promises to foster the most "trade" (7: 461); however, at the same time, he voices profound reservations about the emphasis upon wealth, both personal and national. Monarchy's "aim is to make the people, wealthie indeed perhaps and well fleec't, for thir own shearing and the supplie of regal prodigalitie; but otherwise softest, basest, vitiousest, servilest, easiest to be kept under" (7: 460). Wealth is a sign of, and mechanism for, subjection of an ethically ungoverned populace easier to tyrannize because of its plenty. Milton's remarks closing *The Ready and Easy Way* are worth quoting at length since they help demonstrate his difficulty with this question of national prosperity, and allow us to locate the transitional instabilities fracturing his work. "[I]f the people be so affected," Milton writes,

> as to prostitute religion and libertie to the vain and groundless apprehension, that nothing but kingship can restore trade, not remembring the frequent plagues and pestilences that then wasted this citie, such as through God's mercie we never have felt since, and that trade flourishes no where more then in the free Commonwealths of *Italie, Germanie,* and the Low-Countries before thir eyes at this day, yet if trade be grown so craving and importunate through the profuse living of tradesmen, that nothing can support it, but the luxurious expences of a nation upon trifles or superfluities, so as if the people generally should betake themselves to frugalitie, it might prove a dangerous matter, least tradesmen should mutinie for want of trading, and that therefor we must foregoe & set to sale religion, libertie, honor, safetie, all concernments Divine or human to keep up trading, if lastly, after all this light among us, the same reason shall pass for current to put our necks again under kingship, as was made use of by the *Jews* to returne back to *Egypt* and to the worship of thir idol queen, because they falsly imagind that they then livd in more plentie and prosperitie, our condition is not sound but rotten, both in religion and all civil prudence; and will bring us soon, the way we are marching, to those calamities which attend alwaies and unavoidably on luxurie, all national judgments under forein or domestic slaverie. (7: 461–62)

Milton argues that those who think the nation will flourish under monarchy not only have forgotten the way things were under the Stuarts, but also have ignored the contemporary examples of the prosperity enjoyed by other commonwealths; however, if the national desire for invigorated trade and all the benefits it is supposed to bring can lead England to submit to monarchy, perhaps the criterion of wealth is itself misguided. I offer this reading for the sake of summary clarity, though the almost torturous density of Milton's prose resists synopsis: its grammatical intricacy threatens to collapse into absolute confusion. The proliferation of "if"s and subordinate clauses signals a contest between the premise that the Commonwealth should be maintained because it generates the most trade and the view that decisions based on trade indicate the nation's slavery to "luxurie." Monarchy is a dangerous form of servitude that will not restore vital trade; the luxury that trade propagates is a form of subjugation that will restore monarchy. The specter of plague, furthermore, implicitly equates populousness of the nation with the healthy vigor of trade, and thereby generates a concern about loss of the country's numbers. At the same time, the scornful dismissal of mutinous traders signals an indifference to loss of persons, especially those who would construe Puritan "frugalitie" to be a danger to the nation (7: 462).

Bearing Multitudes

I trace the outlines of this crux to set up a reading of *Paradise Lost* attentive to the difficult relationship between Milton's and political arithmetic's accounts of human procreation. Conflicting views of prosperity as a divine gift to be celebrated or as an abusive excess to be avoided figure in the epic's effort to render the bearing of children an urgent obligation in Eden. Unlike Petty and Graunt—for whom the urgency of generating numbers stems from a simple equation of numbers and wealth and, in turn, of wealth and national prosperity—Milton situates prelapsarian reproductive capacity in two incommensurable dynamics. On the one hand, future offspring are one among many elements of divine wealth, a part of Eden's abundance; on the other hand, Eve's children are implicated in the management of Eden's abundance, understood not as wealth but as potential waste.[16]

When God announces his plan to "create . . . a Race / Of men innumerable," he implicitly places extraordinary emphasis upon human reproductive capacity.[17] Indeed, in remembering the earliest moments of her existence, Eve foregrounds how God lured her away from her "wat'ry image" with assurances of hyperbolic fertility (4.480). Showing her Adam, God promised her that

to him [thou] shalt bear
Multitudes like thyself, and thence be call'd
Mother of human Race.
(4.473–75)

Raphael reinforces and elaborates the implications of God's words by asserting that the institution of gender difference as such derives from the imperative to generate. As he tells Adam, "Male he created thee, but thy consort / Female for Race" (7.529–30).[18] The angel's greeting of Adam's "consort" is consistent on this point. "Hail Mother of Mankind," Raphael exclaims upon first meeting Eve,

whose fruitful Womb
Shall fill the World more numerous with thy Sons
Than with these various fruits the Trees of God
Have heap'd this Table.
(5.388–91)

The archangel's gesture celebrates Eve's fecundity by favorably comparing it to Eden's arboreal abundance, and simultaneously reduces Eve to her role as mother by attributing agency to the trees, which somehow have set the table without her help.[19] Thus Milton's Eve looks like as perfect a teeming-woman as Petty or Graunt could have imagined, capable of generating inconceivable numbers.

The analogy Raphael draws between Eve and the trees reinforces the central assumptions of political arithmetic by rendering the persons Eve will produce as simply another form of Edenic wealth. Prior to Raphael's arrival, the trees' luxuriant growth threatens to outpace the capacity of the first couple to stay on top of their agricultural responsibilities. When Raphael descends from heaven, however, the trees are suddenly transformed into a source of divine "Abundance" (5.315), signifying no longer more work but holy plenty. Anticipating the archangel's visit, Adam asks his wife to fix lunch, justifying the lavish spread by asserting:

well we may afford
Our givers thir own gifts, and large bestow
From large bestow'd, where Nature multiplies
Her fertile growth, and by disburd'ning grows
More fruitful, which instructs us not to spare.
(5.316–20)

Anything less extravagant would be not simply ungracious but unnatural, out of keeping with the precedent set by the trees, which grow ever more fruitful with harvesting. Theirs is an abundance that when enjoyed unsparingly, only multiplies.[20] This understanding of the trees clarifies the equivalence that Raphael's salutation produces between Eden's numbers and riches: Eve's progeny are constituted as God's lavish bounty. Although it may be difficult to imagine Eve's own "fertile growth" increasing each time she gives birth, the archangel's attentiveness to her "fruitful Womb" places considerable pressure on her fecundity as both a manifestation of and a means of producing an inexhaustible abundance.

If Eden serves as the repository of "Nature's whole wealth" (4.207), it does so especially insofar as it is the home of God's offspring. A series of allusions early in book 4 portray Eden as a place for hiding children. The garden is likened to Nysa where Jove hid Bacchus and his mother (4.275–79 and n), and to Mount Amara, "where *Abassin* Kings thir issue Guard" (4.280).[21] Echoes of political arithmetic proliferate in the account of Satan's entrance into Eden. The devil sneaks into the garden:

As when a prowling Wolf,
Whom hunger drives to seek new haunt for prey,
Watching where Shepherds pen thir Flocks at eve
In hurdl'd Cotes amid the field secure,
Leaps o'er the fence with ease into the Fold:
Or as a Thief bent to unhoard the cash
Of some rich Burgher, whose substantial doors,
Cross-barr'd and bolted fast, fear no assault,
In at the window climbs, or o'er the tiles:
So clomb this first grand Thief into God's Fold.
(4.183–92)

The repetition of "Fold" poetically folds together the alternative characterizations of Adam and Eve, and implicitly all of their offspring, as God's livestock and his treasure. The collapse of the two similes likewise figures Satan as both predator and burglar; however, the final line quoted replaces the former term with the latter, insisting that Satan comes not to devour God's stock (an activity assigned to Death) but to pilfer it. Thus the garden is depicted as a bank in which God shepherds persons who count as treasure.

To attribute all wealth to God seems pious enough. However, to the extent that treasure constitutes in political arithmetic a measure of security and national health, we may wonder how far this representation of God's relationship to Eden and Eve's offspring is to be taken. What does it mean for God to have a human savings account? What are we to make of the notion that God's initial act of generation and the first couple's subsequent procreation ensure the stability of his dominion? As troubling as these questions may be to an understanding of divine omnipotence, they simply elaborate upon the idea that the reproductive imperatives of political arithmetic drive God's creation of mankind. Inasmuch as they suggest that populating the new world is a response to Satan's rebellion, these questions also tie our discussion of Eve's procreative capacity to the contradiction inherent in God's postrebellion census: the simultaneous relevance and insignificance of the number of the divine monarch's subjects. While implying the connection between human progeny and God's apparent defense strategy, the poem gives voice to attempts to deny such an equation. Milton's angels provide a response to the implications of the equivalence between Eve's offspring and wealth by seeking actively to refute the idea that God creates people because they are the treasure that makes his rule secure. From the angels' perspective, which takes in the entire universe, the creation of mankind and the future generation of people indicate not a God engaged in strategic planning but a God of infinite generosity. The angels reinforce the connection between people and wealth but remove human reproduction from the sphere of governmental calculation.

A key aspect of the angels' account is the contrast it offers to the poet's suggestion that God, like a "Burgher," hoards the human race. They instead celebrate God's creation, as an extraordinary expenditure, an overwhelming distribution of wealth. God has answered the "Spirits apostate" (7.610) who

> impiously . . . thought
> Thee to diminish, and from thee withdraw
> The number of thy worshippers.
>
> (7.611–13)

The rebellion has given God the opportunity to demonstrate his omnipotence by creating more numbers. "[T]o him," the angels sing,

Glory and praise, whose wisdom had ordain'd
Good out of evil to create, instead
Of Spirits malign a better Race to bring
Into their vacant room, and thence diffuse
His good to Worlds and Ages infinite.
(7.186–91)

The angels share with Satan the view that God has created mankind to fill "vacant room." At the gates of Hell, the devil suggests to Sin that God's generation of Adam and Eve may serve as a means of carefully repeopling heaven (a point he also repeats to Uriel while asking for directions to earth [3.678–80]). As he tells his spouse and daughter, earth is rumored to house:

A race of upstart Creatures, to supply
Perhaps our vacant room, though more remov'd,
Lest Heav'n surcharg'd with potent multitude
Might hap to move new broils.
(2.834–37)

In contrast to the angels, however, Satan links the commonplace theory of why God created mankind to a frequently rehearsed argument, founded on a perceived superabundance of persons at home, for establishing English colonies in the New World.[22] He sees numbers not as the foundation of monarchical strength but as inherently explosive and unstable. His conjecture that God may be repopulating heaven by cultivating a plantation implies that the divine monarch rules through *policy* and so has been compelled to engage in prudential calculation to check a capricious "potent multitude." Indeed, the fallen angel intimates that the revolt in heaven was the consequence of God's mismanagement of his kingdom, the result of the pressure of too many people, an error God seeks to avoid through his colonial project.

Although the angels share Satan's assumption that God goes to the trouble of making a new world to fill the room vacated by the rebellious angels, they nevertheless oppose absolutely the notion that he does so out of insecurity. They assert that the evil of revolt can only occasion an overwhelming display of God's unassailable strength and of his divine benevolence. But what precisely does the chorus mean by their elliptical formulation "and thence diffuse / His good to Worlds and Ages infinite"? That is, how will God replace heaven's numbers? The chorus clarifies any vagueness by turning its attention to the "Stars / Numerous" (7.620–

21) of God's new universe spread before them and by wondering if these might not offer a limitless field in which to house and to propagate future subjects, "every Star perhaps a World / Of destin'd habitation" (7.621–22). In discursive terms, the speculation here extends the questions of political arithmetic to the domain of astronomy by broaching the possibility of other inhabited worlds, a topic then under active consideration.[23] Many of Milton's contemporaries—for example, his former classmate Henry More, the minister and subsequently bishop John Wilkins, and Robert Boyle—insisted that the notion of extraterrestrial life was consistent with, indeed magnified, God's glory.[24] In a text presented to Sir Kenelm Digby and translated into English in 1658, Pierre Borel, physician to the king of France, characteristically argued that positing the existence of other worlds acknowledged God's infinite strength and abundance: "Is it not . . . more meet and convenient to his goodnesse and Divine glory, to have made . . . an Empire adorned with varieties of worlds, as with Provinces and Cities; and that these divers worlds be the habitations of so many Citizens and numberlesse Inhabitants of divers kinds, and that all these things be created for the praise and everlasting glory of their Maker?"[25] In sum, "God's creation, in order to be perfect and worthy of the Creator, must therefore contain all that is possible, that is innumerable individual beings, innumerable earths, innumerable stars and suns."[26]

Like contemporary astronomers, Milton allows that the heavens contain a plurality of worlds—Raphael is described on his journey to earth as "Sail[ing] between worlds and worlds" (5.268)—and, as the angels praising God's distribution of "good to Worlds and Ages infinite" indicate, such a view is corollary to the belief in God's infinite abundance.[27] Crucially, however, Milton differs with his contemporaries on the role of human generation. As he speculates (3.459–63), the heavens are not created populous but will be populated in the future.[28] The angels' conjecture about the stars, with respect to the discussion about, and the rationale for, a plurality of worlds, thus substantially raises the stakes of procreation. The angels' assertions implicitly acknowledge the account of Eve's fecundity as a lavish dispensing of God's abundance; thus the imagined future generations of Adam and Eve become intelligible not as a means of combating Satan but as the form in which God chooses to distribute his wealth throughout creation. The chorus repeats Satan's idea that God is engaging in a colonial enterprise, but it resists the implication that God is showing that he is worried about an explosive multitude in heaven by radically multiplying the lands he will one day people. These worlds do not furnish God with a way to manage his unruly numbers or stabilize his reign; rather, they are a sign of his omnipotence. Indeed, the angels defuse the implication that God need have concern for his numbers by attributing to him the "wisdom" of foresight (7.187) and the ability to turn any assault to his own ends. For them, the populating of the universe represents an "infinite" dispersion of God's omnipotent goodness, and thus, in the terms detailed above, an "infinite" multiplication of wealth through the generation of endless numbers.

"More Hands Than Ours": Procreation and Waste Management

As I have been suggesting, the angels subscribe to the basic equation underwriting political arithmetic, the equivalence between people and wealth, and indeed take the argument about generation for abundance as far as can be imagined. However, they do so in a way that actively resists the implication that God produces the human race out of any felt need to. God, by their account, puts in play the generation of the inconceivable numbers who will one day populate the universe simply because he is God and because he is extraordinarily generous. Although God is like "some rich Burgher," he is not actually one, and he distributes his wealth in a way no real merchant could or would.

But the angels do not have the last word on God's genesis of humankind. As evidenced in Milton's *Ready and Easy Way,* wealth also carries negative valences, and *Paradise Lost* remains ambivalent in its depiction of reproduction. The first couple's procreative activity is rendered an urgent obligation, but in a manner sharply different from the supramundane vision advanced by the angelic chorus or, a fortiori, by Petty's political arithmetic. In this second account of procreation, human fecundity does not relate to God's generous distribution of wealth but instead is coordinated with—indeed is organized by—an imperative to prevent waste.

Prior to Raphael's arrival on earth, as will be remembered, Eden's trees represent not divine gifts but an occasion for work. Critics have long noted the way in which Milton's Paradise structurally requires Adam and Eve's labor.[29] J. M. Evans observes that in Eden agricultural effort, although "pleasant," is "also absolutely necessary."[30] Milton depicts "not just abundance but overabundance, a 'wilderness' in which the trees are 'overwoodie' and reach 'too farr' with their 'branches overgrown.'"[31] Indeed, the endless work the first couple must undertake is a bit too endless. God has been both excessively generous and not generous enough; he has provided plenty to do but too few workers to do it. Adam tells Eve that the very trees "mock our scant manuring, and require / More hands than ours to lop thir wanton growth" (4.628–29), and Eve repeats his complaint in her argument for a division of labor (9.207–12).[32] Even as God's garden requires more laborers to prevent it from turning into a wasteland, it also requires more people to consume the fruits of their labor. Paradise is "For us too large," the two explain to God in prayer, "where thy abundance wants / Partakers, and uncropt falls to the ground" (4.730–31). The threat of unharvested fruit falling off the trees prompts in Adam and Eve an urgency about their lack of numbers and in turn, a reformulating of God's injunction to multiply into a divine obligation to provide more. They quickly remind their maker of his commitment to redress this "want":

> But thou hast promis'd from us two a Race
> To fill the Earth, who shall with us extol
> Thy goodness infinite.
>
> (4.732–34)

They will praise him, certainly, but they will also toil constantly to check Eden's growth and to prevent God's bounty from going to waste.

The urgency of procreation receives an added twist when the specter of unharvested fruit and implicit decay is subsequently dismissed. As Eve tells the serpent,

> in such abundance lies our choice,
> As leaves a greater store of Fruit untoucht,
> Still hanging *incorruptible,* till men
> Grow up to thir provision, and more hands
> Help to disburden Nature of her Birth.
>
> (9.620–24, emphasis mine)

In contrast to the fear that edenic produce will fall "uncropt," there is now a suggestion that the trees in Paradise will reserve God's abundance until it is needed, however many generations away that may be. In his prose works, Milton puts into play a similar antinomy between England's numbers and the national agricultural effort. In his *Proposalls for Certain Expedients,* he justifies the enclosure of England's so-called wastelands as a means of making the nation "much more industrious, rich & populous" (7: 338). Diligent cultivation of the nation's talents would generate an attendant plenty. (Indeed, the metonymic relationship among "industry," wealth, and numbers is perfectly consistent with the discursive aims of political arithmetic.) In *De Doctrina,* Milton approaches the problem of squandered talents from another perspective. Defending polygamy as a technique for generating large populations, he observes that it was practiced by many of the biblical patriarchs but has been dismissed by "our modern Europeans, who allow the fields to go to waste instead, in many places, for want of labor" (6: 367).[33] Together, these two statements trace a mutually confirming relation between lands and hands: efficient utilization of England's land will eliminate waste and increase the country's numbers, and increasing numbers will allow England to reduce the wasteful underutilization of its arable resources. Milton inscribes the same reciprocal dynamic in Eden, a place abundant enough to accommodate future generations and where abundance requires generation in order to be utilized efficiently.

Justifying a policy of open immigration for England, Samuel Fortrey, a member of Charles II's household, offered the following concise formula: "People and plenty are commonly the begetters the one of the other, if rightly ordered."[34] My account of the relation between Eden's abundance and human numbers might be summarized in immediate contrast: people and waste prevention justify and accommodate one another. Eve's reproductivity drives and is required by the domestic economy of an Eden in which the concept of wealth has no discursive standing or operative meaning. For Adam and Eve, Eden's luxuriance provides only an opportunity for waste management, and therefore both enables and incites the generation of earthly multitudes.

I have suggested that alternative accounts of human procreation—that generation produces divine wealth, or that it prevents waste—engage and rework the conflicted apprehension of wealth in Milton's prose writing. To elaborate, I turn now to a highly charged moment in *Paradise Lost,* the famous astronomy lesson of book 8 in which the volatile relationship between producing wealth and preventing waste is broached and provisionally managed through a consideration of interstellar populations. In his colloquy with Raphael, Adam extends his concern about managing waste to the heavens by observing that the multitude of stars in their "incomprehensible" expanse (8.20) seems to exceed the need of providing light to earth. Assuming that the heavenly bodies all rotate around the "sedentary Earth" (8.32), Adam wonders if God might not have come up with a more efficient way to illuminate and heat it: "wise and frugal" nature (8.26) operates here with a "superfluous hand" (8.27). When the angels look at the heavens, they see a glorious expenditure of divine abundance; when Adam surveys the same sky, he sees an uncharacteristic and puzzling extravagance.[35]

Raphael offers Adam a number of explanations; significantly, one of these acknowledges the possibility that the skies contain other planets and other beings. Although the archangel dismisses the emphasis upon the procreative diffusion of human wealth throughout an "Edifice too large for [mankind] to fill" (8.104), he grants that the "terrestrial Moon" (8.142) may be inhabited. Lunar spots may indicate an earth-like terrain and climate and thus the presence of vegetation and people (8.145–48). This inference could in turn be extended to all the stars, "other Suns perhaps" (8.148) that have their own satellites and inhabitants, as well (8.152).

As fascinating as such speculation no doubt is to Adam, he has expressed no interest in the populousness of the heavens; he has asked only about stellar light, heat, and motion. Raphael oddly provides more answer than the immediate question requires. This discursive excess is less a response to Adam, however, than to Milton's contemporaries. The Cambridge Platonist Ralph Cudworth, for example, believed it unreasonable "to think that all this immense vastness should lie waste, desert, or uninhabited, and have nothing in it that could praise the Creator thereof, save only this one spot of earth."[36] Raphael himself rehearses a version of this argument:

> such vast room in Nature unpossest
> By living Soul, desert and desolate,
> Only to shine, yet scarce to cóntribute
> Each Orb a glimpse of Light, convey'd so far
> Down to this habitable, which returns
> Light back to them, is obvious to dispute.
> (8.153–58)

The questions that Raphael's statement puts forward recapitulate Adam's concerns: If the stars were created solely to light a single inhabited planet, rather than planets closer to them, why does so little light reach it? Does not the assumption that there are no other living beings to benefit from this light impute to God an extravagance that tends to wastefulness?[37] Raphael raises the notion that the skies must be peopled in a way that sustains the astronomical argument that God conforms to the imperative to prevent waste, but the archangel does so only to dismiss such speculation as inconsequential, useless—"obvious to dispute" but irrelevant.

The gesture of broaching an argument only to reject it anticipates Raphael's subsequent commands to Adam. Although the angelic chorus has understood the limitless field of stars not as a problem but as an opportunity for God to distribute his bounty to infinite ages and worlds, Raphael forecloses consideration of the issue with his famous injunction:

> Solicit not thy thoughts with matters hid,
> Leave them to God above, him serve and fear;
> Of other Creatures, as him pleases best,
> Wherever plac't, let him dispose: joy thou
> In what he gives to thee, this Paradise
> And thy fair *Eve.*
>
> (8.167–72)

Tactfully refusing to answer the questions Adam has never asked about God's wanting or needing to make more subjects, the archangel continues:

> Think only what concerns thee and thy being;
> Dream not of other Worlds, what Creatures there
> Live, in what state, condition or degree,
> Contented that thus far hath been reveal'd
> Not of Earth only but of highest Heav'n.
>
> (8.174–78)

These imperatives disconnect life on earth from the rest of the universe in two complementary ways. First, Adam is not to worry about the structure and government of the universe. What people are there and why God might have created them are none of his business. Second, by implication humanity's actions have no impact on God. That is, Raphael's instructions prevent the apprehension of a relationship between the conduct of life on earth and God's administration of his creation. Although the angelic chorus seems to suggest that human reproduction is essential because it is the key to God's universal largesse, the first couple never reaches this conclusion. Children may be an important component of God's riches; however, the need to produce wealth is never explicitly formulated as a reason to generate them. Furthermore, Raphael is careful not to describe procreation in this way. He certainly praises

Eve's fruitfulness when he first meets her, but he prohibits the kind of reflection that might lead either Eve or Adam to believe that God actually needs them to reproduce to fulfill his governmental purposes.

As Adam and Eve's sense of obligation to tend the garden of Eden indicates, the need to produce children is not the less urgent because of Raphael's intervention; in fact, his statements compound the urgency. Although the archangel may consider it folly to wonder whether God's design of the universe is frugal, the "obviousness" of the possibility suggests that there is one domain within which the imperative is quite relevant: Paradise, to which Raphael recalls Adam's attention at the end of the astronomy lesson. Following the shift in subject, Adam begins to sing the virtues of "know[ing] / That which before us lies in daily life" (8.192–3). Having dispelled Adam's worry that God's creation is wasteful or that his actions conform to a need to be frugal, Raphael reorients his listener to a sphere of action, the "daily life" of Eden's domestic economy, in which waste management is paramount. In so doing, the archangel effectively endorses the second account of why reproduction is vital: more laborers are needed to prevent the waste of Eden's agricultural abundance.

Governing Reproduction

Although both *Paradise Lost* and political arithmetic place great emphasis on labor, Milton and Petty envision different objectives for it.[38] In Milton's epic, work is a theological issue. God calls men and women to a vocation, and so they are obliged to perform it as an integral part of a regulated existence conducted in anticipation of the day of reckoning.[39] In Petty's project, by contrast, work is understood primarily in relation to the nation, whose health and strength vis-à-vis other nations it sustains. This is to say that political arithmetic simply follows through on the dislocation glimpsed in our reading of Sir Thomas Smith's *Discourse of the Commonweal;* the concern with wealth and trade retains the vocational emphasis of the Protestant ethic but dislodges work from a primarily theological frame of reference.

The reconceptualization of labor was but one element of a broad reorganization of the post-Restoration discursive terrain. One response to the Civil War was to cordon off and subordinate the questions, forms of debate, and modes of investing political practice associated with the theological controversy of the preceding decades.[40] Indeed, by quantifying the English people and their activities, Petty and Graunt sought to guarantee that their information and recommendations were free of "private interest" and would instead promote the national interest by providing an objective foundation for policy.[41] Political arithmetic does not represent an absolutely secular form of knowledge, but it does illustrate (and helped bring about) the diminishment of theology's place in national government, and consequently of its dominance as a means of thinking about and authorizing human relations and actions. This shift underpins Milton's concerns, elaborated in *The Ready and Easy Way,* about using the criterion of national prosperity to judge which form of government is best.

In *Paradise Lost,* Milton's reaction to the realignment of discourses is registered in the poem's well-known description of Adam and Eve in their blissful bower. Rather than follow them into their bedroom, the poet discreetly directs attention elsewhere by engaging a contemporary doctrinal controversy over whether or not they had intercourse before the Fall.[42] He asserts that once settled in "thir inmost bower" (4.738) husband and wife performed "the Rites / Mysterious of connubial Love" (4.742–43), despite the opinions of "Hypocrites" who

> austerely talk
> Of purity and place and innocence,
> Defaming as impure what God declares
> Pure, and commands to some, leaves free to all.
> (4.744–47)

He then punctuates these lines with a question that raises the stakes by firing up the rhetorical heat: "Our Maker bids increase, who bids abstain / But our Destroyer, foe to God and Man?" (4.748–49). Although offered as a pointed response to (among others) the Catholic apologists for celibate priesthood, who justified it by insisting that Adam and Eve did not engage in intercourse in Eden, or would not have done so later had they not fallen, these lines accomplish something more.[43] Because Milton takes male-female intercourse to be the same as reproduction, he is able to counter his adversaries by referring them to God's first command to humans, "Be fruitful, and multiply" (Gen. 1.28). He effectively turns a debate about the purity or impurity of sexual congress between man and woman into a confrontation between those who would obey and those who would resist God's reproductive imperative.

Having thus reconfigured the argument, Milton invests procreation with as much urgency as he possibly can. First, he produces a strategic identification with Adam and Eve at the moment that they receive God's injunction to multiply. The possessive adjective and the present tense of the directed imperative—"Our Maker bids increase"—imply a transhistorical collective subject, a "we" that encompasses not only the first parents but all of their progeny including the speaker and his contemporaries. Second, Milton redefines the adversary. The "Hypocrites" are transformed at the end into "our Destroyer," as if they simply were being unmasked. Together, these gestures elevate a doctrinal controversy to a theo-political agon. Taken on its own, the final line sets up a chiasmus that broadens the implied "we" to include "God" as well as "Man." Underscoring God's investment in the contest with Satan, this formulation suggests that preventing human generation could put God at risk.

To develop this line of argument, we can note the way that the poet's enthusiastic insistence that only an enemy "bids abstain" actively engages a later textual moment in which Eve—the only one who counsels "wilful barrenness" (10.1042) in the poem—considers the merits of abstention. After the fall, Eve argues to her husband that if they are concerned about the fate of their offspring, doomed to being food for Death, then perhaps they could cheat Death of his destructive consumption by not producing any children at all. "[I]n thy power," she tells her spouse,

> It lies, yet ere Conception to prevent
> The Race unblest, to being yet unbegot.
> Childless thou art, Childless remain: So Death
> Shall be deceiv'd his glut, and with us two
> Be forc'd to satisfy his Rav'nous Maw.
> (10.986–91)

If abstention proves too hard or too painful, she adds, then they alternatively could commit suicide (10.992–1006). Adam praises his wife for her "contempt of life and pleasure" (10.1013); he worries however that such a course of action would not only further irritate God (who could not be tricked so easily and who would most likely make their punishment even worse [10.1022–28]), but also would let Satan off scot free. That is, like the poet (10.182–92) and Michael (12.546–51), Adam interprets God's oracular decree against the serpent as providing generation with a retributive function. He explains to his spouse that God's curse, "thy Seed shall bruise / The Serpent's head," would be:

> piteous amends, unless
> Be meant, whom I conjecture, our grand Foe
> *Satan*, who in the Serpent hath contriv'd
> Against us this deceit: to crush his head
> Would be revenge indeed; which will be lost
> By death brought on ourselves, or childless days
> Resolv'd, as thou proposest; so our Foe
> Shall 'scape his punishment ordain'd.
> (10.1031–39)

Milton's rhetorical question—"who bids abstain But our Destroyer, foe to God and Man?"—anticipates the language of Adam's defense of procreation here, in which Satan is twice named "our Foe." Accordingly, even though Satan never bids abstain in the poem, and comes to Eden for the purpose of glutting Hell with numbers and not to prevent generation,[44] I think, with Diane Kelsey McColley, that it is right to infer that the "Destroyer" is Satan; the verbal echoes imply what the polemical intensity of Milton's tirade against the hypocrites demands.[45] The poet attempts to capitalize on the urgency granted procreation both by God before the Fall *and* by Adam afterward, by opposing God's imperative at Genesis 1:28 to a Satanic effort to implement Eve's proposed elective barrenness, pursued not to cheat death but for Satan's own destructive ends.

While Milton utilizes Adam's defense of generation, he also implicitly modifies it. As Adam and Eve learn, the bruise on the head of the serpent will come from Christ, the "Promis'd Seed" who, Eve asserts after her slumbering lesson at the close of the poem, "shall all restore" (12.623). In the poet's historical moment (well after Christ's nativity) it is logically speaking too late for an anti-generational project to stop Satan's punishment. Once Christ is born, regardless of whether or not humans continue procreating, it is simply a matter of time until the devil gets his due. The Destroyer's efforts against generation therefore must advance with reference to and in opposition to some other finality beyond generating Christ. To be sure, Eve's formulation recapitulates God's edict that only through his son's mediation will any return to his good graces; as he tells Christ, "in thee . . . shall be restor'd / As many as are restor'd, without thee none" (3.287–89). However, it also allows that Christ's punitive mission is a salvage operation, restoring otherwise destroyed numbers to God. The latter approves of Christ's plan to pay man's debt, in order "to save, / By losing thee a while, the whole Race lost" (3.279–80). Accordingly, Christ promises to return, stating that after judging the quick and the dead and defeating Satan, he "with the multitude of my redeem'd / Shall enter Heav'n long absent" (3.260–61). That operation completed, Christ will relinquish his monarchy: "thou thy regal Sceptre shalt lay by," God promises, "For regal Sceptre then no more shall need, / God shall be All in All" (3.339–41). In spite of God's post-rebellion insistence (noted at the outset of this chapter) that his creation of humanity had nothing to do with increasing his own numbers—an implicit denial that his rule was in any way correlated with the magnitude of his host—it is not until the restoration of his multitudes that God will be "All in All." The poet's effort to refute the hypocritically pious opponents of reproduction presses on this latter sense of "all restore" by intimating that human generation is necessary to God. If "bidding abstain" counts as an act of aggression, then actually abstaining would amount to siding with the enemy.

The theological urgency granted procreation, surprisingly, opposes the considerable efforts made elsewhere in the poem to separate the reproduction of persons and the security of God's kingdom and so edges close to violating Raphael's injunction against speculating about God's disposition of his subjects. Where the angels work to dispel the suggestion that creating people has anything to do with a divine need to reduce risk, the poet implies that it has everything to do with a need to counter Satan's assault on God. The poet seems to have painted himself into a corner: he authorizes procreation by linking it to God's agon with the Destroyer but runs up against the very problem God has encountered in his post-rebellion census, the idea that Satan may represent a threat to him. Of course, Milton does not say precisely how the new subjects would be of use to God or, conversely, what would happen if Satan prevented their generation. Indeed, the following lines reinforce his silence by changing the subject and again reconfiguring the operative conceptual grid.[46] Having countered those who insist that Adam and Eve did not have intercourse in Eden, by shifting from one opposition (the purity or impurity of intercourse) to another (generation or abstinence), Milton now offers yet another pair of alternatives with his celebration of "wedded Love, mysterious Law, true source / Of human offspring" (4.750–51). The notion of a "true source" of numbers implies the existence of a false one—Milton names it "Casual fruition" (4.767)—

which radically qualifies his insistence that any opposition to intercourse is tantamount to an act of destruction.

Many critics have argued that Milton endorses a modern regime of heterosexuality, although, as my reading of his hymn to marriage indicates, the discursive cathexis of marriage makes no appeal to a need to ensure that men desire only women and vice versa.[47] Instead, the hymn specifies conjugal relations as the proper means for complying with the theological imperative to procreate. It does so not by vilifying same-sex eros but by projecting a specter of ungoverned eros. Milton's insistence upon the difference between the "true source" of children and "casual fruition" widens the scope of his polemic to encompass a broad array of dissolute activity:

> Here Love his golden shafts imploys, here lights
> His constant Lamp, and waves his purple wings,
> Reigns here and revels; not in the bought smile
> Of Harlots, loveless, joyless, unindear'd
> Casual fruition, nor in Court Amours,
> Mixt Dance, or wanton Mask, or Midnight Ball,
> Or Serenate, which the starv'd Lover sings
> To his proud fair, best quitted with disdain.
> (4.763–70)

Milton, maintaining the polemical intensity leveled at the Destroyer who would impede generation, turns it on a newly configured target. The vilified alternative to the "true source" is not simply "casual fruition" but a libertinage encompassing both meretricious generation and various nongenerational practices: mixed dancing, masques, balls, serenading. The proper monarch is love; the proper court is marriage. Milton's definition of marriage appeals back to the opposition with which he began between a view of intercourse as pure and a view of it as impure, and produces a new distinction between regulated and unregulated eros, between "Love" that is properly generational, the "true source" of numbers, and a general debauchery indicative of the depravity of the times. With this new distinction, the poet strikes a delicate balance between the urgency to procreate and an equally urgent imperative to govern eros. Hence Milton can stress the absolute necessity of producing offspring even as he restricts generation by defining a single allowed form, associating all other forms with an illicit eros that serves as both sign and symptom of a widespread failure of government.

To clarify what is at stake in the poet's maneuvers, it is helpful to examine Graunt's endorsement of conjugal relations. Unlike Petty, who was willing to consider nonmonogamous arrangements, Graunt decried "Adulteries and Fornications," for "a Woman, admitting ten Men, is so far from having ten times as many Children, that she hath none at all" (*Natural and Political Observation* 373; see also 377). Instead, Graunt counseled support for marriage, since it produced the most offspring: "States, by encouraging Marriage, and hindering Licentiousness, advance their own Interest, as well as preserve the Laws of God from contempt and violation" (377–78). Graunt thought religious effects important enough to remark, but his formulation is further evidence of the reorganization of discourses authorizing generational activity.[48] Obedience to God's mandates is almost an afterthought, secondary to the nation's interests.

Graunt's statements thus bring the theological emphasis of Milton's intervention into even greater relief. Where political arithmetic offers Charles II a set of tools for administering the nation at the expense of theology and the enthusiasm associated with it, Milton's effort theologically to cathect marriage as the "true source of human offspring" sustains a pointed critique of national government and the post-Restoration dispensation of rule. Metonymically drawing attention to the ways the behavior of those surrounding the monarch is antithetical to the governed eros Milton associates with marriage, the poet sets up textual resonances that link his critique to an earlier moment of anti-court rhetoric. The hymn to wedded love picks up themes introduced in the parade of devils of book 1, namely the description of Belial. Although this "lewd[est]" of demons has no place of worship dedicated to him, he may be found:

> In Courts and Palaces . . .
> And in luxurious Cities, where the noise
> Of riot ascends above thir loftiest Tow'rs,
> And injury and outrage: And when Night
> Darkens the Streets, then wander forth the Sons
> Of *Belial,* flown with insolence and wine.
> Witness the Streets of *Sodom.*
>
> (1.497–503)

In this passage, the abusive behavior spills outside of the court and into the city streets ruled by Belial's offspring, who engage in drunken "riot."

Sodom is both a specific case of where Belial's children engage in their marauding activity, and the biblical precedent that provides a way of comprehending the enormity of the sins committed by the contemporary "Courts and Palaces" and "luxurious Cities." It is difficult to imagine a more damning or more zealous condemnation of Charles II than is implied in the semantic nexus these references establish. Just as the crime of sodomy was understood to be antithetical to the "created order," indeed "part of its dissolution," Sodom figures as, and comes to serve as shorthand for, a polity that fails to govern its members.[49] Although the poet does not, in his celebration of marriage, explicitly denounce the monarch or monarchy, the links noted here only serve to heighten the tension between what Milton takes to be the debauched behavior at court and the ideal of governed generation in marriage. Political arithmetic seeks to advance a technology for knowing and manipulating the reproductive resources of the nation to ensure its more effective government, and does so in such a way as to mitigate against religious zeal. *Paradise Lost,* by contrast, implicitly argues that an ideal of governed generation only takes on meaning within a theological frame of reference.

Poetic Reproduction

How do the poem's elaborate efforts to render marital reproduction an urgent obligation impact Milton's understanding of poetic practice—that is, his own production of "apt Numbers"? This question seeks to modify this chapter's discussion of biological procreation by situating human fecundity within a larger field of reproductive practices. Although Milton's account of poetry's effects certainly coordinates with God's reproductive imperatives, it also qualifies the profound emphasis on married procreation as the single allowed form for producing offspring, by embracing practices of cultural reproduction and fantasies of masculine parthenogenesis. To begin to see this, we can note the complex relation between the poet and Orpheus. Famously, in the invocation that opens book 7, Milton raises the specter of Orpheus's fate, a violent assault comparable to that with which he feels threatened and that he hopes to prevent. Blind, alone, "with dangers compast round" (7.27), writing for no more than a "fit audience . . . though few" (7.31), Milton commands his muse to:

> drive far off the barbarous dissonance
> Of *Bacchus* and his Revellers, the Race

Of that wild Rout that tore the *Thracian* Bard
In *Rhodope,* where Woods and Rocks had Ears
To rapture, till the savage clamor drown'd
Both Harp and Voice.

(7.32–37)

In *The Ready and Easy Way,* Milton worried about the agencies of syphilitic "tigers of Bacchus" (7: 452–53) who yearned after monarchy and would bring about its return. This reference brings into view the manner in which the poet's anxieties about the Bacchic "revelers" draws on the animus leveled in book 4 against the Restoration court, criticized for similar ethical abuse. So doing, Milton's complex reference to the fate of Orpheus implicitly reinforces the prominence granted "wedded Love" and its emphasis upon governed reproduction, in contrast to the libertinage at court. However, his appeal to his muse also suggests a certain distance from the celebration of marriage described above. The maenads besetting Orpheus were angered by his refusal to marry following the death of Eurydice and his withdrawal into a pederastic community.[50]

Milton's reference to Orpheus serves as a kind of apotrope, the mythical poet invoked that his fate may be avoided, so consequently it would be difficult to say that Milton identifies absolutely with Orpheus. However, given the latter's status as paradigmatic educator, whose songs civilized their hearers, it is possible to say that although Milton would avoid the classical poet's fate he shares his pedagogic mission. (Indeed, we may recall that it is precisely this aspect of Orpheus that Milton invokes in his letter to Hartlib when he competitively suggests that the "harp of *Orpheus* was not more charming" than his proposed syllabus and regimen.) *Paradise Lost* announces its pedagogic objectives in its opening sentence, where Milton invokes the muse that "didst inspire" Moses, "who first taught the chosen Seed" (1.7–8).[51] I wish to suggest that just as *Of Education* outlined a technique for governing generation pedagogically, the educational objective of *Paradise Lost* dedicates the poet to a reproductive project. Milton's writing stance at the close of *The Ready and Easy Way* offers a precedent for such a claim. There he imagines that if there is not an "abundance of sensible and ingenuous men" to hear his monitory recommendations and secure the Commonwealth against the "general defection of a misguided and abus'd multitude," he can, like Ezekiel, animate the ground he addresses: Milton hopes that "God may raise of these stones to become children of reviving libertie" (7: 463).[52] *Paradise Lost,* through its pedagogic designs reworks this hope insofar as its stated project of "justify[ing] the ways of God to men" (1.26) contributes to the proselytizing mission of Christ's disciples envisioned by Michael. "All Nations they shall teach," the archangel explains to Adam in previewing future history, "Not only to the Sons of *Abraham's* Loins / Salvation shall be Preacht, but to the Sons / Of *Abraham's* Faith wherever through the world" (12.446–49). Christian educators with a capacity for generation, the disciples through their missionary zeal expand the family of the patriarch beyond what his loins could produce. Michael's words treat the "Faith" as pre-existing the moment of its inculcation; the instruction that makes one a son of Abraham's faith simply renders self-evidently transparent the putative basis of common humanity in Christianity, generates for Abraham "Great numbers of each Nation" (12.503) through an apparently effortless educational revision of genealogy.

Locating this alternative form of reproduction in *Paradise Lost* does not resolve or fully account for the tensions noted between the allusion to Orpheus and the celebration of marriage, however. In fact, this account of the disciples' Christian instruction contributes to these tensions insofar as the generative effects attributed to their educational activities take place as if without women; in the account's attribution of procreative force to "Abraham's loins," women seem to play no part either as wives or as daughters in the generation of "the Sons / Of *Abraham's* Faith." Because belief acts as a form of cultural reproduction, educational generation takes place within what looks like an exclusively male domain.

I bring attention to the gender implications here by way of noting that the poem does not simply present a plurality of generational alternatives; instead, the alternatives define a field of reproductive forms, arrayed in a tense relation of coordination and contest. To make such an observation is to do no more than to consider the ramifications of Adam's postlapsarian diatribe against God and Eve, in which he voices a desire for alternative modes of generation and explicitly situates these alternatives in an antagonistic relation. Adam greets his spouse, come to venture reconciliation, with the following invective:

> O why did God,
> Creator wise, that peopl'd highest Heav'n
> With Spirits Masculine, create at last

This novelty on Earth, this fair defect
Of Nature, and not fill the World at once
With Men as Angels without Feminine,
Or find some other way to generate
Mankind? this mischief had not then befall'n,
And more that shall befall, innumerable
Disturbances on Earth through Female snares,
And strait conjunction with this Sex.
(10.888–98)

Himself "not of Woman born" (11.496), Adam wishes either for an all-male community or an alternative form of generating men, one that has nothing to do with "strait conjunction" with women.[53] James Grantham Turner notes the cultural purchase of alternative fantasies of reproduction in early modern England: church fathers, hermeticists, and purveyors of folk wisdom actively considered fantasies of self-sufficient generation.[54] Thus establishing the contemporary relevance for Adam's regret that God did not come up with another form of procreation, Turner argues that the poem gives voice to these alternatives in order to reject them out of hand. Adam's diatribe against Eve, he asserts, "is revealed as a counsel of despair, inimical both to the eagerness of Paradisal Eros and to the more sober love that reunites the man and the woman, 'hand in hand', at the close of the poem."[55] The closing reconciliation of husband and wife, and the reconfirmation of Eve's procreative capacities as the basis for hope ("By mee the Promis'd Seed shall all restore" [12.623], Eve states) seems, Turner insists, to seal off alternative forms of generation as possibilities only raised to be rejected or demonized. According to Turner, Milton delineates an ideal of married procreation by "dramatic opposition" to "[f]orbidden sexuality" and associates the fantasy of male genesis in the poem with "sexual abominations"[56] and marital procreation with generational "responsibility."[57] "Gnostic fantasies of alternative methods of birth," Turner argues, "are put decisively in their place—the allegory of Sin."[58]

Although I think Turner correct to read Adam's diatribe as a problem, a textual moment where discursive tensions are voiced and formulated in explicitly antagonistic terms, the distinction Turner offers between marriage and parthenogenesis is a false one; in fact, the fantasy of autogeneration circulates within accounts of the reproductive capacities of the two parties to the first marriage. To counter the notion that the poem "decisively" associates parthenogenesis with "sexual abomination," we can remark the way such a fantasy informs the letter of God's statement that he intends to "create . . . out of one man a Race / Of men innumerable" (7.154–56); God himself insists that the genesis of humanity will occur through a raw multiplication of men as if out of Adam. Likewise, God's promise to Eve of a hyperbolic fertility is not a simple exposition of biological process. Showing her Adam, God tells Eve that "to him shalt bear / Multitudes like thyself, and thence be call'd / Mother of human Race" (4.474–75). Eve's version of her creation here situates the generation of multitudes not in opposition to her relation to her "wat'ry image" (4.480)—not as a redirection from narcissistic fascination to desire for Adam—but as another version of that relation: God's promise to Eve figures generation as a superabundant multiplication of images of herself.[59] The poem's depiction of the couple's contrite appeal to God after the Fall picks up on the parthenogenetic fantasy: Adam and Eve are compared to "*Deucalion* and chaste *Pyrrha*" facing the problem of how "to restore / The Race of Mankind drown'd" (11.12–13). (In Ovid's *Metamorphosis,* the two succeeded in their task of repeopling the world after the deluge by throwing stones over their shoulders; those that Deucalion threw produced men, Pyrrha's women.)[60]

The foregoing examples suggest that the poet's endorsement of marriage as the divinely sanctioned form of generation, "true source / Of human offspring" (4.750–51), neither exhausts nor resolves the strained tensions in the poem's consideration of reproductive alternatives. Here I want to elaborate upon my observation that educational generation stands in a relation of both coordination and conflict with the ideal of conjugal procreation. Some possibilities for a mutually reinforcing linkage may be noted by examining the angel Michael's pedagogic ministrations on earth. The angel's instruction is, in fact, figured as a version of the educational genesis of Christ's disciples that he depicts in his lesson. Sent to earth to ready Adam and Eve for life after the Fall, the "Heav'nly instructor" (11.871) repeats a scene of creation. Upon his arrival in Eden, he invites Adam to a lecture on future history: "Ascend / This Hill," he commands, "let *Eve* . . . Here sleep below while thou to foresight wak'st, / As once thou slep'st, while Shee to life was form'd" (11.366–69). What is being repeated here? Or rather, who is repeating what? The ambiguity in Michael's formulation allows for at least two readings.

On one hand, Michael suggests that Eve will be made to sleep just as was Adam when God anaesthetized him in order to make his wife. Instead of receiving a wife from a rib, however, Eve will receive a lesson that reinstitutes domestic government. "Her also I with gentle Dreams have calm'd / Portending good," the angel tells Adam, "and all her spirits compos'd / To meek submission" (12.595–97). This recomposition of Eve to a willful acceptance of sole responsibility for the Fall (12.619), to never departing from her husband (12.615–16), also places Eve within a domestic educational regime supervised by Adam, one that restores the usurped hierarchy of knowledge following Eve's consumption of the forbidden fruit; the angel instructs Adam to relate to his spouse what she needs to know, "what thou hast heard, / Chiefly what may concern her Faith" (12.598–99). It is from within this reinstituted domestic government that Eve's procreative activity will salvage hope from the ruins, that, as she declares, "the Promis'd Seed shall all restore" (12.623).

On the other hand, Michael's association of his educational mission with God's creation of Eve can also be read as securing the fantasy of male parthenogenesis within marriage. Taking the clause beginning "As once thou slep'st" to modify "while thou to foresight wak'st," Michael's invitation suggests that where, before, Adam was put to sleep during the creation of Eve, he now will remain awake and watch the panorama of the future spring from him. Thus, Adam construes the vision of the horror wrought by the deluge as a punitive form of generation: "The burd'n of many Ages, on me light / At once," Adam exclaims, "by my foreknowledge gaining Birth / Abortive, to torment me ere thir being" (11.767–69). Adam's education presents him all of future history as his offspring. This future, moreover, as the specific instance of Noah illustrates, is one that proceeds through male generation. By Michael's account, Noah figures as "The one just Man alive" (11.818), commanded to "build a wondrous Ark . . . To save himself and household from amidst / A World devote to universal rack" (11.819–21). Adam's reaction to the future after the "Depopulation" (11.756) wrought by the annihilating flood performatively collapses the household into the man, and then attributes to Noah the capacity to regenerate mankind, as if it proceeded from him alone. "I rejoice," Adam exclaims, "For one Man found so perfet and so just, / That God voutsafes to raise another World / From him, and all his anger to forget" (11.876–78). Adam's synecdochic reduction of the man and "household," a collapse that elides the place of women within post-Edenic oeconomies, allows him to subsume female procreation into male.

Although Michael's lesson provides these resolutions to the tension between parthenogenesis and married procreation, the poem also engages another register in which the fantasy of pedagogic generation is enlisted in a project of circumventing marital government altogether. While, in the invocation to book 1, Milton asks to be placed in the position of instructor, he also asks to be taught, commanding his muse to "Instruct" (1.19) him. Such a request provides an occasion to consider that the desire to be instructed comes from one already pedagogically formed; prior to the composition of *Paradise Lost,* Milton was the subject of a grammar school, university, and private education that enabled the writing of the poem by making possible a poetic vocation. As detailed in previous chapters, vocation provided the means not only through which persons were accountable for the disposition of their talents, but also through which persons were constituted as useful. This is the case as well in *Paradise Lost.* Consistent with Protestant doctrine, angelic numbers become intelligible to God through their vocational activity. Recall that in his post-rebellion census, God emphasized that "Number sufficient" remained in heaven "to possess her Realms / Though wide, and this high Temple to frequent / With Ministeries due and solemn Rites" (7.146–49). To the extent that they matter, numbers matter insofar as they are directed toward theocratic ends, regimentally disposed and vocationally employed toward keeping the empire intact and maintaining worship.

Milton's poetic vocation therefore renders him, like the angels, useful to God, though it is important that such a perspective was not universally held. This is not merely to say that there were "poet haters" of the sort Sidney addressed who questioned the piety of poetry in Milton's day, but rather, that the vocation-form made it possible to invalidate poetry as a way of spending one's life. William Petyt a few years after the initial publication of *Paradise Lost* would dismiss the "ways of living by meer *Literature and the Pen*" as "add[ing] no Treasure to the Nation."[61] Implicit here is a perspective (glanced at in our reading of Smith's *Discourse,* but more fully elaborated in Petty's *Political Arithmetic*) that some vocations are more important to the nation than others because of their ability to generate wealth and thus to bolster the "Health of the Kingdom."[62] For example, Petty argues that "[t]he Husbandman of *England* earns but about 4 *s. per* Week, but the Seamen have as good as 12 *s.* in Wages, Victuals (and as it were housing) with other accommodations, so as a Seaman is in effect three Husbandmen."[63] Quantitatively specifying the differential effects of alternate vocations, through which Petty constitutes the populace as an object to be manipulated and optimized, provides the basis for policies aimed at augmenting national prosperity. For Petty, encouragement of sea trade would realign vocational distribution within the national household, and, according to his calculations, would provide more wealth for the nation by effectively creating people.

As we have seen, Milton voices strong reservations about the assumptions underlying these statements, namely that wealth should be the single criterion guiding policy decisions, and construes such an approach to national governance an illegitimate displacement of theological concerns. His poetic commitments reaffirm this view to the extent that he seeks not only to be like the angels—vocationally useful to God—but also to number among them by joining their chorus of praise. Milton details the angelic multitudes' effusive celebration following Christ's intervention with God on humankind's behalf, an effusion to which he implicitly dedicates *Paradise Lost.* "Hail Son of God," the poet exclaims, "Savior of Men, thy Name / Shall be the copious matter of my Song / Henceforth, and never shall my Harp thy praise / Forget, nor from thy Father's praise disjoin" (3.412–15). This "copious matter," what Andrew Marvell would call in his introductory poem a "vast expense" of verse, contributes to God's treasure by vocationally miming his "copious" generosity: at the feast in heaven, God himself is an "all bounteous King, who show'r'd / With copious hand" (5.640–41).[64] Milton's expenditure of verse, as an activity through which he situates himself among the heavenly "numbers without number" (3.346), amounts to an effort to rewrite his genealogy, to become one of the "Progeny of Light" (5.600) generated by God himself. This is to say that the poet, through his vocation, seeks to achieve the wish Adam voiced in his postlapsarian diatribe—to take a place among a multitude of "Spirits Masculine" generated spontaneously by God.

Conclusion

Although after the Restoration theological concerns come to be partitioned off from policymaking, this does not mean that theology loses completely its governmental relevance or that it stops being capable of providing tools with which people organize their lives or their relationships to others. Consequently, although Milton diverges from the assumptions and objectives of political arithmetic, he cannot be said simply to resist a rising tide of modernity, a dispensation in which the governance of populations is founded on a purely secular administrative rationality. As a coda to my discussion of Milton, and to this book as a whole, I wish to return to Thomas Malthus's *Essay on the Principle of Population,* and his passing allusion to Milton's epic, to demonstrate the complexity and the unevenness of the transformations to which I gesture. As I described at this book's outset, Malthus provides a brief history of the progress of mankind through a series of forms of social organization, from nomadic to shepherding to farming, and so forth. Describing the way the advantages of the shepherd life put in play the forces that would overwhelm this mode of being, Malthus posits that population growth is the key to social change. Here again is Malthus's description of the response to the misery that follows from population pressures:

> Want pinched the less fortunate members of society, and, at length, the impossibility of supporting such a number together became too evident to be resisted. Young scions were then pushed out from the parent-stock and instructed to explore fresh regions and to gain happier seats for themselves by their swords. "The world was all before them where to choose."[65]

As suggested in the introduction, Malthus's quotation from the close of *Paradise Lost* offhandedly dispenses with the elaborate theological explanation of the 10,561 lines that come before this one, and the 3 that come after. This stunningly efficient redaction of the poem reconfigures the first couple, rewrites and reconstitutes them within the parameters of a new account of human fecundity. Rather than search out "Thir place of rest" (12.647), as Milton suggests, Adam and Eve number among the restless offspring whom Malthus likens to "famished wolves in search of prey"; cast off from their original communities, they coalesced into the "clouds of Barbarians" that annihilated the very society that had generated them.[66]

It will be instructive here to note that Milton figuratively distanced Adam and Eve from the barbarians by associating the latter with Satan's troops, who when called into formation constitute:

> A multitude, like which the populous North
> Pour'd never from her frozen loins, to pass
> *Rhene* or the *Danaw*, when her barbarous Sons
> Came like a Deluge on the South, and spread
> Beneath *Gibraltar* to the *Lybian* sands.
>
> (1.351–55)

Although Adam and Eve choose to generate humanity rather than commit suicide or remain barren, and thus stand as the "Grand Parents" (1.29) of all who follow, Milton's construction of the Vandal family tree elides this basic premise of the poem by attributing reproductive agency to a geographical region, the "North," which "Pour[s]" its offspring from its "frozen loins." The poet's depiction manages the implication that complying with the divine imperative to generate numbers, even within the institution of marriage, could produce—however many generations in the future—uncontrollable effects, could generate and put in play the dissolute agencies of numbers out of control. Malthus, on the other hand, collapses Adam and Eve into their Vandal progeny. Thus wrenching them from Milton's poem, he recasts them as both the historical precedent for and the first instance of the hyperfecundity that he views as a threat to late eighteenth-century England, the overwhelming "power of population" he sought to specify and to curb.[67]

Certainly Malthus operates within a conceptual vocabulary and practical dispensation that differs sharply from that utilized and confronted by Milton, although this is not to say that anything like an absolute epistemological rupture separates the two writers. Malthus did not simply reject the kinds of views Milton advances, in favor of Petty's or Graunt's arithmetical science of government, which remained in relative abeyance until the explosion of interest in statistics in the nineteenth century. Although it is clear Malthus's apprehension of the population was made possible by the stigmatization of theology that took place at the end of the seventeenth century, his vision is nevertheless informed by a providentialism that would limit the scope of national governments. As he speculates, the oscillation of the magnitude of the population may in fact simply be the process through which God works out his elaborate and inscrutable designs.[68] The effect of such an account, *pace* Petty, is to reinforce a sense of the limit of national government in the face of God's administrative agencies. Similarly, in contrast to Edmund Spenser, whose *View* claimed an administrative capacity to accomplish God's providential mission, Malthus insists that any effort to administer policies to curb or augment the population would certainly backfire or produce unintended effects exacerbating the devastating imbalances between people and agricultural resources. Instead, consistent with a liberal mode of governmentality, Malthus emphasized "moral restraint," a practical capacity for "prudential" deliberation and self-regulation.[69] Of course, the masculine prudential subject endorsed by Malthus chooses *not* to marry if he cannot foresee the means to support a family. Nevertheless, Malthus's privileging of this governed personality may be understood as an elaboration of the connection Milton forges between appropriate reproduction and self-control: governed generation requires each person to govern his or her own desires. To observe this link not only locates Malthus's relation to Milton, but our relation to Malthus—if not to his model of geometrically growing populations outstripping arithmetically growing agricultural resources, at least to the vision of government upon which he relied. The emphasis on the capacity for self-government, which, especially in the realm of erotic behavior, carries with it the imperative to regulate oneself, is a linchpin of the neoliberal dispensation and the attendant sexual regimes that characterize our contemporary moment.

Notes

Introduction

1. Thomas Malthus, *An Essay On the Principle of Population* (1798), ed. Anthony Flew (Harmondsworth: Penguin, 1985), 83–84.

2. Douglas Bruster, *Drama and the Market in the Age of Shakespeare* (Cambridge: Cambridge University Press, 1992), 20–21.

3. The phenomenon described here is widespread, so it seems somewhat unnecessary to pinpoint specific instances. But to mention a few important examples of work that insists on the relevance of demographic changes to cultural production, I note the following studies, for which I have considerable admiration. Richard Halpern, *Poetics of Primitive Accumulation* (Ithaca: Cornell University Press, 1991); Jean Howard, *The Stage and Social Struggle in Early Modern England* (London: Routledge, 1994), William C. Carroll, *Fat King, Lean Beggar: Representations of Poverty in the Age of Shakespeare* (Ithaca: Cornell University Press, 1996).

4. Fernand Braudel, "The Weight of Numbers," chapter 1 of *The Structures of Everyday Life: The Limits of the Possible,* vol. 1 of *Civilization and Capitalism: 15th–18th Century,* trans. Siân Reynolds (New York: Harper and Row, 1981), 31–103.

5. Bruster, *Drama,* 21.

6. Lorraine Daston, "Historical Epistemology," in *Questions of Evidence: Proof, Practice, and Persuasion Across the Disciplines,* ed. James Chandler, Arnold I. Davidson, and Harry D. Harootunian (Chicago: University of Chicago Press, 1994), 282. See also Mary Poovey, *A History of the Modern Fact: Problems of Knowledge Production in the Sciences of Wealth and Society* (Chicago: University of Chicago Press, 1999), 7. Although not understanding his efforts in these terms, Philip Kreager advances a similar call for historical awareness from within the discipline of demography in "Histories of Demography: A Review Essay," *Population* 47 (1993): 519–39. See also his essay "Demographic Regimes as Cultural Systems" in *The State of Population Theory: Forward From Malthus,* ed. David Coleman and Roger Schofield (Oxford: Basil Blackwell, 1986), 131–55.

7. The term "back projection" and the methodology it describes figure prominently in the monumental work of E. A. Wrigley and R. S. Schofield, *The Population*

History of England, 1541–1871: A Reconstruction (Cambridge, Mass.: Harvard University Press, 1981).

8. An important study upon which I seek to elaborate in discussing questions of population in relation to literature is James Holstun's brilliant analysis of utopic discourse, *A Rational Millenium: Puritan Utopias of Seventeenth-Century England and America* (Oxford: Oxford University Press, 1987). Holstun reads a number of utopias as advancing a reformative practice that transforms "anomic" masses of people into disciplined populations. My argument, in many ways enabled by Holstun's project, develops this analysis in two directions. First, it examines an array of texts that are not explicitly utopic. Second, it attempts to specify in greater genealogical detail than does Holstun the conceptual vocabularies through which numbers of people are rendered culturally intelligible. The emphasis here is on the "commonwealth" as a terrain of governmental action and as a site of governmental obligation. I argue that, throughout the century and a half upon which I focus, a (by no means static) understanding of the common weal organizes the ways numbers of people come to be defined as objects of knowledge and subjects of governmental concern, policy intervention, or collective action.

9. Michel Foucault, *The History of Sexuality,* vol. 1, *An Introduction,* trans. Robert Hurley (New York: Vintage, 1990), 26. Future references are noted internally.

10. See Ian Hacking, "Biopower and the Avalanche of Printed Numbers," *Humanities in Society* 5 (1982): 279–95.

11. Colin Gordon, "Governmental Rationality: An Introduction" in *The Foucault Effect: Studies in Governmentality,* ed. Graham Burchell, Colin Gordon, and Peter Miller (Chicago: University of Chicago Press, 1991), 3 and 5. See also Michel Foucault, "The Politics of Health in the Eighteenth Century," *Power / Knowledge: Selected Interviews and Other Writings, 1972–1977,* ed. Colin Gordon (New York: Pantheon, 1980), 171–72; and "Omnes et Singulatim: Towards a Criticism of 'Political Reason,'" in *The Tanner Lectures on Human Values II,* ed. Sterling McMurrin (Salt Lake City: University of Utah Press, 1981), 223–54.

12. Michel Foucault, "Governmentality" in *Foucault Effect,* 99–101.

13. This question structures the famous "Brenner debate," with the eponymous scholar vigorously contesting what he sees as a neo-Malthusian vision of history that fails to account for the role class plays in demographic transformations. *The Brenner Debate: Agrarian Class Structure and Economic Development in Pre-Industrial Europe,* ed. T. H. Aston and C. H. E. Philpin (Cambridge: Cambridge University Press, 1985). For another account of population as last-instance determinant of social transformation, see Jack Goldstone, *Revolution and Rebellion in the Early Modern World* (Berkeley and Los Angeles: University of California Press, 1990).

14. The summary that follows—indeed, much of my thinking about government—is indebted to these authors. The works that I have drawn upon include the essays collected in *The Foucault Effect* and in *Foucault and Political Reason,* ed. Andrew Barry, Thomas Osborne, and Nikolas Rose (Chicago: University of Chicago Press, 1996); Peter Miller and Nikolas Rose, "Governing Economic Life," *Economy and Society* 19, 1 (February 1990): 1–31; Nikolas Rose and Peter Miller, "Political Power Beyond the State: Problematics of Government," *British Journal of Sociology* 43, 2 (June 1992): 173–205; Mitchell Dean, *Critical and Effective Histories: Foucault's Methods and Historical Sociology* (London: Routledge, 1994); and Ian Hacking, "Making Up People," *Reconstructing Individualism: Autonomy, Individuality, and the Self*

in Western Thought, ed. Thomas C. Heller, Morton Sosna, and David E. Wellberry (Stanford: Stanford University Press, 1986), 222–36. I have also profited from Mary Poovey's reflections on the reconfiguration of numbers of persons as an object of knowledge under the aegis of William Petty's *Political Arithmetic* (in Charles Henry Hull, ed., *The Economic Writings of Sir William Petty* [1899; reprint, Fairfield, N.J.: Kelley 1986], 232–313), in the latter seventeenth century, "The Social Constitution of 'Class': Towards a History of Classificatory Thinking," *Rethinking Class: Literary Studies and Social Formations,* ed. Wai Chee Dimock and Michael T. Gilmore (New York: Columbia University Press, 1994): 15–56, and from Poovey's more recent work, *A History of the Modern Fact* (Chicago: University of Chicago Press, 1998).

15. Barbara Cruikshank, *The Will to Empower: Democratic Citizens and Other Subjects* (Ithaca: Cornell University Press, 1999), 20.

16. Michel Foucault, "The Subject and Power," afterword to Hubert L. Dreyfuss and Paul Rabinow, *Michel Foucault: Beyond Structuralism and Hermeneutics* (Chicago: University of Chicago Press, 1982), 221.

17. Foucault, "Governmentality," *Foucault Effect,* 88.

18. Ibid., 103.

19. The point advanced here suggests a rereading of G. R. Elton's extraordinary *Tudor Revolution in Government* (Cambridge: Cambridge University Press, 1966). Elton's work has been criticized strongly for the narrative of rupture upon which it relies, and its attribution of a too central role to the genius of Cromwell as the primary if not sole agent responsible for the advent of state power in Henrician England. Although he does tend to straightjacket his evidence into all too stark a narrative, the evidence he adduces actually tells a story of administrative improvisation, ad hoc problem solving, creative borrowing of administrative techniques, uneven and unplanned development, and transformation of offices, positions, commissions, councils, departments, and so forth. For a similar call for reevaluating Elton's work, see John Guy, *Tudor England* (Oxford and New York: Oxford University Press, 1988), 156–58.

20. Gordon, "Governmental Rationality," 2.

21. Mitchell Dean, *Critical and Effective Histories,* 176–77.

22. Foucault, "Governmentality," 90.

23. Foucault outlines the transition from domestic economy to national economy in "Governmentality," and the effects of the model of pastoral power in his lecture "Omnes et Singulatim."

24. Recent studies include (in chronological order): Richard Helgerson, *Forms of Nationhood: The Elizabethan Writing of England* (Chicago: University of Chicago Press, 1992); Andrew Hadfield, *Literature, Politics, and National Identity: Reformation to Renaissance* (Cambridge: Cambridge University Press, 1994); Claire McEachern, *The Poetics of English Nationhood, 1590–1612* (Cambridge: Cambridge University Press, 1996); and David Baker, *Between Nations: Shakespeare, Marvell, and the Question of Britain* (Stanford: Stanford University Press, 1997).

25. This argument is most forcefully and compellingly advanced by Baker in *Between Nations.*

26. It is important to emphasize that the scholars who have written about English nationhood do not completely ignore questions of governance, and they frequently remark the way the nation form imposes various kinds of order. The distinction I draw is primarily a matter of emphasis, although the focus on the pro-

duction of exclusive or inclusive identities tends to displace a more elaborated or nuanced analysis of dynamics of government.

27. Foucault, *Introduction,* 104–5, 154.

28. Pierre Bourdieu and Jean-Claude Passeron, *Reproduction in Education, Society, and Culture,* trans. Richard Nice (London: Sage Publications, 1977). For useful surveys of educational reproduction theory, see Michael W. Apple, "Reproduction and Contradiction in Education: An Introduction," *Cultural and Economic Reproduction in Education: Essays on Class, Ideology and the State* (London: Routledge and Kegan Paul, 1982), 1–31, and Margaret Ferguson, "Teaching and/as Reproduction," *Yale Journal of Criticism* 1, 2 (spring 1988): 213–22.

29. Jonathan Goldberg, *Writing Matter: From the Hands of the English Renaissance* (Stanford: Stanford University Press, 1990), and Halpern, *Poetics of Primitive Accumulation.*

30. I use the gender-neutral term "persons" to acknowledge that women could be included in humanist fantasies of cultural reproduction; it is important to note, however, that the subject of humanist pedagogy is generally assumed to be gendered male. On the ideal of pedagogic generation, see Jonathan Goldberg, *Sodometries: Renaissance Texts, Modern Sexualities* (Stanford: Stanford University Press, 1992), and Elizabeth Pittenger, "Dispatch Quickly: The Mechanical Reproduction of Pages," *Shakespeare Quarterly* 42, 4 (winter 1991): 389–408, who brilliantly links the pedagogic program of generating men to the disciplinary regime, the fantasies of pure multiplication, and the dream of perfect textual and sexual transmission, all organized through and around the printing press.

31. I borrow the notion of "governmental optimism" from the work of Rose and Miller.

32. Stuart Hall, "Rethinking the 'Base and Superstructure' Metaphor," *Class, Hegemony, and Party,* ed. Jon Bloomfield (London: Lawrence and Wishart, 1977), 71, as quoted by Michael Apple, "Reproduction and Contradiction," 16. Pittenger makes a similar point in "Dispatch Quickly," 395–96n.25.

33. Bourdieu and Passeron, *Reproduction,* 19.

34. Wrigley and Schofield, *Population History of England,* 528. For an overview of subsequent work on Western European population, see L. R. Poos, "The Historical Demography of Renaissance Europe: Recent Research and Current Issues," *Renaissance Quarterly* 42, 4 (winter 1989): 794–811.

35. For example, see Paul Slack, *Poverty and Policy in Tudor and Stuart England* (London: Longman, 1988), 43–44, which argues that the marked population growth Wrigley and Schofield observe placed a strain on material resources and food supplies, increasing vagabondage and creating the preconditions for the explosive political disruptions at mid-seventeenth century; and A. L. Beier, *Masterless Men: The Vagrancy Problem in England, 1560–1640* (London: Methuen, 1985), 19–20.

1. "Making Up People"

1. Ian Hacking, "Making Up People," 228. Hacking's argument finds confirmation in Judith Butler's assertion that "the 'coherence' and 'continuity' of 'the person' are not logical or analytical features of personhood, but, rather, socially instituted and maintained norms of intelligibility." Judith Butler, *Gender Trouble: Feminism*

and the Subversion of Identity (New York: Routledge, 1990), 17. See also Ian Hunter, "Personality as a Vocation: The Political Rationality of the Humanities," *Economy and Society* 19, 4 (1990): 401–05.

2. Mary Dewar, ed. *A Discourse of the Commonweal of This Realm of England, Attributed to Sir Thomas Smith* (Charlottesville: University Press of Virginia, 1969). I have also consulted Elizabeth Lamond's 1893 edition, *A Discourse of the Common Weal of This Realm of England* (1893; reprinted New York: Burt Franklin, 1971). Lamond favors John Hales as the most probable author (xxv–xxix); Dewar spells out her case for Smith in "The Authorship of the 'Discourse of the Commonweal," *Economic History Review* 2d ser., 19, 2 (August 1966): 388–400. On Smith's life and career, see also Dewar's *Sir Thomas Smith: A Tudor Intellectual in Office* (London: Athlone Press, 1964). Dewar's attribution generally has been accepted by recent scholars, and I follow suit here, though my argument does not stand or fall on the question of authorship.

3. For a definitive study of sixteenth- and seventeenth-century dissidence, see Roger Manning, *Village Revolts: Social Protest and Popular Disturbances in England, 1509–1640* (Oxford: Clarendon Press, 1988).

4. See for example, Stephen Greenblatt, "Murdering Peasants: Status, Genre, and The Representation of Rebellion," *Representations* 1, 1 (February 1983): 1–29; and Christopher Hill "The Many-Headed Monster in Late Tudor and Early Stuart Political Thinking," in *From the Renaissance to the Counter-Reformation: Essays in Honor of Garrett Mattingly*, ed. Charles H. Carter (New York: Random House, 1965), 296–324.

5. Dewar, *Tudor Intellectual*, 52.

6. Peter H. Ramsey, "Introduction" to Peter H. Ramsey, ed., *The Price Revolution in Sixteenth-Century England* (London: Methuen, 1971), 1–17.

7. Joseph A. Schumpeter, *History of Economic Analysis*, ed. Elizabeth Boody Schumpeter (New York: Oxford University Press, 1954), 166–67.

8. Annabel Patterson, *Reading Holinshed's Chronicles* (Chicago: University of Chicago Press, 1994), 76.

9. Neal Wood, "The Foundations of Political Economy: The New Moral Philosophy of Sir Thomas Smith," in *Political Thought and the Tudor Commonwealth: Deep Structure, Discourse, and Disguise*, ed. Paul A. Fideler and T. F. Mayer (London: Routledge, 1992), 140–68, stands as an interesting possible exception to such an approach. Wood reads Smith not against the example of economists, but as the first economist, and takes *A Discourse* to be the origin of political economy. My difficulty with this effort is that it continues to endorse the teleology implied in the economic perspective. Consequently, Wood tends to overstate Smith's distinction from his contemporaries in order to read him as an early incarnation of Adam Smith.

10. Patterson, *Reading*, 76.

11. For a lucid overview of Renaissance moral philosphy, see Paul Oskar Kristeller, "Humanism and Moral Philosophy," in *Renaissance Humanism: Foundations, Forms and Legacy*, ed. Albert Rabil, 3 vols. (Philadelphia: University of Philadelphia Press, 1988), 3: 271–309.

12. Helpful here are Mary Poovey's varied and extensive contributions to a genealogy of political economy, which are also crucial to the argument of this chapter as a whole: *A History of the Modern Fact;* "The Social Constitution of 'Class'"; "Aesthetics and Political Economy in the Eighteenth Century: The Place of Gender in

the Social Constitution of Knowledge," in *Aesthetics and Ideology*, ed. George Levine (New Brunswick, N.J.: Rutgers University Press, 1994), 79–105.

13. Kraye, "Moral Philosphy," in Charles B. Schmitt et al., eds., *The Cambridge History of Renaissance Philosophy* (Cambridge: Cambridge University Press, 1988), 303–4.

14. Ernst Kantorowicz, *The King's Two Bodies: A Study in Mediaeval Political Theology* (Princeton: Princeton University Press, 1957), 177.

15. Ibid., 96.

16. Arthur B. Ferguson, *The Articulate Citizen and the English Renaissance* (Durham: Duke University Press, 1965), 244, 365. I also make reference here to Gaines Post, "A Romano-Canonical Maxim, 'Quid Omnes Tangit,' in Bracton," *Traditio* 4 (1946): 197–251, upon which Kantorowicz draws. Post demonstrates the ways Roman and Canonical law contributed to the development of a sense of national community, to the implicit assumption or explicit articulation of spheres of communal life that concerned and affected all.

17. See, in addition to Ferguson, Whitney R. D. Jones, *The Tudor Commonwealth, 1529–1559* (London: Athlone Press, 1970). The work of David Starkey on this topic ("Which Age of Reform?" in *Revolution Reassessed: Revisions in the History of Tudor Government and Administration*, ed. Christopher Coleman and David Starkey [Oxford: Oxford University Press, 1986], 13–27, as well as his concluding remarks to the same volume, "After the 'Revolution,'" 199–208) has been extremely useful, as well. See also William H. Sherman's fine essay, "Anatomizing the Commonwealth: Language, Politics, and the Elizabethan Social Order," in *The Project of Prose in Early Modern Europe and the New World*, ed. Elizabeth Fowler and Roland Greene (Cambridge: Cambridge University Press, 1997), 104–21.

The discursive focus of the scholars above, which emphasizes the shared terms through which knowledge about the polity was constituted, distributed, or applied by England's "articulate citizenry," departs from a dominant approach of Tudor historians of the commonwealth literature. The primary objective of the latter has been to establish the links between a commonwealth "party" and the reign of a particular monarch (say, that of Edward VI) or specific royal officials (Thomas Cromwell or Protector Somerset). G. R. Elton provides a brief survey of the literature advancing such a view, although he generally disagrees with it in spite of his own lionization of Cromwell, in "Reform and the 'Commonwelth-Men' of Edward VI's Reign," in *The English Commonwealth, 1547–1640: Essays in Politics and Society*, ed. Peter Clark, Alan G. R. Smith, and Nicholas Tyacke (New York: Barnes and Noble Books, 1979), 23–38.

18. David Starkey, "Which Age," 19; see in general 19–23.

19. Ferguson, *Articulate Citizen*, 143.

20. Starkey, "After the 'Revolution,'" 208, emphasis his.

21. Ferguson, *Articulate Citizen*, 201.

22. Foucault, "Governmentality," 92. For discussions of the purchase of the household analogy in early modern thought, see Wood, "Foundations," 153–55; Jonathan Goldberg, *James I and the Politics of Literature: Jonson, Shakespeare, Donne, and Their Contemporaries* (Baltimore: Johns Hopkins University Press, 1983), 85–112; Constance Jordan, "The Household and the State: Transformations in the Representation of an Analogy from Aristotle to James I," *Modern Language Quarterly* 54, 3 (September 1993): 307–26

23. Jeffrey Minson, *Genealogies of Morals: Nietzsche, Foucault, Donzelot, and the Eccentricity of Ethics* (New York: St. Martin's Press, 1985), 103.

24. Gerhard Oestreich, *Neostoicism and the Early Modern State,* ed. Brigitta Oestreich and H. G. Koenigsberger, trans. David McLintock (Cambridge: Cambridge University Press, 1982), 156. On the concept of police, see also Pasquale Pasquino, "Theatricum Politicum," 105–18; and Franz-Ludwig Knemeyer, "Polizei," *Economy and Society* 9, 2 (May 1980): 172–96. For an early example of English policy recommendations, see *The Libel of English Policy* (1436), an abridged and edited version of which appears in *Complaint and Reform in England: 1436–1714,* ed. William Huse Dunham Jr. and Stanley Pargellis (New York: Oxford University Press, 1938; reprinted New York: Octagon Books, 1968), 3–30.

25. Knemeyer, "Polizei," 179–80; Quentin Skinner, *The Foundations of Modern Political Thought,* 2 vols. (Cambridge: Cambridge University Press, 1978), 1: 50. I regret that Peter Biller's study *The Measure of Multitude: Population in Medieval Thought* (Oxford: Oxford University Press, 2000) came to my attention after *Increase and Multiply* had gone to press. This is an extraordinary examination of demographic and reproductive themes across a vast array of intellectual sites. One of the many strengths of this book is its analysis of the impact Aristotle's *Politics* had on medieval vocabularies for conceptualizing the growth, decline, and possible management of "multitudes."

26. J. G. A. Pocock, *The Machiavellian Moment: Florentine Political Thought and the Atlantic Republican Tradition* (Princeton: Princeton University Press, 1975), 28. See also Oestreich; and Victoria Kahn, *Rhetoric, Prudence, and Skepticism in the Renaissance* (Ithaca: Cornell University Press, 1985), offers considerable insight into these issues as well.

27. Ferguson, *Articulate Citizens,* 59 et passim. See also John Guy, *Tudor England.*

28. See, in addition to Jordan and Ferguson, Paul Slack, "Social Policy and the Constraints of Government, 1547–1558," *The Mid-Tudor Polity, c. 1540–1560,* ed. Robert Tittler and Jennifer Loach (Totowa, N.J.: Rowman and Littlefield, 1980), 94–115; in the same volume, Robert Tittler, "The Emergence of Urban Policy, 1536–58," 74–93; Joan Thirsk, *Economic Policy And Projects: The Development of a Consumer Society in Early Modern England* (Oxford: Clarendon Press, 1978).

29. Felix Raab, *The English Face of Machiavelli: A Changing Interpretation, 1500–1700* (London: Routledge and Kegan Paul, 1964). Chapters 1 and 2 are particularly relevant; see also p. 111, and p. 166 for especially pointed examples of such an understanding of "policy."

30. Paul Viroli, *From Politics to Reason of State: The Acquisition and Transformation of the Language of Politics, 1250–1600* (Cambridge: Cambridge University Press, 1992), 71.

31. Richard Tuck, *Philosophy and Government, 1572–1651* (Cambridge: Cambridge University Press, 1993). Helpful here as well is Poovey, *Modern Fact,* 85–91. See also Ferguson, *Articulate Citizen,* 201–2.

32. On parish registers, see J. Charles Cox, *The Parish Registers of England* (Totowa, N.J.: Rowman and Littlefield, 1974) and John Southerden Burn, *The History of Parish Registers in England* (London: J. R. Smith, 1862). For the survey of people and foodstuff in Coventry, see *Tudor Economic Documents,* ed. R. H. Tawney and Eileen Power, 3 vols. (London: Longmans, Green, 1924), 1: 141–43. On registration of the poor, see John F. Pound, *The Norwich Census of the Poor, 1570* (Norfolk Record

Society, 1971) and "An Acte for the Punishement of Vacabondes, and for Relief of the Poore and Impotent" in Tawney and Power, *Tudor Economic Documents,* 2: 329–31. Examples of orders to enumerate resident aliens, as well as correspondence relating to the distribution of "strangers" around the country, may be found in *Acts of the Privy Council of England,* ed. John Roche Dasent (1893; Nendeln/Liechtenstein: Kraus Reprint, 1974), 8: 50, 198, 306, 336–37, 345–46, 22:506–8. For the bills of mortality, see *Acts of the Privy Council,* 24: 442, and *Reflections on the Weekly Bills of Mortality* in *A Collection of Very Valuable and Scarce Pieces Relating to the Last Plague in the Year 1665* (1721), 53–82, esp. 54–55.

33. See also Colin Gordon, "Governmental Rationality," *Foucault Effect,* 10. For a discussion of the epistemological transformation that renders the domain of particularity a valid object of philosophical inquiry, see Pocock, *Machiavellian Moment,* 3–113. Of course, the administrative recording of persons is by no means new to English governance. Quantifying people had been a concern for royal or civic administrators long before the 1500s, primarily for military calculation or for levying taxes. The widespread and dispersed efforts to register and to count people in sixteenth-century England signals the application of writing practices central to medieval administration to new areas of existence, the adaptation of older modes of knowledge production to changed circumstances. For a study of the relation between writing and administrative activity in medieval England, see M. T. Clanchy, *From Memory to Written Record: England, 1066–1307* (Cambridge, Mass.: Harvard University Press, 1979).

34. *A Dialogue between Pole and Lupset,* ed. T. F. Mayer (London: Royal Historical Society, 1989), 98.

35. Tawney and Power, *Tudor Economic Documents,* 3: 314.

36. Nikolas Rose and Peter Miller, "Political Power Beyond the State," 190. See also their essay "Governing Economic Life," 1–31, esp. 10–11.

37. Rose and Miller, "Political Power," 190.

38. My discussion of the Antrim plantation is indebted to David Beers Quinn, "Sir Thomas Smith (1513–1577) and the Beginnings of English Colonial Theory," *Proceedings of the American Philosophical Society* 89, 4 (December 1945): 543–60, whose account of the troubles encountered by the colony I summarize. See also Dewar, *Tudor Intellectual,* 156–70; and Lisa Jardine, "Encountering Ireland: Gabriel Harvey, Edmund Spenser, and English Colonial Ventures," in *Representing Ireland: Literature and the Origins of Conflict, 1534–1660,* ed. Brendan Bradshaw, Andrew Hadfield, and Willy Maley (Cambridge: Cambridge University Press, 1993), 60–75.

39. The "indenture" dated October 5, 1571, is quoted in Quinn, "Sir Thomas Smith," 551.

40. Quinn, "Sir Thomas Smith," 552. For an overview of the argument for colonial endeavor as a means of addressing overpopulation, see Howard Mumford Jones, "The Colonial Impulse: An Analysis of the 'Promotion' Literature of Colonization," *Proceedings of the American Philosophical Society* 90, 2 (May 1946): 146–52.

41. For more on the effort to people Ireland, see chapter 3, which discusses Edmund Spenser's *View of the State of Ireland* and his policy recommendations for peopling that land.

42. In Starkey, the nation is beset both by "consumptyon"—a lack of people—and "palsy"—a superfluity of idle persons who contribute nothing to the commonweal. Starkey, *A Dialogue,* 96–103. See also G. R. Elton, *Reform and Renewal: Thomas*

Cromwell and the Common Weal (Cambridge: Cambridge University Press, 1973), 126.

43. Smith separates out this kind of enclosure, and not others, for censure. See William C. Carroll, "'The Nursery of Beggary': Enclosure, Vagrancy, and Sedition in the Tudor-Stuart Period," in *Enclosure Acts: Sexuality, Property, and Culture in Early Modern England,* ed. Richard Burt and John Michael Archer (Ithaca: Cornell University Press, 1994), 37.

44. This point is repeated frequently. For a forceful instance, see the anonymous *Pyers Plowmans Exhortation* (London, 1550), Sig. A7r–A7v.

45. Smith's observations echo the complaints of numerous writers. Relevant here is Raphael Hythlodaeus's acerbic comment that England's sheep were "so greedy and wild that they devour human beings themselves and depopulate fields, houses, and towns," St. Thomas More, *Utopia,* ed. Edward Surtz (New Haven: Yale University Press, 1964), 24. Robert Powell, writing several decades after Smith, made explicit the logic underpinning this position. "Depopulation . . . robbes and pilles the people of their due maintenance, and thereby disables them both in body and state from performing their service, and liege obedience, immediately to their Prince, and mediately to the Common-weale. . . . And it alters the quality of the people; from good Husbands, it makes them houselesse and thriftlesse, puts them in a course of idleness (the mother of mischiefe, and bane of all rule and order.) So as they become aliens and strangers to their nationall government, and the kingdome by that meanes in a manner dispeopled and desolated." *Depopulation Arraigned, Convicted and Condemned* (London, 1636), 6–7.

46. Michel Foucault, *The Use of Pleasure,* vol. 2, *The History of Sexuality,* trans. Robert Hurley (New York: Vintage, 1990), and *The Care of the Self,* vol. 3, *The History of Sexuality,* trans. Robert Hurley (New York: Vintage, 1988). For an important discussion of Foucault's work on ethos, see Arnold I. Davidson, "Ethics as Ascetics: Foucault, the History of Ethics, and Ancient Thought," in *The Cambridge Companion to Foucault,* ed. Gary Gutting (Cambridge: Cambridge University Press, 1994), 115–40.

47. See, for example: Max Weber, *The Protestant Ethic and the Spirit of Capitalism,* trans. Talcott Parsons (New York: Charles Scribner's Sons, 1958); Norbert Elias, *The History of Manners,* vol. 1 of *The Civilizing Process,* trans. Edmund Jephcott (1939; New York: Pantheon, 1982), who attributes a crucial role to Erasmian humanism in the transformation of human behavior in the direction of *civilité;* Oestreich's *Neostoicism* details a pan-European neo-Stoicism in the latter decades of the sixteenth century that serves as a source of ethical ideals serviceable to an emergent modern state; Margo Todd, *Christian Humanism and the Puritan Social Order* (Cambridge: Cambridge University Press, 1987); R. Po-Chia Hsia, *Social Discipline in the Reformation: Central Europe 1550–1750* (London: Routledge, 1992); and Stephen Greenblatt's *Renaissance Self-Fashioning* (Chicago: Chicago University Press, 1980). R. H. Tawney, *Religion and the Rise of Capitalism* (New York: New American Library, 1954), 11–60, provides an overview of ethical formulations in the English Middle Ages, which in many ways lay the groundwork for the ethical intensification of the sixteenth and seventeenth centuries. These precursors qualify one potential implication of Hacking's account of "making up people": one drawback of this phrasing is to suggest that acts of descriptive specification are wholly new, drawn out of the air; instead, it is important to understand that such acts take place within, and work upon, given categories and practices.

48. Oestreich, *Neostoicism,* 5.

49. Todd, *Christian Humanism,* 30. See also Oestreich, *Neostoicism,* 127.

50. Oestreich, *Neostoicism,* 127.

51. Anon., *The Prayse and Commendacion of Suche as Sought Comenwelthes* (1548), A4r.

52. Robert Crowley, *The Way to Wealth,* (1550) in *Selected Works,* ed. J. M. Cowper (1550: London, 1872), 132.

53. Thomas Becon, *The Jewel of Joy,* in *The Catechism of Thomas Becon . . . With Other Pieces Written By Him in the Reign of King Edward the Sixthe* (1844), 432.

54. Richard Morison, *A Lamentation in Which is Showed What Ruin and Destruction Cometh of Seditious Rebellion* (1536), in *Humanist Scholarship and Public Order: Two Tracts against the Pilgrimage of Grace by Sir Richard Morison,* ed. David Sandler Berkowitz (Washington, D.C.: Folger Shakespeare Library, 1984), 86.

55. Weber, *Protestant Ethic,* 95.

56. Todd, *Christian Humanism,* passim.

57. Ian Hunter, "Aesthetics and Cultural Studies," in *Cultural Studies,* ed. Lawrence Grossberg, Cary Nelson, and Paula A. Treichler (New York: Routledge, 1992), 351.

58. John Barston, *Safegarde of Societie,* as quoted in Markku Peltonen, *Classical Humanism and Republicanism in English Political Thought, 1570–1640* (Cambridge: Cambridge University Press, 1995), 62–63. As Peltonen details, Barston was a city official of the town of Tewkesbury.

59. William Perkins, *The Workes of the Famous and Worthy Minister of Christ in the Universitie of Cambridge, Mr. William Perkins* 3 vols. (London, 1635), 1: 764

60. John Hales, "Bill on the Decay of Tillage," printed in an appendix to the introduction of the Lamond edition of *A Discourse,* xlvi.

61. See chapter 5.

62. Starkey, *A Dialogue,* 31.

63. Peltonen, *Humanism and Republicanism,* 39–40.

64. *Dialogue,* 4–5.

65. John Poynet, *A Short Treatise of Politike Power* (1556; facsimile reprint Amsterdam: Theatrum Orbis Terrarum, 1972), D7r.

66. Mervyn James, *Society, Politics, and Culture: Studies in Early Modern England* (Cambridge: Cambridge University Press, 1986), 215 and 284. See also Jones, *Tudor Commonwealth,* 54.

67. Perhaps the clearest illustration of this is Edmund Dudley's 1509–1510 *Tree of Commonwealth,* ed. D. M. Brodie (Cambridge: Cambridge University Press, 1948). For an illuminating discussion of Dudley's work in the context of early commonwealth writers, see Raymond Lurie, "Some Ideas of Commonwealth in Early Modern England," in *Reformation, Humanism, and "Revolution",* ed. Gordon Schochet (Washington, D.C.: Folger Institute, 1990), 293–306.

68. Pocock, *Machiavellian Moment,* 348; Jones, *Tudor Commonwealth,* 39–40. Jones cites correspondence from Sir Anthony Aucher to Cecil: "under the pretence of simplicity and poverty," Aucher wrote in 1549, "there may be much mischief. So do I fear there doth in these men called Common Wealths and their adherents."

69. Sir Thomas Elyot, *The Boke Named the Gouernour,* 2 vols. (1531; New York: Burt Franklin, 1967), 1: 1–2. McEachern, *Poetics of English Nationhood,* 86–106, addresses Elyot's reaction, and provides an excellent discussion of the potentially destabilizing implications of an appeal to national commonality.

70. Sir Thomas Smith, *De Republica Anglorum* (London, 1583; Amsterdam: Da Capo Press, 1970), D2r–D2v. On the governmental functions—service as jurors, as church officers, or in various civic offices—that Smith notes were available to artificers, copyholders, merchants, day laborers, and the like, see F1r. Although *De Republica* is frequently characterized as merely descriptive, it is, I think it important to note, as much hortatory as an actual depiction of the way things were. Recent work by Mihoko Suzuki foregrounds the forging of political agencies by apprentices and women in early modern England. Stephen Orgel notes a striking example in Patricia Crawford's discussion of female voting in parliamentary elections during the first half of the seventeenth century, Stephen Orgel *Impersonations: The Performance of Gender in Shakespeare's England* (Cambridge: Cambridge University Press, 1996), 74. Orgel cites Crawford's "Gender and Politics in Seventeenth-Century England," a paper delivered at a conference of the Australian Historians of Medieval and Early Modern Europe, University of Tasmania, Hobart, in February 1994. As Orgel reports, this paper represents an early précis of much more extensive research done in collaboration with Sara Mendelson. See Mendelson and Patricia Crawford, *Women in Early Modern England, 1550–1720* (Oxford: Clarendon Press, 1998), esp. 345–430.

71. Morison, *Remedy*, 116.

72. For an important discussion of expertise that builds on Foucault's account of "governmentality," see Nikolas Rose, "Expertise and the Government of Conduct," *Studies in Law, Politics and Society* 14 (1994): 359–97. On early modern expertise, see Poovey, "Accomodating Merchants: Double-Entry Bookkeeping, Mercantile Expertise, and the Effect of Accuracy," chapter 2 of *Modern Fact*, 29–91; and Lisa Jardine, *Worldly Goods: A New History of the Renaissance* (1998; New York: Norton, 1996), especially chapter five, "New Expertise for Sale," 231–74.

73. Wood, "Foundations," 143–44. This aspect of *A Discourse* might be compared usefully to Jürgen Habermas's account of the "bourgeois public sphere," which, he argues, emerges in England with the coffeehouse and periodical print culture of the late seventeenth century. (Jürgen Habermas, *The Structural Transformation of the Public Sphere: An Inquiry into a Category of Bourgeois Society*, trans. Thomas Burger [1962; Cambridge: MIT Press, 1991]). Habermas understands this public sphere to be a realm of association based on critical rational exchange, informed debate about issues of concern to society as a whole. While *A Discourse*, especially in its dialogue form, evidences characteristics of this kind of public discussion (informed exchange and intelligent debate), the differences between the critical forms of association that Habermas studies and the forum of expert discussion that Smith depicts are important to emphasize. According to Habermas, the bourgeois public sphere exists independently of the state and stands in a critical relation to it; the public sphere Smith imagines is one in which the critical energies are incorporated into the functioning of government, and hence directly contribute to national and local administration. Where Habermas views administrative expertise as antithetical to the communicative rationality that grounds and enables the bourgeois public sphere, by Smith's account it is precisely expertise that allows persons access to a public discussion, that authorizes their interventions as governmentally valid and useful.

74. On the obligation to critique, and challenges of critiquing, rulers, see F. W. Conrad, "The Problem of Counsel Reconsidered: The Case of Sir Thomas Elyot," in Fideler and Mayer, *Political Thought*, 88–89.

75. On this ideal in Roman rhetorical theory, see Quentin Skinner, "'*Scientia Civilis*' in Classical Rhetoric and in the Early Hobbes," in *Political Discourse in Early Modern Britain,* ed. Nicholas Phillipson and Quentin Skinner (Cambridge: Cambridge University Press, 1993), 67–93.

76. In this regard, it is significant to note that the only mention of a wife in *A Discourse* stands as an example of the inability to distinguish between primary and secondary causes of any given problem. Just as removing a secondary cause will not fix anything, so "the wife of Ajax, that lost her husband in the ship called Argos, wished that those fir beams had never been felled in Peleius wood, whereof the said ship was made; when that was not the efficient cause of the losing of her husband, but the wildfire cast in the said ship which did set it on fire" (97). As Dewar notes, Smith errs here in placing Ajax among the Argonauts; this error notwithstanding, the comparison has the effect of associating femininty with analytical incompetence.

77. In the 1581 version of *A Discourse,* Smith modifies his thinking about the debasing of coin as the exclusive cause of "dearth." (In the Dewar edition, the changes from manuscript are printed in appendix A, part 2, 143–46.) Needless to say, although the content of the analysis is changed, the form remains the same, and the Doctor maintains his position of intellectual superiority.

78. Pocock, *Machiavellian Moment,* 25.

79. Desiderius Erasmus, *De Pueris Statim ac Liberaliter Instituendis,* printed in William Harrison Woodward, *Desiderius Erasmus Concerning the Aim and Method of Education* (New York: Bureau of Publications, Teachers College, Columbia University, 1964), 192.

80. See, for example, *Pyers Plowmans Exhortation* (A4r–A5r).

81. Richard Mulcaster, *Positions,* ed. Robert Hebert Quick (London: Longmans, Green, and Co., 1888), 148. Future references to this text are noted internally.

82. Starkey advances a similar proposal in the face of what he took to be a vocational imbalance, a poor distribution of people in occupations. What was needed, he states in *A Dialogue,* were "experts" (105) who could channel people to the occupations to which they were most "apte" (106).

2. Defending Poetic Generation

1. On the conditions of educational overproduction more generally, see Frank Whigham, *Ambition and Privilege: The Social Tropes of Elizabethan Courtesy Theory* (Berkeley and Los Angeles: University of California Press, 1984), 9–20.

2. Sir Philip Sidney, *The Defence of Poesie,* in *The Prose Works of Sir Philip Sidney,* ed. Albert Feuillerat, 4 vols. (Cambridge: Cambridge University Press, 1923), 3: 10. All references are to this edition and are cited in the text.

3. Samuel Daniel, *A Defence of Ryme,* in *The Great Critics: An Anthology of Literary Criticism,* ed. James Harry Smith and Edd Winfield Parks (New York: Norton, 1951), 240–41.

4. Stephen Gosson, *The Schoole of Abuse* (1579; facsimile reprint, New York: Da Capo Press, 1972), B1r.

5. Norbert Elias, *The History of Manners,* esp. 73–84.

6. These complaints about the effects of poetry may be compared to Gosson's censure of fencers in the same text: although their art was in some instances useful,

more often than not it led to civil discord, violence, and their own or others' death. "The wood is eate[n] by the woorme, [that] breedes within it" (D5r–D5v). "The adders death," Gosson notes a few lines later, "is her owne broode" (D5v), referring to the belief that young snakes feed on their mother. (Sidney uses this same figure to describe poetry's critics, who would use knowledge against the source of knowledge: "will you play... the Vipers, that with their birth kill their parents?" [4].) Gosson's metaphorics imply both that fencers breed their own destruction through lack of government, bringing about their own demise by their dissolute swashbuckling, and that the policies that allow fencing in the commonwealth will bring forth a threat to national stability.

7. Although Musophilus, the eponymous participant in the dialogue, answers Philocosmus with a strident appeal for the necessity of poetry and learning, he nevertheless acknowledges the validity of the points Philocosmus makes.

8. See S. K. Henninger Jr., *Touches of Sweet Harmony: Pythagorean Cosmology and Renaissance Poetics* (San Marino, Calif.: Huntington Library, 1974), 287–88; D. H. Craig, "A Hybrid Growth: Sidney's Theory of Poetry in *An Apology for Poetry*," in *Essential Articles for the Study of Sir Philip Sidney*, ed. Arthur F. Kinney (Hamden, Conn.: Archon Books, 1986), 113–34; and, in the same volume, John C. Ulreich Jr., "'The Poets Only Deliver': Sidney's Conception of *Mimesis*," 135–54. E. N. Tigerstedt, "The Poet as Creator: Origins of a Metaphor," *Comparative Literature Studies* 5, 4 (1968): 455–88, traces the neoplatonic, hermetic, and patristic sources of the analogy of poetic production to God's creation.

9. See, for example, Fran Dolan, "Taking the Pencil out of God's Hand: Art, Nature, and the Face-Painting Debate in Early Modern England," *PMLA* 108, 2 (March 1993): 224–39; Katharine Eisaman Maus, "A Womb of His Own: Male Renaissance Poets in the Female Body," chapter 6 of *Inwardness and Theater in the English Renaissance* (Chicago: University of Chicago Press, 1995), 182–209; Elizabeth Harvey, "Matrix as Metaphor: Midwifery and the Conception of Voice," chapter 3 of *Ventriloquized Voices: Feminist Theory and English Renaissance Texts* (London: Routledge, 1992), 76–115; Elizabeth Sacks, brief discussion of Sidney in the introduction to her *Shakespeare's Images of Pregnancy* (New York: St. Martin's Press, 1980). (An exception to the effort to read the parthenogenetic metaphorics in terms of contest and antagonism is M. J. Doherty, *The Mistress-Knowledge: Sir Philip Sidney's Defence of Poesie and Literary Architectonics in the English Renaissance* [Nashville: Vanderbilt University Press, 1991], which praises Sidney's irenic "*good* will" [xxxi, emphasis Doherty's] towards women.) The above critics argue that the dream of self-sufficient masculine reproduction that Sidney advances lays claim to a properly feminine capacity as a way of confirming once more an invidious gender hierarchy that subordinates men to women. Certainly the appeal to a language of procreation and fecundity to characterize a given set of activities must bear some relation to the multiple, overlapping, discontinuous, and tensely articulated efforts to authorize gender hierarchies. And certainly such a claim participates in the complex efforts to enable specific kinds of activities and to disable others. However, the relation between the capacity of some bodies, and the figurative uses to which such capacity is put in its discursive reformulation, is not self-evident. Neither are the effects of the reproductive claims exhaustively accounted for by the metaphorics of "propriety" and "appropriation" to which this argument appeals. Recognizing that a set of tropes *derives* from certain bodies is one thing; gauging the effect of appeal to that trope is

another. Although the claim of a generative capacity can indeed be consistent with feminine subordination, it need not be, and this caveat prompts further study of the relations and effects the reproductive metaphorics seeks to describe and to impact.

It is worth emphasizing here, since not generally acknowledged in the criticism that pursues this line of argument, that fecundity cannot be taken as an essential characteristic of femininity, cannot be said to define "the feminine." Not all bodies gendered female were, or are, capable of giving birth. Further, the description of certain practices as forms of generation is not necessarily limited to masculine activity, and indeed could serve to authorize the efforts of women. For example, Katherine Duncan-Jones relates that Philip Sidney's maternal aunt Catherine "had no children of her own, but seems in effect to have run a kind of boarding school for well-born orphans, especially girls. She boasted in old age that 'I think there will none question but I know how to breed and govern young gentlewomen.'" (*Sir Philip Sidney: Courtier-Poet* [New Haven: Yale University Press, 1991], 10.) I shall have more to say about this fantasy of educational generation; for now, this anecdote serves as a counter-example that begins to suggest the limits of both the "appropriation" account and the notion that the figure inherently serves to limit female agency.

10. Sir Philip Sidney, *The Countess of Pembroke's Arcadia*, ed. Maurice Evans (London: Penguin, 1977), 711.

11. Mary Ellen Lamb, "Apologizing for Pleasure in Sidney's *Apology for Poetry:* The Nurse of Abuse Meets the Tudor Grammar School," *Criticism* 36 (fall 1994): 512. On the pervasive emphasis on imitation within continental and English humanist theory and practice, see Thomas M. Greene, *The Light in Troy: Imitation and Discovery in Renaissance Poetry* (New Haven: Yale University Press, 1982); and Timothy Hampton, *Writing From History: The Rhetoric of Exemplarity in Renaissance Literature* (Ithaca: Cornell University Press, 1990), 4, and see also 15–16. On pedagogic mimesis in early-modern grammar schools see Goldberg, *Sodometries,* 79–80; Pittenger, "Dispatch Quickly," 397–99; and Richard Halpern, *Poetics of Primitive Accumulation,* 29–38. For a classical precedent for mimetic pedagogy, see Quintillian's argument that a teacher both should instruct students in things suitable for imitation and should be upright, gentle, and interesting, worthy of the love of his pupils: "it is scarcely possible to say how much more readily we imitate those whom we like." Quintillian, *Institutio Oratoria,* 4 vols., trans. H. E. Butler (London: William Heinemann, 1920), 1: 215.

12. We might compare Sidney's claim here to Thomas Sackville's praise of Castiglione's *Courtier.* In his poem commemorating Hoby's translation, Sackville understands the author's production as a form of masonry superior to the ostentatious construction generally undertaken by kings in building elaborate palaces:

> The prince he raiseth huge and mightie walles,
> Castilio frames a wight of noble fame:
> The king with gorgeous Tissue clads his halles,
> The Count with golden vertue deckes the same.

The poetic framing here is an alternative to the luxurious and hence suspect construction project of the king, and so represents an equivalent kind of construction—the implication being that building men is as effective as, if not more appropriate than, the standard use of monarchical resources. Thomas Sackville, "To the

Reader," in Baldassare Castiglione, *The Book of the Courtier,* trans. Sir Thomas Hoby (1928; London: J. M. Dent and Sons, 1948), 1.

13. Judith Butler, *Bodies That Matter: On the Discursive Limits of "Sex"* (New York: Routledge, 1993).

14. Laura Levine observes that, in his subsequent tract, aimed specifically at the theater, Gosson produced a similar account of "the way the audience can be made compulsively to imitate what happens in the play." *Men in Women's Clothing: Antitheatricality and Effeminization, 1579–1642* (Cambridge: Cambridge University Press, 1994), 13. My next chapter focuses specifically on the purchase of the fantasy of mimetic generation within the polemic surrounding the popular stage; for now I focus on plays, and their culturally reproductive effects, as falling within Sidney's expansive definition of "poesie."

15. Levine, *Men in Women's Clothing,* 16.

16. Ibid.

17. This point is indebted to Robert Matz's fine discussion of Sidney and Gosson in his *Defending Literature in Early Modern England: Renaissance Literary Theory in Social Context* (Cambridge: Cambridge University Press, 2000), 56–87.

18. Margaret Ferguson, *Trials of Desire: Renaissance Defenses of Poetry* (New Haven: Yale University Press, 1983), 146.

19. For an important discussion of these issues, see Andrew Weiner, *Sir Philip Sidney and the Poetics of Protestantism: A Study of Contexts* (Minneapolis: University of Minnesota Press, 1978), 28–50.

20. Sidney's use of the classical hero participates in a complex and conflicted tradition of narratives about Hercules—a figure, as Stephen Orgel shows, who could stand in for either virtue or voluptuousness, for order or rebellion. He was the "embodiment of brute strength and destructive passion, but also the civiliser and defender of mankind; Stoic hero and paragon of virtue, but the archetype also of lechery and gluttony; comic grotesque and tragic hero." Stephen Orgel, "The Example of Hercules," in *Mythographie der frühen Neuzeit: ihre Anwendung in den Künsten,* ed. Walther Killy (Wiesbaden: In Kommission bei O. Harrassowitz, 1984), 25.

21. On the instabilities of Renaissance exemplarity, see Stephen Orgel, "Gendering the Crown," in *Subject and Object in Renaissance Culture,* ed. Margareta de Grazia, Maureen Quilligan, and Peter Stallybrass (Cambridge: Cambridge University Press, 1996), 146; and Hampton, *Writing from History,* 26–27.

22. Margaret Ferguson insightfully reads the way the Pugliano narrative anticipates the *Defence*'s definition of the "role" of a "critical reader, who, as logician and historian, resists being swayed by an image of desire." *Trials of Desire,* 153. For a primarily deconstructive reading attuned to the importance and rhetorical complexity of the Pugliano material, see Catherine Barnes, "The Hidden Persuader: The Complex Speaking Voice of Sidney's *Defence of Poetry,*" in Kinney, ed. *Essential Articles,* 155–65.

23. *The School of Cyrus: William Barker's 1567 Translation of Xenophon's Cyropaedeia (The Education of Cyrus),* ed. James Tatum (New York: Garland Publishing, 1987), 8.

24. Joel Altman, *The Tudor Play of Mind: Rhetorical Inquiry and the Development of Elizabethan Drama* (Berkeley and Los Angeles: University of California Press, 1978), 87–106. See also Kahn, *Rhetoric,* 41.

25. On the way the ambiguity of Pyrocles's motto evokes rival views of Hercules' crossdressing, see Laura Levine, *Men in Women's Clothing,* 155n.9.

26. Such a view engages a contemporary sense of the constitutive effects of clothing, a capacity most recently studied by Peter Stallybrass. This effectivity is most forcefully acknowledged by the anti-theatrical "fear [of...] the power of clothes to *produce* new subjects" (author's emphasis) by changing actors into their roles. (It is, consequently, relevant that Musidorus accuses the younger prince of being "like an ill player" [132].) Peter Stallybrass, "Transvestism and the 'Body Beneath": Speculating on the Boy Actor," *Erotic Politics: Desire on the Renaissance Stage,* ed. Susan Zimmerman, (New York: Routledge, 1992), 76. According to Stallybrass, the practice of dressing boys to portray women on the Renaissance stage foregrounds the constructedness of sexual differences by locating difference in "prosthetic devices," arbitrary markers such as hair or clothes. By the same token, frequent scenes of undressing or stage directions that call for breast baring serve to materialize the body as the site of "signs of absolute difference" (73). Plays, in particular those that foreground their use of actors for women's roles, thus present an "oscillation between a sense of the absolute difference of the boy from his role and the total absorption of the boy into the role" (74). My understanding of the textual representation of Pyrocles' cross-dressing is analogous to Stallybrass's analysis here; the text presents Pyrocles both as undergoing a transformation into a woman (for example, Zelmane is referred to as "she" almost exclusively) and as maintaining an identity outside of the habits he assumes. Stallybrass also emphasizes the central role clothes play in the early modern construction of persons, how clothes embody subjects within a complex web of social relations, a network of obligations and entitlements, in his "Worn Worlds: Clothes and Identity on the Renaissance Stage," in *Subject and Object,* 289–320.

For a recent reading of *The Old Arcadia* that similarly capitalizes on Stallybrass's work, emphasizing the implications of Pyrocles' femininity on the sexualities depicted in the text, see Kathryn Schwarz, *Tough Love: Amazon Encounters in the English Renaissance* (Durham: Duke University Press, 2000), 176–201.

27. Helpful here is Roger Howell's emphasis, in his biography of Sidney, on the extent to which Sidney was committed to the Protestant activist policies of his uncle, the Earl of Leicester, and his future father-in-law, Sir Francis Walsingham. *Sir Philip Sidney: The Shepherd Knight* (Boston: Little, Brown and Company, 1968).

28. Thomas Moffet, *Nobilis or A View of the Life and Death of a Sidney and Lessus Lugubris,* trans. Virgil B. Heltzel and Hoyt H. Hudson (San Marino, Calif.: The Huntington Library, 1940), 87.

29. On the practice of masculine friendship as procreative, see Jeffrey Masten, "My Two Dads: Collaboration and the Reproduction of Beaumont and Fletcher," *Queering the Renaissance,* ed. Jonathan Goldberg (Durham: Duke University Press, 1994), 280–309.

30. Compare the formulation here with that in Shakespeare's *The First Part of King Henry the Sixth.* Lord Talbot saves his son during battle with the French, in thanks for which the young John Talbot declares, "O twice my father, twice am I thy son!" (IV.vi.6). *Complete Works,* Alfred Harbage, gen. ed. (New York: Viking Penguin, 1969).

31. Christopher Hill, *Society and Puritanism in Pre-Revolutionary England* (London: Secker and Warburg, 1964), 443. For a broad overview of the transition from the feudal standard, in which the household contained a relatively large number of members—extended family, wards, retainers—to the small "nuclear" family con-

sisting exclusively of immediate kin, see Lawrence Stone, *The Family, Sex, and Marriage In England, 1500–1800* (New York: Harper and Row, 1979). See also Jonathan Goldberg, *James I and the Politics of Literature*, 85–112. Nancy Armstrong and Leonard Tennenhouse provide a useful survey of the social-historical research around the early modern family, and offer an important critique of Stone's thesis that the reorganization of the family represents a "humanization" of family relations, in chapter 3 of their *The Imaginary Puritan: Literature, Intellectual Labor, and the Origins of Personal Life* (Berkeley and Los Angeles: University of California Press, 1992), 69–88.

Certainly the dynamic I outline here produced destabilizing effects, especially, but not exclusively, in the domain of religious practice; the privilege granted to household government could be taken as overriding the governmental claims advanced within other domains. This is an antagonism, for example, exacerbated on the eve of civil war in England, when pious householders would complain of the intrusiveness of church officials. I take up this point in the following chapter; for now, I am interested simply in the definition of this governmental logic.

32. Aristotle, *Nichomachean Ethics*, trans. David Ross (Oxford: Oxford University Press, 1980), 1.

33. Spenser similarly emphasizes the poet's maternal lineage—his mother was a Dudley, and hence of higher rank than the Sidneys—in his elegy for Sidney, "Astrophel": "For from the time that first the Nymph his mother / Him forth did bring, and taught her lambs to feed, / A sclender swaine excelling far each other, / In comely shape, like her that did him breed, / He grew up fast in goodnesse and in grace." Edmund Spenser, "Astrophel," *Poetical Works*, ed. J. C. Smith and E. De Selincourt (1912; Oxford: Oxford University Press, 1970), 547.

34. Constance Jordan, *Renaissance Feminism: Literary Texts and Political Models* (Ithaca: Cornell University Press, 1990), 220–40; and Stephen Orgel, *Impersonations*.

35. Hugh Languet, letter to Sidney dated 2 May 1577, cited by Katherine Duncan-Jones, *Sir Philip Sidney*, 153; on Languet's urgency towards Sidney's procreation, see Howell, *Shepherd Knight*, 44.

36. Basilius and Gynecia are married, certainly, but their love is directed at others, in a way that belies Geron's optimism about the regulatory effects of marriage; Dametas and Miso, servants to the royal family, can hardly be said to be either happy or exemplary; Geron himself praises his wife of fifty years (712), but she is never introduced into the narrative and they are never pictured together.

37. William Craft, "Remaking the Heroic Self in the New Arcadia," *Studies in English Literature* 25 (1985): 45–67, aptly reads Parthenia and Argalus as an important conjunction of both heroism and love (65–66). The ideal they represent becomes the site of considerable investment, especially in Puritan doctrines of marriage; with respect to the argument of this book, the ideal will gain its greatest polemical visibility in Milton's account of Adam and Eve in *Paradise Lost*.

38. Maurice Evans explains that the *Old Arcadia* marginally notes, at another moment in the text, that palms were the arboreal emblem of "happy marriage" (853–54 n14). Elsewhere, Evans provides a detail that makes explicit the reproductive implications of the symbol, by remarking that palm trees "were believed only to produce fruit when growing in pairs" (854, n2.2).

39. Although Schwarz and I approach the issue from somewhat different directions, my reading of the Argalus and Parthenia episode reinforces her point that the

text's "system of desire" seems inconsistent with hetero-trajectories. Schwarz, *Tough Love,* 201.

40. As Rich McCoy aptly observes, the conclusion of the Arcadia, specifically the trial of Musidorus and Pyrocles, provides "an occasion for retrospective organization of the preceding events." Rich McCoy, *Rebellion in Arcadia* (New Brunswick, N.J.: Rutgers University Press, 1979), 124.

41. Such a move might be compared to the fact that, in the *Defence,* the only time human procreation is an issue is when it appears as a violation of generic unity: dramatizing the life of a poetic subject from birth onwards is a tedious burden on one's audience, transgressing the Aristotelian unity of time.

42. On the disruptiveness of the imagination, and the effort of English aesthetics to accommodate the imagination, see John Guillory, *Poetic Authority: Spenser, Milton, and Literary History* (New York: Columbia University Press, 1983), 1–22.

43. Halpern, *Primitive Accumulation,* 50.

44. For general discussion of Sidney's representation of rebellion, see, in addition to Greenblatt, "Murdering Peasants," W. Gordon Zeeveld, "The Uprising of the Commons in Sidney's Arcadia," *Modern Language Notes* 48, 4 (April 1933): 209–17; and Richard M. Berrong, "Changing Depictions of Popular Revolt in Sixteenth-Century England: The Case of Sidney's Two Arcadias," *Journal of Medieval and Renaissance Studies* 19 (1989): 15–33.

45. For a reading of Sidney's relationship to Mary that takes seriously the kind of eroticism implicit in this statement, see Jonathan Crewe, *Hidden Designs: The Critical Profession and Renaissance Literature* (New York: Methuen, 1986), 70–88.

46. Evans, "Introduction," 9.

47. Hannay, *Philip's Phoenix: Mary Sidney, Countess of Pembroke* (New York: Oxford University Press, 1990), 70.

48. Ibid., 69. See also Wendy Wall's brilliant study, *The Imprint of Gender: Authorship and Publication in the English Renaissance* (Ithaca: Cornell University Press, 1993), 311–19, esp. 318–19.

49. Hannay, *Philip's Phoenix,* 81.

50. For a fine account of the negotiations surrounding Sidney's "life narrative," see Kevin Pask, *The Emergence of the English Author: Scripting the Life of the Poet in Early Modern England* (Cambridge: Cambridge University Press, 1996), 53–82.

51. Sir Fulke Greville, *The Life of the Renowned Sir Philip Sidney,* ed. Nowell Smith (Oxford: Clarendon, 1907), 18; cited in McCoy, *Rebellion,* 22.

52. Pask, *Emergence of the English Author,* 58–60.

53. Thomas Moffet, *Nobilis,* 91. Latin quotation from p. 40.

54. On this text's claims to exemplarity, see Peter C. Herman, *Squitter-wits and Muse-haters: Sidney, Spenser, Milton, and Renaissance Antipoetic Sentiment* (Detroit: Wayne State University Press, 1996), 17.

55. *The First Part of the Return from Parnassus,* III.i.928–31 and 934–39, printed in *The Three Parnassus Plays, 1598–1601,* ed. J. B. Leishman (London: Nicholson and Watson, 1949).

56. For example, see Alan Sinfield, *Faultlines: Cultural Materialism and the Politics of Dissident Reading* (Berkeley and Los Angeles: University of California Press, 1992), 210–11.

3. Staging Government

1. E. K. Chambers reprints the correspondence pertaining to this plan—initiated by complaints of the lord mayor and aldermen of London in mid-1597, but never carried out by the justices of the peace of Middlesex and Surrey—in *The Elizabethan Stage,* 4 vols. (Oxford: Clarendon Press, 1923), 4: 320–33, passim. Richard Dutton briefly discusses this episode in *Mastering the Revels: The Regulation and Censorship of English Renaissance Drama* (Iowa City: University of Iowa Press, 1991), 107–8.

2. The quote is from correspondence from the lord mayor and aldermen of London to the Privy Council, reprinted in Chambers, *Elizabethan Stage,* 4: 321. As Katharine Eisaman Maus has pointed out, the opponents of the stage seemed incapable of envisioning play audiences as other than "an undifferentiated multitude, whose disorder projects the breakdown of hierarchy [the anti-theatricalists] find so threatening." Katharine Eisaman Maus, "'Playhouse Flesh and Blood': Sexual Ideology and the Restoration Actress," *ELH* 46 (1979): 606–7.

3. Henry Crosse, *Vertues Common-wealth: or The Highway to Honour* (1603), Q1r.

4. See also John Northbrooke, *A Treatise wherein Dicing, Dauncing, and Vaine Playes or Enterluds... are Reproved* (London: George Byshop, 1577). Northbrooke's text is also excerpted briefly in Chambers, *Elizabethan Stage,* 4: 196–7. Like Crosse, Northbrooke laments the threatening abundance of "infamous persons" (K3v) pestering England: "ydle Roges... Dicers, Carders, Mummers & Dauncers... and filthy livers [who] are spred about in every quarter" (a1r–v). Although he blames England's fathers for failing properly to educate their children, and thus allowing them to waste their lives and debase the nation with filthy living, he also provides an alternative genealogy of these "multitudes" who, among other things, attend the theater. "Ye are of your father the deviil [sic]," insists Northbrooke, addressing all of England's "infamous persons," "and the lust of your father ye will doe" (B3r). Their origins, according to Northbrooke and Crosse alike, explain their actions; the sins of the flesh are bred in the bone.

5. For this view, see, in addition to Maus's essay, Laura Levine, *Men in Women's Clothing,* 10–25, esp. 13, where she explicitly addresses the imitative dynamic as formulated by Stephen Gosson; and Jean Howard, *The Stage and Social Struggle,* passim. The following, too, provide important background on the anti-theatrical polemic: Jonas Barish, *The Antitheatrical Prejudice* (Berkeley and Los Angeles: University of California Press, 1981); Colin MacCabe, "Abusing Self and Others: Puritan Accounts of the Shakespearian Stage," *Critical Quarterly* 30, 3 (autumn 1988): 3–17; and Jeffrey Knapp, "Preachers and Players in Shakespeare's England," *Representations* 44 (fall 1993): 29–59.

6. The figurative dynamic put in play here participates in and localizes the invective Thomas Dekker used to describe the suburbs in general (the location of the popular stages at the outskirts of London); the suburbs were, he asserted, "caves where monsters are bred up to devour cities themselves." (Thomas Dekker, as quoted in A. L. Beier, *Masterless Men,* 43).

7. Gosson, *Playes Confuted in Five Actions* (London: Thomas Gosson, 1582), B8r. Date proposed by Pollard and Redgrave in their *Short Title Catalogue,* entry 12095.

8. Philip Stubbes, *The Anatomy of Abuses* (1583), L6r.

9. Thomas White, *A Sermon preached at Pawles Crosse on Sunday the thirde of November 1577 in the time of the Plague,* in Chambers, *Elizabethan Stage,* 4: 197.

10. White, *A Sermon,* 4: 197. Crosse similarly asks, "is not Vice set to sale on open Theaters? is there not a *Sodome* of filthinesse painted out?" (P2v). A few pages later, he asserts that the punishment meted out to Sodom awaits England: "were it not for some fewe that stand in the gap, fire and brimstone would fall from heaven & consume the wicked like *Sodome* and *Gomorrah* " (Q4r). On Sodom as a privileged biblical locus representing God's judgment on a polity that failed to govern its members, see Michael Warner, "New English Sodom," in *Queering the Renaissance,* 330–58; and Jonathan Ned Katz, "The Age of Sodomitical Sin, 1607–1740," in *Reclaiming Sodom,* ed. Jonathan Goldberg (New York and London: Routledge, 1994), 43–58. See also, Goldberg's discussion of William Bradford's account of sodomy in colonial America in *Sodometries,* 223–46.

11. Critics have noticed the shared assumptions of the pro- and anti-theatricalist positions, although they have tended to dismiss this similarity as a sign of the putatively anemic defense of the stage. See, for example, Maus, "Playhouse Flesh and Blood," 608.

12. Thomas Heywood, *An Apology for Actors in 3 Books* (1612), C1r.

13. For Gosson, that the theater was the site of the rape of the Sabine women is no defense but, rather, proof plain and simple of the "whoredome" licensed there, evidence that "Theaters are snares unto faire women." *Playes Confuted,* G5v–G6r. See also Northbrooke, *Treatise,* I2v.

14. This apt characterization belongs to Michael Bristol, *Carnival and Theater: Plebeian Culture and the Structure of Authority in Renaissance England* (London: Methuen, 1985), 108.

15. Heywood especially insists upon the pedagogic effectivity of the theater for those without access to grammar school education or even basic literacy: "playes have made the ignorant more apprehensive, taught the unlearned the knowledge of many famous histories, instructed such as ca[n]not reade in the discovery of all our *English* Chronicles" (F3r). Ultimately, he insists, they "teach the subjects obedience to their king" (F3v).

16. Thomas Lodge, *A Defence of Plays* (1580), C5r.

17. Though only in passing, Levine perceptively notes the "genealogy of heroes" Heywood provides, *Men in Women's Clothing,* 144n21.

18. Gosson, *Playes Confuted in Five Actions* (1582), C7v–C8r.

19. See also Northbrooke's "Preface to the Reader," *Treatise,* a1r–v.

20. I here follow the lead of Robert Weimann, who has drawn attention, in "Thresholds to Memory and Commodity in Shakespeare's Endings," *Representations* 53 (winter 1996): 1–20, to epilogues as an important place where the playwright seeks to anticipate and to manage audience response and thus to promote the future success of the stage.

21. William Shakespeare, *Love's Labor's Lost* (I.i.13), in Alfred Harbage, gen. ed. *The Complete Works* (New York: Viking Penguin, 1969). All future references to Shakespeare's texts, except where indicated, will be to this edition.

22. On the ideal, especially as a model for Puritan subjectivity, of the warfaring Christian who conducted battle against his or her "own affections / And the huge

army of the world's desires," see William Haller, *The Rise of Puritanism* (1938; New York: Harper and Row, 1957).

23. Such a formulation is not inconsistent with classical ethical theories. As Aristotle asserts, intellectual voracity is removed from the question of whether one is in control of one's desires or the subject of them: "men who are concerned with such pleasures [honor, learning] are called neither temperate nor self-indulgent." Aristotle, *Nichomachean Ethics,* 72.

24. For a reading of these lines that focuses on questions of property, inheritance, and aristocratic identity, see Katharine Eisaman Maus, "Transfer of Title in *Love's Labor's Lost:* Language, Individualism, Gender," in Ivo Kamps, ed. *Shakespeare Left and Right* (New York and London: Routledge, 1991), 205–223.

25. To be sure, contemporary dictionaries lend support to Harbage's gloss. For example, John Minsheu's 1599 Spanish/English dictionary equates the Spanish "Hospitalid['a]d" with "hospitalitie, keeping of a good house." The linkage of the latter two terms suggests that hospitality and good housekeeping are the same thing. However, Thomas Thomas's rendering of the Latin "Res familiares" "Domestical busines, housekeeping" suggests the sense I wish to emphasize. If the latter term could conceivably encompass hospitality, clearly the sense of "domestical busines" with which Thomas associates it implies a much wider variety of functions, activities, responsibilities, and objectives for "housekeeping" than simply entertaining the occasional visitor. (These references are derived from Ian Lancashire's Early Modern English Dictionaries Database on the World Wide Web, and the "Patterweb" search engine located at *www.chass.utoronto.ca/english/emed/patterweb.html*).

26. Although I use the Princess's response to the king's actions as a point of departure for my remarks, she cannot be taken as merely an advocate for household government. We can specify, at least in outline, the kind of dispensation the Princess would endorse. Boyet asks:

> Do not curst wives hold that self-sovereignty
> Only for praise' sake, when they strive to be
> Lords o'er their lords?
>
> (IV.i.36–38)

The Princess answers that intractable and independent wives are so "Only for praise; and praise we may afford / To any lady that subdues a lord" (39–40). This is a traditional household government turned upside down, a domestic economy in which a self-governing woman lords it over her subordinate husband.

Some time ago, Peter Erickson observed the intractable tensions between the party of the Princess and that of Navarre, in "The Failure of Relationship Between Men and Women in *Love's Labor's Lost,*" *Women's Studies* 9 (1981): 65–81. In this essay, Erickson comprehends the gender dynamics of the play in terms of patriarchal power and its destabilization. The focus of what follows seeks to qualify this totalizing critical apparatus by situating one form of governmental activity, domestic economy, in relation to other relatively autonomous sites of governmental practice.

27. Gayle Rubin, "The Traffic in Women: Notes on the 'Political Economy' of Sex," in Rayna R. Reiter, ed. *Toward an Anthropology of Women,* (New York: Monthly Review Press, 1975), 157–210.

28. Karen Newman, "Directing Traffic: Subjects, Objects, and the Politics of Exchange," *differences* 2, 2 (1990): 47. See also Judith Butler's call for a submission to Foucauldian critique of Rubin's essay, specifically its reliance upon a sexuality that pre-exists and is repressed by the transcultural taboo against incest, in *Gender Trouble,* 72–77. Stephen Orgel (*Impersonations,* 124–26) has endorsed Newman's view, as well, providing a caveat that we not simply take at face value patriarchal representations of society.

29. My emphasis and approach here draws on the latter two volumes of Michel Foucault's *History of Sexuality,* which address the place of economics in Greek and Roman moral reflection and view the *oikos* as the site for the production and maintenance of ethical effects. See *Use of Pleasure,* 143–84; and *Care of the Self,* 146–85. For recent work on the status and obligations conferred by the wedding ceremony, see David Cressy, *Birth, Marriage, and Death: Ritual, Religion, and the Life-Cycle in Tudor and Stuart England* (Oxford: Oxford University Press, 1997), 285–88.

30. R. Cleaver, *A Godly Forme of Household Government* (1598), 168–69. Pollard and Redgrave's *Short Title Catalogue,* which I follow here, attributes authorship to Cleaver. Christopher Hill, "Spiritualization," 451n1, attributes this text to R. Cawdrey, and lists J. Dod and R. Cleaver as editors of subsequent printings.

31. Peter de la Primaudaye, *The French Academie,* trans. T. B. (London: George Bishop, 1602), 496.

32. La Primaudaye, *French Academie,* 493.

33. The wife, according to Cleaver, operated as an agent of frugality, constantly monitoring the flow of money and goods, noted and adjusted for the daily accidents of household life. "She must be wise, to marke and see, what needlesse burthens, unnecessarie expences, and losses, there do upon occasions fall out within doores, and prevent such occasions afterwards. Shee must knowe the best waies of doing things to great use, with least charges. Brieflie, shee must knowe which way to save a penny, and lay about her, to save it, for many a little maketh a great deale. Shee must knowe what is meete for servants, what for worke-men, and what not" (85–86).

34. T. K. makes a similar point in *The Housholders Philosophie* (1588), included in Frederick Boas's edition of *The Works of Thomas Kyd* (Oxford: Clarendon Press, 1955), 258. (Thanks to Jeff Masten for this reference.) See also Cressy, *Birth, Marriage, and Death,* 290.

35. T. K., *Householders Philosophie,* 263. The analogy is extraordinarily rich and much more complex than my use of this passage can demonstrate. The immediate point being made is that the servant, likened to appetite, receives impressions from the master, compared to reason; this dynamic is associated in turn with the lover/beloved dynamic Petrarch describes in the following lines: "I am become hir liege man and hir thrall, / That made impressions in my hart, and printed hyrs withall."

36. Cleaver, *Godly Forme,* 86.

37. For instance, see Thomas Elyot, *The Education or bringinge up of children/ translated out of Plutarche* (1533), facsimile reprint in Robert D. Pepper, *Four Tudor Books on Education* (Gainesville, Fla.: Scholars' Facsimiles and Reprints, 1966), Sig. B3v.

38. Patricia Parker notes the pederastic innuendo of this passage in her essay "Preposterous Reversals: *Love's Labor's Lost,*" *Modern Language Quarterly* 54, 4 (December 1993): 476–77, 481. Parker's argument substantially qualifies the operative

premise of Mark Breitenberg, "The Anatomy of Masculine Desire in *Love's Labor's Lost*," *Shakespeare Quarterly* 43, 4 (winter 1992): 430–49, that the only kind of desire the play addresses is the "heterosexual" love of a man for a woman.

39. Parker, "Preposterous Reversals," 449.

40. Harbage, "Note on the Text," *Complete Works*, 178.

41. See also *Venus and Adonis*, ll.163–74, where Venus attempts to woo the uninterested Adonis by telling him "By law of nature thou art bound to breed" (171).

42. I follow here Harbage's note on this passage, IV.iii.364n.

43. The constitution of love as a form of war resolves an intractable contradiction—an understanding of love between man and a woman as natural, as opposed to a view of a man's love for a woman as somehow degenerate—the oppositions I discussed in relation to Musidorus's response to seeing Pyrocles crossdressed. Berowne offers the following account of the effect of women on his companions, castigating them for their loss of self-control and their ungoverned expressions of love:

> O me, with what strict patience have I sat,
> To see a king transformèd to a gnat;
> To see great Hercules whipping a gig,
> And profound Solomon to tune a jig,
> And Nestor play at push-pin with the boys,
> And critic Timon laugh at idle toys!
> (IV.iii.160–65)

Here, love for women undermines the imagined martial ideal of ethical self-combat, transforms a monarch into an insect, reverts adulthood to childhood, and sobriety to mirth. Love for a woman is construed, against the ideal regimen of studious self-government, as an infantilizing force, in violation of the protocols of a thoroughly governed masculinity. Othello similarly comprehends erotic dalliance with women as having a "corrupt[ing]" (I.iii.271) effect on the ability to fulfill civic obligations, and opposes military masculinity to the household domain; such is the implication, at least, of his promise that if Desdemona distracts him while at war, "Let housewives make a skillet of my helm" (272). I thank Peter Stallybrass for drawing my attention to the latter example.

44. The obverse of the Princess's poetics of comedy, which finds humor in miscarriage, is a linkage suggested by the juxtaposition of the announcement of Jacquenetta's pregnancy to the news (delivered almost immediately after) of the death of the Princess's father, the king of France. Where the play opened on an attempt to reconfigure "house-keeping" as a way of overcoming the voracious appetite of "cormorant devouring time" through extending the austere and learned persons into the future, obviating the need for generation with women, the play near its close gives way to a prospective female generation associated with death.

45. Breitenberg, "Anatomy of Masculine Desire," 446–48, ably reads the fear of cuckoldry voiced here, but suggests that this is the only concern of the closing. As I emphasize, the debate between Winter and Spring does not focus exclusively on a "masculine economy of desire" (433) but instead provides an unfavorable account of the workings and failures of domestic economy.

46. Mary Beth Rose, *The Expense of Spirit: Love and Sexuality in English Drama* (Ithaca: Cornell University Press, 1988), 36, as quoted by Breitenberg, "Anatomy of Masculine Desire," 447n27.

47. Compare also with Falstaff's muster in *The First Part of King Henry the Fourth* (IV.ii.12–40), in which, impressing unfit soldiers, he displays a sorcerer's skill for reanimating the dead, paying the ragged soldiers less than their allotted wages and skimming off the top for his own purposes.

48. Valerie Traub discusses Falstaff's generative capacity, though she focuses on the manner in which he is associated with an abjected maternality. Valerie Traub, *Desire and Anxiety: Circulations of Sexuality in Shakespearean Drama* (London: Routledge, 1992), 56.

49. Compare Edmund's defense of bastards in *King Lear.* "Why brand they us / With base? . . . / Who, in the lusty stealth of nature, take / More composition and fierce quality / Than doth, within a dull, stale, tirèd bed, / Go to th' creating a whole tribe of fops / Got 'tween asleep and wake" (I.ii.9–15).

50. On Falstaff's appetite, see Barish, *The Anti-theatrical Prejudice,* 128. The Hostess anticipates the king here by describing the destruction following Falstaff's overwhelming consumption. Having made the mistake of letting him run up a tab, she complains of the knight that "He hath eaten me out of house and home" (*2H4* II.i.70). The Chief Justice makes a similar point, punning on the size of his belly. "Your means are very slender," he tells the knight, "and your waste is great" (*2H4* I.ii.134): what goes into Falstaff's waist is wasted and—because of the magnitude of his consumption—has laid waste.

51. Willy Maley, *Salvaging Spenser: Colonialism, Culture, and Identity* (New York: St. Martin's Press, 1997), 52

52. Edmund Spenser, *A View of the State of Ireland,* ed. Andrew Hadfield and Willy Maley (Oxford, U.K.: Blackwell, 1997), 11.

53. David Scott, "Colonial Governmentality," *Social Text* 43 (fall 1995): 204.This essay also appears in modified form as chapter 1 of Scott's brilliant book *Refashioning Futures: Criticism After Postcoloniality* (Princeton: Princeton University Press, 1999), 23–52. For a compelling account of the politics of colonial space in Ireland, see "Thinking Territorially: Spenser, Ireland, and the English Nation-State," chapter 2 of Bruce McCleod, *The Geography of Empire in English Literature, 1580–1745* (Cambridge: Cambridge University Press, 1999), 32–75.

54. On England's barbarian past, see Deborah Shuger, "Irishmen, Aristocrats, and Other White Barbarians," *Renaissance Quarterly* 50 (1997): 495–525.

55. The work on Ireland and the second tetralogy is extensive. Most recently, see David Baker, *Between Nations,* 17–65, and Christopher Highley, *Shakespeare, Spenser, and the Crisis in Ireland* (Cambridge: Cambridge University Press, 1997).

56. Despite the horrifying brutality Irenius would visit on those who resist his program, it is not undertaken (as is frequently argued) genocidally to kill all the Irish, but to increase commerce, enrich the nation, augment the population (Spenser, *A View,* 123, 155), and provide for English national security.

57. In this, the Old English are like young Irishmen who fall under the influence of the Bards, whom Irenius both admires and despises. These Irish poets do not "instruct . . . yong men in morall discipline" and do not "choose unto themselves the doings of good men for the arguments of their poems," but instead "whomsoever they finde to be most licentious of life, most bolde and lawlesse in his doings, most dangerous and desperate in all parts of disobedience and rebellious disposition, him they set up and glorifie in their rithmes, him they praise to the people, and to

yong men make an example to follow" (76). The Old English deformation is thus like the degenerative education the Irish "yong men" receive from the Bards.

58. It is relevant as well that the practice of marrying women from a colonized population amounts to the imitation of an inappropriate classical precedent. Telamon, Alexander the Great, and Julius Caesar provide an "example [of marrying women from conquered populations that] is so perilous, as it is not to be adventured" (71).

59. The Talal Asad quote is from his essay "Conscripts of Western Civilization" and is cited by Scott, "Colonial Governmentality," 191.

60. Michael Neill, "The Exact Map or Discovery of Human Affairs: Shakespeare and the Uses of the Past," Shakespeare Association of America annual meeting, March 1998, in Cleveland, briefly touched on the issue of Hal's military instruction.

61. See David Scott Kastan's incisive discussion of this scene in his "'The King Hath Many Marching in His Coats,' or, What Did You Do in the War, Daddy?" *Shakespeare Left and Right,* ed. Ivo Kamps (New York and London: Routledge, 1991), 241–58, esp. 252–53.

62. McEachern provides an insightful reading of this passage in her *Poetics of English Nationhood,* 120–21.

63. My reading here qualifies somewhat critical accounts of the Fluellen scenes as parodically disarming comedy. David Quint, "'Alexander the Pig': Shakespeare on History and Poetry," *Boundary 2* 10 (spring 1982): 49–67, argues that the representation of Fluellen comedically deflates humanist valorization of the past in the face of an emergent skepticism about history as a source of precedents. Joel Altman, 'Vile Participation': The Amplification of Violence in the Theater of *Henry V, Shakespeare Quarterly* 42 (spring 1991): 1–32, argues that Fluellen provides a kind of comedic deniability, acknowledging the destructive violence of monarchy even while allowing the acting company to claim that the episode parodies the act of drawing historical parallels (23–24).

64. I follow Jonathan Goldberg's powerful account of the prince's violent self-constitution through engrossing both Hotspur and Falstaff, in *Sodometries,* 150–52.

65. Thus in *The First Part of Henry the Sixth,* which opens upon the funeral procession of Henry V, the dead king is remembered for his military exploits, and is compared favorably to a dragon, a monster that both hoards and wastes. (*1H6* I.i.11).

66. This hierarchical account of differences between kinds of men underwrites the chronicle histories' division (in Holinshed, for instance) of troops into sheer numbers and specific nobles, listed by name; the set piece account of the death of the French in *Henry V* is a clear example (*H5* IV.viii.76–96). Within this logic, the strength of any contingent of numbers hinges on the presence of the titled, their virtue, courage, and composure. Hence, Morton remembers Hotspur as a singular soldier who when slain takes the valor of his men with him, leaving them dispersed chaotically on the field after his death (*2H4* I.i.112–25).

Phyllis Rackin, *Stages of History: Shakespeare's English Chronicles* (Ithaca: Cornell University Press, 1990), 225–29, emphasizes the tension between "anonymous enumeration" and "naming" in these plays, arguing that such differences demonstrate the extent to which Shakespeare participates in, but also remarks, the "ideologically motivated exclusions of historical writing" (229).

67. For a similar instance of this logic see Robert Burton, *Anatomy of Melancholy*

(Oxford, 1621; Amsterdam and New York: Da Capo Press, 1971), F1r–F1v (part 1, sect. 2, memb. I, subs. 6). Thanks to Mary Floyd-Wilson for this reference.

68. Such a distinction displaces the critical interest in reading the play as giving us insight into, and participating in, the operations of monarchical power or the early modern state understood as a unified agent. I have in mind here, to name only a few of the more recent notable examples, Stephen Greenblatt, "Invisible Bullets," chapter 2 of *Shakespearean Negotiations,* 21–65; the reading of *Henry V* as demonstrating and enacting the contradictory "logic of absolutism" by Chris Pye, *The Regal Phantasm: Shakespeare and the Politics of Spectacle* (London: Routledge, 1990), 30; and Jonathan Dollimore and Alan Sinfield, "History and Ideology: The Instance of *Henry V,*" in *Alternative Shakespeares,* ed. John Drakakis (1985; London: Routledge, 1990), 206–27. Rather than focus on the way the play works to locate "a single source of power in the state" (220), as Dollimore and Sinfield would have it, I concentrate on the tensions between various governmental activities that constitute the monarch's field of action and domain of effectiveness.

69. Karen Newman, *Fashioning Femininity and English Renaissance Drama* (Chicago: University of Chicago Press, 1991), 104.

70. Katherine Eggert, "Nostalgia and the Not Yet Late Queen: Refusing Female Rule in *Henry V,*" *ELH* 61 (1994), 535.

71. See Eggert, "Nostalgia," 539–40, Newman, *Fashioning Femininity,* 101–08, and Traub, *Desire,* 61–64, for insightful discussions of the play's treatment of Princess Katherine.

72. See this chapter's note 43.

73. On the Chorus's emphasis here upon failed rule, see Rackin, *Stages,* 247.

74. Altman, "Vile Participation," 16.

75. To this extent, my argument here coordinates with Robert Weimann's observations in "Bifold Authority in Shakespeare's Theatre," *Shakespeare Quarterly* 39 (winter 1988): 401–17. David Scott Kastan ("Proud Majesty Made a Subject: Shakespeare and the Spectacle of Rule," *Shakespeare Quarterly* 37 [winter 1986]: 459–75) provides an important qualification of readings that view plays as entirely coopted into the project of reinforcing monarchy, at the same time that he voices an awareness of the dangers of simply turning the tables of such readings by romanticizing the theater's putatively subversive effects (473).

76. See, in addition to Eggert's insightful reading of the gender dynamics of the Chorus's reproductive ideal ("Nostalgia," 527–28 and 538–41), David Willbern, "Shakespeare's Nothing," in *Representing Shakespeare: New Psychoanalytic Essays,* ed. Murray M. Schwartz and Coppelia Kahn (Baltimore: Johns Hopkins University Press, 1980), 255–57.

77. Of course, I here draw upon Steven Mullaney's important study of the location of the stage in the "liberties" of London, *The Place of the Stage: License, Play, and Power in Renaissance England* (Chicago: University of Chicago Press, 1988). On the Swan's proximity to Paris Garden, and for an important discussion of theater audiences more generally, see Andrew Gurr, *Playgoing in Shakespeare's London* (Cambridge: Cambridge University Press, 1987), esp. 13.

78. An important exception to this dominant critical view is that of Ivo Kamps, who, in *Historiography and Ideology in Stuart Drama* (Cambridge: Cambridge University Press, 1996), 91–139, provides a provocative and insightful reading of Cranmer's prophecy from the perspective of the politics of Stuart historiography.

79. Kim Noling, "Grubbing Up the Stock: Dramatizing Queens in *Henry VIII*," *Shakespeare Quarterly* 39, 3 (fall 1988): 291–306.

80. Ibid., 305.

81. Such a strategy mirrors James's own manipulations of his genealogy, as discussed by Jonathan Goldberg, *James I and the Politics of Literature*, 16–17; Goldberg notes that, when it suited James, he referred to Elizabeth as his "dearest mother." See also Stephen Orgel's discussion of James's "insecur[ity]" about his lineage in "Prospero's Wife," in *Rewriting the Renaissance: The Discourses of Sexual Difference in Early Modern Europe*, ed. Margaret W. Ferguson, Maureen Quilligan, and Nancy J. Vickers (Chicago: University of Chicago Press, 1986), 58–59.

82. See, for example, R. A. Foakes, "Introduction," to the Arden edition of *King Henry VIII*, ed. R. A. Foakes (London: Methuen, 1957), lv; and Leonard Tennenhouse, "Strategies of State and Political Plays: *A Midsummer Night's Dream, Henry IV, Henry V, Henry VIII*," in *Political Shakespeare: New Essays in Cultural Materialism*, ed. Jonathan Dollimore and Alan Sinfield (Ithaca and London: Cornell University Press, 1985), esp. 124–25.

83. Lee Bliss, "The Wheel of Fortune and the Maiden Phoenix of Shakespeare's *King Henry the Eighth*," *ELH* 42 (1975): 1–25; and Edward I. Berry, "*Henry VIII* and the Dynamics of Spectacle," *Shakespeare Studies* 12 (1979): 229–46, stand as relatively rare exceptions in the criticism of the play insofar as they read Cranmer's prophecy as "hortatory" (Bliss, 23), to both Henry VIII and James I, as a vision of what should be rather than what will be or what is.

84. For an account of Elizabeth's reputation as a superb student of Latin and Greek, see Roger Ascham's *The Scholemaster* (1571; New York: AMS Press, 1966, reprint of Edward Arber's 1870 edition), 95–96.

85. That these words come from Buckingham, convicted and executed for putative treasonous designs on the throne, and that Buckingham's learning is both his finest ornament and a reason for the enormity of his crimes (I.ii.111–24), is not a matter of mere irony. Despite Buckingham's invective, both he and Wolsey—like Clinias from Sidney's *Arcadia*—embody fears that learning enables a deformation of government.

86. John Skelton, "Why Come Ye Nat to Courte?" in *John Skelton: The Complete English Poems*, ed. John Scattergood (New Haven: Yale University Press, 1983), ll.460–77. I am indebted to Jonathan Goldberg for directing my attention to Skelton's anti-Wolsey poems.

87. In addition to the sources listed at this chapter's note 10, see Alan Bray, "Homosexuality and the Signs of Male Friendship in Elizabethan England," *History Workshop Journal* 29 (spring 1990): 1–19. As Goldberg argues, accusations of sodomy were never simply about erotic practice; typically overlooked sexual actions became visible as sodomy only when they occurred in relation to other transgressions of social relations (*Sodometries*, 19).

88. Glynne Wickham perceptively describes Wolsey as the "prime begetter" of the entertainments. "The Dramatic Structure of Shakespeare's *King Henry the Eighth:* An Essay in Rehabilitation," *Proceedings of the British Academy* 70 (1984): 155.

89. These are the very same terms with which Queen Katherine, in the following scene, assesses the impact of the excessively severe taxation for which Wolsey is blamed, and that has pushed the commons to the brink of rebellion: "The back is sacrifice to th' load" (I.ii.50).

90. For a brilliant discussion of the relation between the representation of Caliban and emergent discourses of colonialism and racial difference, see Kim F. Hall, *Things of Darkness: Economies of Race and Gender in Early Modern England* (Ithaca: Cornell University Press, 1995), 141–53.

91. In addition to Beier, *Masterless Men,* see Paul Slack, *Poverty and Policy,* and Peter Clark, "A Crisis Contained? The Conditions of English Towns in the 1590s," in *The European Crisis of the 1590s: Essays in Comparative History,* ed. Peter Clark (London: George Allen and Unwin, 1985), 44–66.

92. On anxieties about women as agents of imitation at theaters—specifically, city women miming women of higher social status—see Gurr, *Playgoing,* 8 and 82.

93. This is Wickham's thesis in "Dramatic Structure."

94. On women in theater audiences see Gurr, *Playgoing,* 56–64, et passim.

95. Compare the Epilogue's efforts here to the similar gesture in the Epilogue to *The Second Part of Henry the Fourth* (*2H4* Epi. 18–21). For the argument that the play was presented as part of celebrations of the marriage of Princess Elizabeth to the Elector Palatine in February of 1613, see Foakes, "Introduction," xxviii–xxxiii.

96. For this argument, see Hugh Richmond, "The Feminism of Shakespeare's *Henry VIII,*" *Essays in Literature* 6 (1979): 11–20, esp. 12.

97. Eric Partridge identifies this pun in his *Shakespeare's Bawdy: A Literary and Psychological Essay and a Comprehensive Glossary* (1955; London: Routledge and Kegan Paul, 1947), 87.

4. The Educational Genesis of Men

1. William Riley Parker, "Education: Milton's Ideas and Ours," *College English* 24, 1 (October 1962): 12.

2. Although a fuller account of Parker's intervention as an analysis of the academy is beyond the scope of this chapter, his polemic anticipates, even as it instantiates, aspects of recent accounts of the university from the left. I have in mind specifically Bill Readings on the university under conditions of global capitalism. See Bill Readings, *The University in Ruins* (Cambridge, Mass.: Harvard University Press, 1996).

3. Ernest Sirluck, introduction to *Complete Prose Works of John Milton,* Don M. Wolfe, gen. ed., 8 vols. (New Haven: Yale University Press, 1953), 2: 184–216. See also Donald Lemen Clark's important *John Milton at St. Paul's School: A Study of Ancient Rhetoric in English Renaissance Education* (New York: Columbia University Press, 1948), esp. 250–51. These two works may stand in for a large critical literature that insists on Milton's relation to a humanist tradition (of the education of gentlemen) circumscribed by a set of vaguely defined religious objectives.

4. Voicing a widely held view of Milton, Oliver Morley Ainsworth similarly consecrated Milton's text as characteristic of a nature that embodied a pure mixture of "the classical spirit with the Christian." *Milton on Education: The Tractate* Of Education *with Supplementary Extracts from Other Writings of Milton,* ed. Oliver Morley Ainsworth, Cornell Studies in English no. 12. (New Haven: Yale University Press, 1928), 15.

5. On Hartlib, Comenius, and Dury, see Charles Webster, ed. *Samuel Hartlib and the Advancement of Learning* (London: Cambridge University Press, 1970); Christo-

pher Hill, *Milton and the English Revolution* (New York: Penguin, 1979), 146–49; G. H. Turnbull, *Samuel Hartlib: A Sketch of His Life and His Relations to J. A. Comenius* (London: Oxford University Press, 1920); also by Turnbull, *Hartlib, Dury, Comenius* (Liverpool: Liverpool University Press, 1947); Frank E. Manuel and Fritzie P. Manuel, *Utopian Thought in the Western World* (Cambridge, Mass.: Harvard University Press, 1979), 309–31; John Lawson and Harold Silver, *A Social History Of Education in England* (London: Methuen, 1973), 153–63. James Holstun provides a compelling reading of the work of Hartlib and Comenius in *A Rational Millennium.*

This emphasis upon Milton's relations to the Hartlibians is one that dissents from the standard critical line of Milton scholars. In this respect, Parker, along with Sirluck, Clark, and most who have written about the pamphlet make much of Milton's stated disinclination to studying the massive programs of Comenius: "to search what many modern *Janua's* and *Didactics* more then ever I shall read, have projected," Milton informs Hartlib, with reference to his associate's most famous works, "my inclination leads me not" (*Of Education,* II: 364–66). The above critics conclude from this statement that Milton's aims and assumptions are completely unrelated, if not diametrically opposed, to those of the Hartlib circle. Certainly Milton's letter of advice cannot simply be collapsed into their works; however, as I elaborate, I think it a mistake to take Milton's statement as evidence of his rejection of Hartlib's agenda.

6. *Of Education,* in John Milton, *Complete Prose Works* 2: 408. All future references to Milton's prose work, except where otherwise indicated, will be to this edition and noted in the text with the title or a short form of the title. I utilize the following: *Of Education = Of Education; Of Reformation = Of Reformation; Animadversions = Animadversions Upon the Remonstrants Defence Against Smectymnuus; Apology = An Apology Against a Pamphlet Call'd A Modest Confutation of the Animadversions upon the Remonstrant Against Smectymnuus; Reason = The Reason of Church-government Urg'd Against Prelaty; Doctrine = The Doctrine and Discipline of Divorce; Second Defense = The Second Defense of the People of England.*

7. *Geneva Bible,* annotations to John 3:3.

8. Quoted in Haller, *Rise of Puritanism,* 73.

9. Christopher Hill provides a helpful summary of Puritan complaints, about the Anglican church hierarchy, that came to crisis in the late 1630s and early 1640s, in *Milton and the English Revolution,* 80–92; William Haller does, also, in *Rise of Puritanism,* passim.

10. "The humble Petition of many of His Majesty's subjects in and about the City of London, and several Counties of the Kingdom," in *The Constitutional Documents of the Puritan Revolution: 1625–1660,* ed. Samuel R. Gardiner (3d ed., Oxford: Clarendon Press, 1906), 143. For accounts of the Root and Branch Petition, see Webster, *Samuel Hartlib,* 27–28; William Haller, *Liberty and Reformation in the Puritan Revolution* (New York: Columbia University Press, 1955), 16–22. David Masson, *The Life of John Milton: Narrated in Connexion with the Political, Ecclesiastical, and Literary History of His Time,* 3 vols. (London, 1873), 2: 199–202, 2: 231–36, provides a detailed chronology of the movement of the petition, and its introduction in the House of Commons as a bill on May 27. Two more recent essays on the Root and Branch Petition and the Grand Remonstrance, in *The Theatrical City: Culture, Theatre, and Politics in London, 1576–1649,* ed. David L. Smith, Richard Streir, and David Bevington (Cambridge: Cambridge University Press, 1995) are extremely valuable:

David L. Smith, "From Petition to Remonstrance," 209–23; and Richard Streier, "From Diagnosis to Operation," 224–43.

11. Businessman and polemicist Henry Robinson similarly fretted over the "clothiers and manufactors in swarmes flocking over into Holland." Henry Robinson, *Englands Safety in Trades Encrease* (1641), Sig. B2r. W. K. Jordan's *Men of Substance: A Study of the Thoughts of Two English Revolutionaries, Henry Parker and Henry Robinson* (Chicago: University of Chicago Press, 1942) provides an apotheosizing summary of the main currents of Robinson's writings.

12. On ecclesiastical control of learning, the Church of England's funding of education, and Bishops' licensing of all teachers, see W. A. L. Vincent, *The State and School Education, 1640–1660, In England and Wales: A Survey Based on Printed Sources* (London: Church Historical Society, 1950), 12; and Christopher Hill, *The Century of Revolution: 1603–1714* (New York and London: W. W. Norton, 1982), 64.

13. Foster Watson, "The State and Education during the Commonwealth," *English Historical Review* 15 (January 1900): 70.

14. Haller, *Rise of Puritanism,* 63. On the more general Protestant imperative to read and rationally come to terms with the Bible, see Lawrence Stone, *Family, Sex, and Marriage,* 103–05

15. Milton harangues his confuter on this point in *Apology:* "while one Prelat enjoyes the nourishment and right of twenty Ministers, how many waste places are left as darke as *Galile*... without preaching Minister, without light" (*Apology,* 1: 932). In answer to church apologists, who argued that the position that the rewards of learning would and had produced scholars enough for the commonwealth (Bishop Hall had answered the Smectymnuans by asserting that "No one Clergie in the whole Christian world yeelds so many eminent schollers, learned preachers, grave, holy and accomplish'd Divines as this Church of *England* doth at this day"), Milton answered with sarcasm: "Ha, ha, ha" (*Animadversions,* 1: 726). Anglican divine Thomas Hacket echoed Hall's defense of Anglican stewardship over education. "Upon the ruins of the rewards of learning," he wrote, "no Structure can be raised up but ignorance: and upon the Chaos of ignorance no Structure can be built but profaneness and confusion." Hacket's architectural metaphor insisted on the validity of the existing system of rewards and incentives that attracted individuals to a life of learning, and attempted to reinforce the church's role in funding schools, ensuring the quality of the teachers, and policing curriculum. Thomas Hacket, *A Century of Sermons Upon Several Remarkable Subjects: Preached by the Right Reverend Father in God, Thomas Hacket, Late Lord Bishop of Litchfield and Coventry,* ed. Thomas Plume (London, 1675), xxi. On Hacket, see Webster, *Samuel Hartlib,* 27–28.

16. Parishes that were able often employed the services of "lecturers" to supplement the preaching of the minister officially assigned by the Anglican Church; such extramural worship could take place with the approval of the pastor, but did not necessarily require it. Laud hated lectureships and saw in them a threat to Anglican church authority, a check on its ability to govern religious worship—as Bishop of London he asked Charles I to curtail lectureships, and as Archbishop he sought to end them altogether. On lecturers, see Haller, *The Rise of Puritanism,* 40, 53, and 230. See also Curtis, "Alienated Intellectuals," 309. An officer of Bishop Wren in 1636 argued that "if his majesty shall in his princely care abolish the ratsbane of lecturing out of his churches... we shall have such a uniform and orthodox Church, as the Christian world cannot shew like" (cited by Curtis, "Alienated Intellectuals," 310).

Rosemary O'Day argues more generally that the "Protestant clergy['s] . . . religious convictions bid them open up the Scriptures," although "their vested interests bade them close them or, as many charged, obscure them." Rosemary O'Day, *Education and Society, 1500–1800: The Social Foundations of Education in Early Modern Britain* (New York: Longman, 1982), 23.

17. Lord George Digby, *The Third Speech of the Lord George Digby, To the House of Commons, Concerning Bishops, and the Citie Petition, the 9th of Febr: 1640* (1640), C1r.

18. John White, *The First Century of Scandalous, Malignant Priests* (London: George Miller, 1643), A2v–A3r. White details only one case of buggery, that of John Wilson, "Vicar of Arlington in the County of Sussex," who, he writes, in addition to attempting the crime with several of his congregation, "hath openly affirmed, *that Buggery is no sinne,* and is a usuall frequenter of Ale-houses and a great drinker" (B1r–B1v). Bray cites this text at several points in *Homosexuality in Renaissance England*—for example, at 66–67 and 117n33. He uses Wilson's defense of his own practice of buggery (that he did it to avoid producing illegitimate children) as evidence of "self-delusion" (66) in confronting one's putatively true sexuality. Elizabeth Pittenger discusses this approach to textual evidence as a kind of historical "outing" that proleptically institutes the structure of the closet in early-modern England, in "'To Serve the Queere': Nicholas Udall, Master of Revels," *Queering the Renaissance,* 162–89.

19. Edward Le Comte, *Milton and Sex* (London: Macmillan, 1978), 48–49, notes Milton's construction of prelates as women; however, Valerie Traub notes that "the gender of the whore was not delimited in early modern culture," in her "The (in)significance of 'lesbian' desire in early modern England," *Erotic Politics,* 151.

20. William E. Paden traces the connection between early ascetic Christianity and Puritanism, mentioning Weber in passing, in "Theaters of Humility and Suspicion: Desert Saints and New England Puritans," *Technologies of the Self,* 64–79.

21. Max Weber, *The Protestant Ethic,* 95. On Weber and the relevance of the Protestant ethic to Milton, see John Guillory, "The Father's House: *Samson Agonistes* in its Historical Moment," *Re-membering Milton: Essays on the Texts and the Traditions,* ed. Mary Nyquist and Margaret W. Ferguson (New York: Methuen, 1987), 148–76; and Laura Lunger Knoppers, "Rewriting the Protestant Ethic: Discipline and Love in *Paradise Lost,*" *ELH* 58 (1991): 545–59. R. H. Tawney's *Religion and the Rise of Capitalism,* although it attempts to qualify his account (261–63n32), nonetheless maintains Weber's basic line of argument and supplements his analysis with much detail.

Colin Gordon argues for the relevance of Weber's work to Foucault's notion of governmentality, in "The Soul of the Citizen: Max Weber and Michel Foucault on Rationality and Government," *Max Weber, Rationality and Modernity,* ed. Scott Lash and Sam Whimster (London: Allen and Unwin, 1986), 293–316.

22. Weber, *Protestant Ethic,* 80.

23. Haller, *Rise of Puritanism,* 97.

24. Weber, *Protestant Ethic,* 36.

25. Milton parted ways with Parliament on the question of "rewards" as incentives to pursue education. Article 186 of "The Grand Remonstrance" asserts the House of Commons' intention to keep in place essentially the Anglican structure of securing learning through adequate financial support for the clergy. (Printed in *The*

Puritan Revolution: A Documentary History, ed. Stuart E. Prall [Garden City, N.Y.: Anchor Books, 1968], 73.)

26. Weber, *Protestant Ethic,* 117.

27. Guillory, "Father's House," 151.

28. Michael Walzer, *The Revolution of the Saints: A Study in the Origins of Radical Politics* (Cambridge, Mass.: Harvard University Press, 1965), 216. Walzer quotes from Perkins, *Works,* 1:755–56.

29. William Petty, *The Advice of W. P. to Mr. Samuel Hartlib, for the Advancement of some particular Parts of Learning,* printed in *The Harleian Miscellany* (London, 1810), 6: 10. All further references are noted parenthetically in the text.

30. Samuel Hartlib, *A Further Discovery of the Office of Publick Address for Accomodations* (London, 1648). Printed in *The Harleian Miscellany,* 6: 25. Hartlib's Office was to have been a clearing house of information enabling a rational distribution of things, money, and people. It would have allowed, for example, those seeking work to meet those needing laborers, those with inventions to find those with available investment capital, those with marketable goods to contact those who wanted to buy, those who needed poor relief to locate those offering jobs or aid. For a discussion of Hartlib's Office of Address, see Webster, *Samuel Hartlib,* 43–52.

31. Jan Amos Comenius, *A Reformation of Schooles* (1642; Menston, England: Scolar Press Limited, 1969), 12. Unless otherwise indicated, further references to Comenius's work are to this text and noted internally.

32. John Dury, *The Reformed School,* ed. H. M. Knox (Liverpool: Liverpool University Press, 1958), 25–26.

33. Dury, *Reformed School,* 25. See also George Snell, *The Right Teaching of Useful Knowledge, to fit Scholars for som honest Profession* (London, 1649), a text dedicated to Hartlib and Dury. Snell proposes instruction in those subjects "as may make them most fit, whether rich or poor, for that calling which they are to profess" (A4v).

34. Sirluck, "Introduction," 2: 189.

35. On the Protestant perspective on the dangers of wasting time, see Weber, *Protestant Ethic,* 157–58.

36. Sirluck, "Introduction," 2: 186; cf. Ainsworth, *Milton on Education,* 20–21.

37. Sirluck, "Introduction," 2: 194.

38. I draw here on John Guillory's reflections on the tensions, in *Paradise Lost,* between waste and superfluity, a dynamic he relates to Weber's discussion of vocation. ("From the Superfluous to the Supernumerary: Reading Gender into *Paradise Lost,*" in *Soliciting Interpretation,* 77–85.)

39. Hughes, ed. *Complete Poems,* 605.

40. Thomas Grantham, who insisted that he could teach most of the Latin language in two weeks, represented a limit of this familiar complaint. See his *A Discourse in Derision of the Teaching in Free-Schooles, and Other Common Schooles* (1644). Brevity of teaching was an abiding concern for Milton, as evidenced by the opening comments of his 1669 *Accedence Commenc't Grammar,* in *The Works of John Milton,* ed. F. A. Patterson, et. al., 20 vols. (New York: Columbia University Press, 1931–1940), 6: 285–86.

Sirluck argues that Milton's complaints about wasted time in the instruction of Latin and Greek go back at least as far as Erasmus's and as Colet's assaults upon the "verbiage of the schools," and therefore have only the most tenuous connection to the similar concerns of the Puritan reformers: they share only a common source

("Introduction," 2: 199). Certainly Milton repeats these century-old complaints; as I am attempting to establish, however, he does not *simply* repeat them.

41. See also *Of Reformation,* 1: 588, 592, 595. In *The Reason of Church Government,* Milton also emphasized the value of having a "populous . . . nation" (*Reason,* 1: 799).

42. See Gary S. Becker, *Human Capital: A Theoretical and Empirical Analysis, with Special Reference to Education,* 2d edition (New York: National Bureau of Economic Research, 1975). Especially suggestive for the current study is the place that education occupies in Becker's analysis, which offers case studies of tertiary and secondary instruction as means of augmenting human capital.

43. Brian Vickers, "The Royal Society and English Prose Style: A Reassessment," in *Rhetoric and the Pursuit of Truth: Language Change in the Seventeenth and Eighteenth Centuries* (Los Angeles: William Andrews Clark Memorial Library, University of California, Los Angeles, 1985), 26 and 40. Vickers provides a trenchant and convincing critique of the influential account of R. F. Jones, who reductively insists, for example, that during the English Civil War "the Anglican humanists" offered the only bastion of learning against "the more ignorant and fanatical puritan sects." R. F. Jones, "The Humanistic Defense of Learning in the Mid-Seventeenth Century," *Reason and Imagination: Studies in the History of Ideas, 1600–1800,* ed. J. A. Mazzeo (New York: Columbia University Press, 1962), 72.

44. For a brief account of Bacon's critique and its currency with Puritan reformers, see Charles Webster's introduction to *Samuel Hartlib,* 17–21 and 53–56. Surveys of the rhetoric of word versus thing may be found in A. C. Howell, "*Res et Verba:* Words and Things," *ELH* 13 (1943): 131–42; and G. A. Padley, *Grammatical Theory in Western Europe, 1500–1700: The Latin Tradition* (Cambridge: Cambridge University Press, 1976), 132–53. Tony Davies, "The Ark in Flames: Science, Language, and Education in Seventeenth-Century England," in *The Figural and the Literal: Problems of Language in the History of Science and Philosophy, 1630–1800,* ed. Andrew E. Benjamin, Geoffrey N. Cantor, and John R. R. Christie (Manchester: Manchester University Press, 1987), 83–102, also addresses the Hartlib circle's Baconian materialism, and seeks to relate and differentiate Milton from this group. His mapping of the cultural terrain onto a Derridean opposition between the spoken and the written, aligning Milton solely with the logocentric voice, the Hartlibians with the written word, seems to me to obliterate the complexities I am trying to trace here.

45. "Erasmus's ideal reader," according to Halpern, "internalizes texts in the hope of mastering them, not of being mastered by them; instead of dutifully reproducing models, he emulates them in a competitive way." Richard Halpern, *Poetics of Primitive Accumulation,* 37. See also Terence Cave, *The Cornucopian Text: Problems of Writing in the French Renaissance* (New York: Oxford University Press, 1979), 3–34, et passim.

46. Halpern, *Poetics of Primitive Accumulation,* 37.

47. On Digby's fears, see Smith, "The Root and Branch Petition," 215.

48. Radical sectarians polemically flayed the schools as the prop and mechanism of illegitimate distinctions that sanctioned some men to preach and disallowed others unmediated access to Christ's spirit (and thus license to teach God's word). Samuel How insisted that, contrary to the "*sound knowledge,* and *sure information* that everie Christian hath in *Jesus Christ* . . . grafted into him by faith," the profane learning of the schools was "that, whereby certain men do excel, and are farre above and beyond other ordinary men," a presumption in the face of a God who was no

respecter of persons. *The Sufficiency of the Spirits Teaching, Without Humane Learning* (London, 1683), B2v, B1v. William Walwyn argued that learning was a tool whereby ministers "engrossed the trade to themselves" by asserting the difficulty of scriptures and institutionalizing the illusory "distinction" conferred by the mastery of foreign languages and the maintenance of arcane and obscure doctrines. Walwyn, *The Compassionate Samaritane* (1644), in William Haller, ed., *Tracts on Liberty in the Puritan Revolution: 1638–1647,* 3 vols. (New York: Columbia University Press, 1934), 3: 31. How and Walwyn, like those who addressed themselves to questions of reforming childhood education, did not argue against all learning, but only insisted on its relevance to a godly life. On the radicals' acceptance of Comenian and Hartlibian ideas, see Hill, *World Turned Upside Down* (1972; London: Penguin, 1984), 289.

49. Holstun, *A Rational Millenium,* 295, 308–10. See also C. B. Macpherson, "The Levellers: Franchise and Freedom," chapter 3 of *The Political Theory of Possessive Individualism: Hobbes to Locke* (Oxford: Oxford University Press, 1962), 107–59.

50. Comenius, *The Great Didactic of John Amos Comenius,* ed. and trans. M. W. Keatinge (New York: Russell and Russell, 1967), 69.

51. Halpern, *Poetics of Primitive Accumulation,* 91. See also Terence Cave, *The Cornucopian Text,* and, on Miltonic copia, Goldberg, *Voice Terminal Echo: Postmodernism and English Renaissance Texts* (New York: Methuen, 1986), 142–47.

52. Milton's identification with a heavenly scribe de- and re-formed his father's vocation—reconfigured the investment and moneylending activities of the scrivener into participation in a godly economy of writing and of learned expenditure. As John Guillory argues, Milton "transform[s] the father's talents, the moneylender's material capital ... into 'talent,' symbolic capital." ("The Father's House," 172.) On the activities and reputation of scriveners, see D. C. Coleman, "London Scriveners and the Estate Market in the Later Seventeenth Century," *Economic History Review* 2d ser., 4, 2 (1951): 221–30.

53. Walzer, *Revolution,* 187–91.

54. See also, on this point, Haller, *Rise of Puritanism,* 257. Stone argues that Puritans displayed a "fierce determination to break the will of the child, and to enforce his utter subjection to the authority of his elders and superiors, and most especially of his parents," *Family, Sex, and Marriage,* 116.

55. See Michael Lieb, "'The Sinews of Ulysses': Exercise and Education in Milton," *Journal of General Education* 36, 4 (1985): 245–56.

56. See Thomas Elyot, *The Education or bringinge up of children,* B3v.

57. Relevant here is that, as noted by D. L. Clark, Milton considered his relation to one of his tutors, Thomas Young, in filial terms. Milton wrote to Young, "I call to God to witness how much in the light of a Father I regard you, with what singular devotion I have always followed you in thought." (Cited in *Milton at St. Paul's,* 29.)

58. Milton in his letter to Hartlib, through the very texts he chooses to give his pupils an introduction to "houshold matters" (*Of Education,* 2: 635), signals instabilities in the coherence of a domestic ideology. These sensibilities are evident in the distance between the violence of the household portrayed in *Trachiniae* and Hercules' efforts to resurrect the integrity of King Admetus's household in *Alcestis.* Sophocles' *Trachiniae* envisioned Hercules' household in turmoil because of his absence and his lack of fidelity to his wife, Deianira. Her unwitting contribution to his gruesome and torturous death invested the domestic space with a darkly inevitable violence. See *Trachiniae,* trans. F. Storr (Cambridge, Mass.: Harvard University Press,

1978), 253–359. Euripides' *Alcestis,* in contrast, emphasized Hercules' role in prolonging the marriage of his host King Admetus. The sudden death of Alcestis, presented as an exemplary woman and wife to the king, left Admetus in hopeless mourning. Hercules, by wrestling with Death, won the release of Alcestis and restored her to her husband, securing the stability of both the king's home and his realm. Euripides, *Alcestis,* trans. Arthur S. Way (Cambridge, Mass.: Harvard University Press, 1964), 399–507.

Coiro notes the interesting and ambiguous conjunction of two plays involving Hercules at this moment in the Miltonic curriculum. However, she does so only to upbraid Milton for providing "a very tentative and insufficient lesson" on women, and complains that "a few plays are to be his [the student's] only introduction to women and marriage." To be sure, the exclusion of women from the Miltonic academy bears remarking, insofar as it provides a gauge of the elitism of his educational plan—and Masson gruffly disapproves of Milton on this point (*Life of John Milton,* 238)—as well as on his primary concern with the educational production of an ideal English masculinity, but Coiro imagines that inclusion of the right things in the curriculum might somehow rectify the implicit misogyny. See Ann Baynes Coiro, "'To Repair the Ruins of our First Parents': *Of Education* and Fallen Adam," *SEL* 28 (1988): 139.

59. Walzer, *Revolution of the Saints,* 187. Stephen Greenblatt also identifies the lability of family identifications within sixteenth-century Protestant fellowship. *Renaissance Self-Fashioning,* 82–83. The persistence of such tensions across a century is a function of the transitional status of the dynamic I am tracing.

60. Keith Thomas points to sectarian resistance to traditional patriarchal authority in "Women and the Civil War Sects," *Past and Present* 13 (April 1958): 42–62, esp. 54; similarly, Christopher Hill discusses freedoms accorded men and women, especially erotic license in the sects, during the turbulence of the Civil War in *The World Turned Upside Down,* 306–23.

61. William Gouge, *Of Domestical Duties* (London, 1622), 17–18; quoted in Walzer, *Revolution of the Saints,* 191.

62. Hezekiah Woodward, *A Childes patrimony laid out upon the good culture or tilling over his whole man. The first part, respecting a childe in his first and second age* (London, 1640), 5.

63. Woodward, *Childes patrimony,* 14.

64. Similarly, the primary task of a parent, under Woodward's tutelage, was to erase his or her own fallen image in the child, and to reproduce himself or herself through a pedagogic refashioning. Woodward required parents to "labour by all meanes, and take all occasions, whereby, through Gods blessing, our *owne* and bad *image* may be defaced; and the *New,* which is after Christ, formed on, and in the Childe" (*Childes patrimony,* 45).

65. See Foucault, "Governmentality," 92; Rose and Miller, "Governing Economic Life."

66. Jonathan Goldberg and Richard Halpern have each made legible the place of handwriting instruction as a site of the violently regularizing inscription of gendered subjects—have recognized, that is, the institution of hands as a complex social function, and thus provide a critical context for Milton's figurative appeal to, and Petty's technological innovation of, scribal production. Jonathan Goldberg, *Writing Matter,* passim; and Halpern, *The Poetics of Primitive Accumulation,* 79–84.

67. John Milton, *Complete Poems and Major Prose,* ed. Merritt Y. Hughes (New York: Macmillan, 1957). All subsequent references to Milton's poetry are to this edition.

68. Stephen Fallon, *Milton among the Philosophers: Poetry and Materialism in Seventeenth-Century England* (Ithaca: Cornell University Press, 1991), 109; as quoted in John Rogers, *The Matter of Revolution: Science, Poetry, and Politics in the Age of Milton* (Ithaca: Cornell University Press, 1996), 111n18.

69. For a fine discussion of this poem, see Stella P. Revard, "*Ad Joannem Rousium:* Elegiac Wit and Pindaric Mode," *Milton Studies* 19 (1984): 205–26.

70. Leonard Barkan discusses humanist reworkings of the myth of Ganymede in *Transuming Passion: Ganymede and the Erotics of Humanism* (Stanford: Stanford University Press, 1991). Gregory Bredbeck also addresses both high and low cultural uses of the myth in *Sodomy and Interpretation: Marlowe to Milton* (Ithaca: Cornell University Press, 1991), 90–91, 152–54; I differ with Bredbeck's guiding assumption that "male-male attraction" could only be "prurien[t]" (11), or, when voiced with approval, nonerotic "ornament" (92).

5. Paradisal Arithmetic

1. John Milton, *Paradise Lost,* 7.145–49.

2. *Milton's God* (London: Chatto and Windus, 1961), 175.

3. Augustine reasoned as follows: "Even if no one had sinned there would have come into being a number of saints sufficient to complete the muster of that Blessed City, as large a number as is now being assembled, through God's grace, from the multitude of sinners, so long as the 'children of this world' beget and are begotten" (St. Augustine, *Concerning the City of God against the Pagans,* trans. Henry Bettenson [Harmandsworth: Penguin, 1984], 585). John Salkeld, following Augustine, asserted that God was not interested in simply replacing the lost numbers, but would generate more than had fallen: "The Citie of God shall not (by the fall of the prevaricating Angels) be defrauded of the multitude or numerositie of her Citizens, but peradventure shall enjoy and raigne with a greater copie, and number" (John Salkeld, *A Treatise of Angels of the Nature, Essence, Place, Power, Science, Will, Apparitions, Grace, Sinne, and All Other Properties of Angels* [London, 1613], 210). The widespread invocation of this notion at the time is noted in Robert H. West, *Milton and the Angels* (Athens: University of Georgia Press, 1955), 126; and Diane Kelsey McColley, *Milton's Eve* (Urbana: University of Illinois Press, 1983), 44. See also Carlo Ginzburg, *The Cheese and the Worms: The Cosmos of a Sixteenth-Century Miller,* trans. John Tedeschi and Anne Tedeschi (New York: Penguin, 1982), 57.

4. Pocock, *Machiavellian Moment,* 424–25. See also R. W. K. Hinton, "The Mercantile System in the Time of Thomas Mun," *Economic History Review,* 2d ser., 7, 3 (1955): 287.

5. Christopher Hill, *The Century of Revolution,* 120–21.

6. On the dating of *Political Arithmetic,* see Hull, *Economic Writings,* 235–38. For brief surveys of Petty's life and work, and of Graunt's, see Hull, xiii–lxxix, and William Letwin, *The Origins of Scientific Economics: English Economic Thought, 1660–1776* (New York: Doubleday, 1964), 123–157. In the account here, I rely on Mary Poovey, "The Social Constitution of 'Class,'" 15–56.

7. Graham Burchell, "Peculiar Interests: Civil Society and Governing 'the System of Natural Liberty,'" in *The Foucault Effect,* 124.

8. See also Keith Tribe, "The Structure of Political Oeconomy," in *Land, Labour, and Economic Discourse* (London: Routledge and Kegan Paul, 1978), 80–109.

9. *The Petty Papers: Some Unpublished Writings of Sir William Petty,* ed. Marquis of Lansdowne, 2 vols. (London: Constable; Boston: Houghton Mifflin, 1927), 2: 48. See also Poovey, "Social Constitution," 30–32; and Erich Strauss, *Sir William Petty: Portrait of a Genius* (London: Bodley Head, 1954), 201–11.

10. See also John Graunt, *Natural and Political Observations... Made Upon the Bills of Mortality* (1665), in Hull, 372–78.

11. For a similar plan to institute a punitive tax on the celibate or unmarried to encourage the production of legitimate children, see Thomas Sheridan, *A Discourse of the Rise & Power of Parliaments* (London, 1677), 179–82. See also Joyce Oldham Appleby, *Economic Thought and Ideology in Seventeenth-Century England* (Princeton: Princeton University Press, 1978), 135–38.

12. Mary Poovey, "Between Political Arithmetic and Political Economy," paper delivered at the conference "Regimes of Description," Stanford University, January 1996; Juri Mykkänen, "'To Methodize and Regulate Them': William Petty's Governmental Science of Statistics," *History of the Human Sciences* 7, 3 (1994): 65–88, esp. 80.

13. Quint, "David's Census: Milton's Politics and Paradise Regained," in *Re-membering Milton,* 143. On the difficulties of the account of state formation upon which Quint relies, see Nikolas Rose and Peter Miller, "Political Power Beyond the State," 173–205, and Miller and Rose, "Governing Economic Life," 3.

14. Armstrong and Tennenhouse, *Imaginary Puritan,* 95–96; see also 89, 101. I wish to thank Dan Denecke for his help in thinking through these authors' model of historical change.

15. In Armstrong and Tennenhouse's narrative of "revolution," the assertion that Petty's assigning a dollar value to each person reflected and furthered the conceptual formation of a national population of laborers engaged in production, overlooks the fact that political arithmetic understood labor in relation to circulation—that is, only insofar as it contributed to international trade (Burchell, 147–48n30). To be sure, Quint qualifies his argument by suggesting that "Milton's refuge in a passive individualism... was, perhaps, responding to a state that did not yet exist" (142); however, such an observation grants Milton the status of prophet, a lone and prescient individual standing at the origin of modernity and warning all subsequent generations of the coming dangers of the state's monolithic and totalitarian control over individual lives. Armstrong and Tennenhouse attribute to Milton similar vatic powers (163).

16. My discussion of waste and abundance in *Paradise Lost* owes much to John Guillory, "From the Superfluous to the Supernumerary: Reading Gender into *Paradise Lost,*" in *Soliciting Interpretation: Literary Theory and Seventeenth-Century English Poetry,* ed. Elizabeth D. Harvey and Katharine Eisaman Maus (Chicago: University of Chicago Press, 1990), 68–88, esp. 80. Armstrong and Tennenhouse similarly identify two mutually exclusive "economies" in Milton's poem: one in which Eden's abundance represents "bounty" (102), "plenitude" (99), and "luxury" (107) and another in which it represents waste. The second economy is organized around the imperatives of "frugal[ity]" (107), in which the luxurious plenitude of the first "appears impractical, wasteful, and decadent" (108).

17. For an overview of the complex thematics of generation in the poem, see Michael Lieb, *The Dialectics of Creation: Patterns of Birth and Regeneration in Paradise Lost* (Amherst: University of Massachusetts Press, 1970).

18. The divine etiology and sanction provided for Eve's reproductive abilities, here and elsewhere in the poem, have prompted both trenchant criticism and staunch defenses of Milton's work. This polemic centers on the question of whether Milton's representation of procreation is repressive or liberating, misogynist in its restricted definition of gender roles or liberally inclusive in its incorporation of Eve into God's design. For the first position, see Marcia Landy, "Kinship and the Role of Women in *Paradise Lost*," *Milton Studies* 4 (1972): 3–18, and Christine Froula, "When Eve Reads Milton: Undoing the Canonical Economy," *Critical Inquiry* 19 (December 1983): 321–47. For the second position see McColley, *Milton's Eve;* Virginia R. Mollenkott, "Milton and Women's Liberation: A Note on Teaching Method," *Milton Quarterly* 7 (1973): 99–103, esp. 101; and Barbara Lewalski's response to Landy, "Milton on Women—Yet Once More," *Milton Studies* 6 (1974): 3–20. Landy answers Lewalski's critique in "A Free and Open Encounter: Milton and the Modern Reader," *Milton Studies* 9 (1976): 3–36. Mary Nyquist responds to both positions by questioning their essentialist assumptions and countering the vision of an extra-discursive femininity that Milton either celebrates or represses by turning to his participation in the differential construction of gender-specific subjectivities that reflected and were answerable to the social forms—those typifying the bourgeois private sphere—that attended the emergence of capitalism in England ("The Genesis of Gendered Subjectivity in the Divorce Tracts and in *Paradise Lost*," in Nyquist and Ferguson, *Remembering Milton*, 99–127). While Nyquist deftly traces Milton's relentless efforts to establish the marital bond in terms of a mutuality that requires voluntary subordination, she does so by rendering the genesis of numbers a non-problem for the poet and polemicist, "a kind of necessary consequence of the conjunction of male and female, but for that very reason . . . a subordinate end" of marriage (118). I share Nyquist's interest in rethinking the terms of the debate, but I regard procreation as central to the poem.

19. On the formation of Eve's "identity" exclusively in terms of reproduction, see Landy, "Kinship," 9.

20. Eden's fruit may usefully be understood in relation to Georges Bataille's account of potlatch, a form of destructive expenditure through which status relations are established and reconfirmed, in "The Notion of Expenditure," *Visions of Excess: Selected Writings, 1927–1939*, ed. Allan Stoekl, trans. Allan Stoekl, with Carl R. Lovitts and Donald M. Leslie Jr. (Minneapolis: University of Minnesota Press, 1985), 116–29. Where potlatch confirms status relations in societies through the spectacle of extraordinary loss, God's expenditure, as imagined in the passages under scrutiny, only enables greater expenditure in the future. See also Jacques Derrida, "From Restricted to General Economy: A Hegelianism without Reserve," *Writing and Difference*, trans. Alan Bass (Chicago: University of Chicago Press, 1978), 251–77.

21. William Empson notes the same allusions, but by way of asserting that they "remind us that children were the result of the fall" (*Some Versions of Pastoral* [New York: New Directions, 1974], 174). But if children in the poem are post hoc, they are not therefore propter hoc.

22. Robert Gray argued that "[t]here is nothing more dangerous for the estate of commonwealths than when the people do increase to a greater multitude and num-

ber than may justly parallel with the largeness of the place and country," and hence that the superabundance should be shipped abroad (*A Good Speed to Virginia* [1609], in *Seventeenth-Century Economic Documents,* 757–58). E. A. J. Johnson provides a survey of primary literature advancing this defense of colonization in *American Economic Thought in the Seventeenth Century* (New York: Russell and Russell, 1961), 49–54.

23. Alexandre Koyré offers a fine introduction to the history of astronomical ideas, especially during early modernity, in *From the Closed World to the Infinite Universe* (Baltimore: Johns Hopkins University Press, 1957). Grant McColley provides an extensive survey of speculation about other planets (a topic of discussion since before Socrates) in "The Seventeenth-Century Doctrine of a Plurality of Worlds," *Annals of Science* 1 (1936): 385–430. Also helpful is Marjorie Nicolson, "The 'New Astronomy' and the English Literary Imagination," *Studies in Philology* 32 (July 1935): 428–62.

24. See Henry More, *Democritus platonissans* (Cambridge, 1646), vv.25–26, 31–32; John Wilkins, *A Discovery of a New World* (London, 1638), 102–3; and Robert Boyle, *Of the High Veneration Man's Intellect Owes to God* (London, 1685), 4–5, 51, 72–77.

25. Pierre Borel, *A New Treatise Proving a Multiplicity of Worlds,* trans. D. Sashott (London, 1658), sig. C6v–C7r. Borel's metaphorical extension of a divine polity into the sky may be compared to the angelological commonplace that follows from Proverbs 14.28: "We must believe that the angels are there in marvellous and inconceivable numbers, because the honor of a king consists in the great crowd of his vassals, while his disgrace or shame consists in their paucity" (Raymonde de Sebonde, *Natural Theology,* quoted in E. M. W. Tillyard, *The Elizabethan World Picture* [New York: Vintage, n.d.], 40).

26. Koyré, *Closed World,* 52. Although Koyré refers specifically to the work of Giordano Bruno, who was writing in the late sixteenth century, a version of the same logic underpins much of the discussion that follows on this point. Indeed, Bruno's assertions represent an early instance and characteristic example of the justification of a point (the possibility of plural worlds) neither stated in the Bible nor subject to empirical confirmation. "Thus is the excellence of God magnified and the greatness of his kingdom made manifest; he is glorified not in one, but in countless suns; not in a single earth, but in a thousand, I say, an infinity of worlds" (*De l'infinito universo e mondi* [1584], quoted in Koyré, *Closed World,* 42).

27. Christopher Hill addresses Milton's attention to astronomy, including his awareness of the principle of a plurality of worlds, in *Milton and the English Revolution* (New York: Penguin, 1979), 398–402.

28. This account of the peopling of the universe effectively responds to the sort of assertion made by Thomas Hobbes, who argued that procreation in Eden would have stopped once the garden was full, "For if Immortals should have generated, as Mankind doth now; the Earth in a small time, would not have been able to afford them place to stand on" (*Leviathan* [1651], ed. C. B. Macpherson [Harmondsworth: Penguin, 1985], 481).

29. Laura Lunger Knoppers insightfully reads the poem's focus on labor in relation to Max Weber's account of the disciplinary effects of the Protestant concept of vocation: "Labor, the curse of fallen man, is placed before the fall as a sign of divine election. Adam and Eve desire to work" ("Rewriting the Protestant Ethic: Discipline and Love in *Paradise Lost,*" *ELH* 58 [1991]: 553).

30. Evans, *Paradise Lost and the Genesis Tradition* (Oxford: Clarendon Press, 1968), 248. See also Joseph E. Duncan, *Milton's Earthly Paradise: A Historical Study of Eden* (Minneapolis: University of Minnesota Press, 1972), 147–61.

31. Evans, *Genesis Tradition,* 249. Evans here quotes from 4.135–37, 4.624–32, 5.212–15 and 5.294–97.

32. McColley astutely notes Milton's association of work with procreation in Eden (*Milton's Eve,* 112, 135).

33. On Milton's endorsement of polygamy, see Hill, *Milton and the English Revolution,* 136–41; Leo Miller, *John Milton Among the Polygamophiles* (New York: Loewenthal Press, 1974); Alan Rudrum, "Polygamy in *Paradise Lost,*" *Essays in Criticism* 20, 1 (January 1970): 18–23.

34. Samuel Fortrey, *Englands Interest and Improvement: Consisting in the Increase of Store, and Trade of This Kingdom* (Cambridge, 1663), B2v.

35. Guillory, "From the Superfluous to the Supernumerary," 81–85.

36. Ralph Cudworth, *The True Intellectual System of the Universe,* 3 vols. (London, 1845), 3: 481. John Glanville's translation of Bernard LeBovier de Fontenelle's *A Plurality of Worlds* (London, 1688) insisted that, since "Nature . . . is fruitful to an excess here," it could not "be so very barren in the rest of the Planets" (sig. G5v). Otherwise, "if we are to believe these vast Bodies are not inhabited . . . they were made to little purpose" (sig. G3v). Fontenelle managed the tension between God's superabundance and his efficiency by arguing that "Nature is a great Huswife," who displays a "frugality . . . accompany'd with an extraordinary magnificence, which shines thro' all her works; that is, she is magnificent in the design, but frugal in the Execution" (sig. C1v).

37. Similarly, Wilkins claims that if God had made the moon only to reflect the sun's light, its recently observed valleys and mountains would imply that he was an incompetent creator, insofar as he did not make a perfect mirror (102). Therefore "we may guesse in generall that there are some inhabitants in that Planet: for why else did providence furnish that place with all such conveniences of habitation?" (*A Discovery of a New World,* 188).

38. The following point qualifies Armstrong and Tennenhouse's assertion that Milton's and Petty's emphasis on labor situates them both squarely within a "world of work" (106).

39. In addition to Knoppers's essay, see the previous chapter's discussion of Weber's *Protestant Ethic.*

40. See Michael McKeon, "Politics of Discourses and the Rise of the Aesthetic in Seventeenth-Century England," in *Politics of Discourse: The Literature and History of Seventeenth-Century England,* ed. Kevin Sharpe and Steven N. Zwicker, (Berkeley and Los Angeles: University of California Press, 1987), 35–51. Sharpe and Zwicker's essay in this volume, "Politics of Discourse: Introduction," is also very useful (1–20).

41. Poovey makes this point in "Social Constitution." See also her discussion of the "Authority of Mathematical Instruments," in *Modern Fact,* 138–43.

42. Some church fathers insisted that the "naturall generation of mankinde" was a product of the Fall (John Salkeld, *A Treatise of Paradise* [1617], quoted in Hughes, 295n744). James Grantham Turner establishes the patristic, philosophical, hermetic, and sectarian contexts for the stand that Milton takes, in *One Flesh: Paradisal Marriage and Sexual Relations in the Age of Milton* (Oxford: Clarendon Press, 1987), 96–

106; see also Peter Lindebaum, "Lovemaking in Milton's Paradise," *Milton Studies* 6 (1974): 277–306, esp. 285.

43. In *De Doctrina,* Milton writes that because "[m]arriage is intrinsically honorable . . . the Papists are wrong to prohibit their priests from marrying" (6: 370).

44. Beelzebub makes this point at the demonic war council; he tells his coadjutors of the "new Race call'd *Man*" (2.348, Milton's emphasis), and proleptically celebrates the day "when [God's] darling Sons / Hurl'd headlong to partake with us, shall curse / Thir frail Original, and faded bliss" (2.373–75).

45. McColley, *Milton's Eve,* 31.

46. Lindebaum observes that the poet effects a "jump" in the argument with the hymn to "wedded Love" (285).

47. Such an account attributes to *Paradise Lost* the terms of a medico-juridical discourse that had no standing for Milton (or, for that matter, anybody else) in seventeenth-century England. See Goldberg, *Sodometries;* Alan Bray, *Homosexuality in Renaissance England;* and Alan Bray, "Homosexuality and the Signs of Male Friendship." For explicit assertions that Milton reflects or seeks to institute a modern regime of (hetero)sexuality, see Armstrong and Tennenhouse, *Imaginary Puritan,* 165; Janet E. Halley, "Female Autonomy in Milton's Sexual Poetics," in *Milton and the Idea of Woman,* ed. Julia M. Walker (Urbana: University of Illinois Press, 1988), 235; Nyquist, "Genesis," 105–6 and 122; and David Aers and Bob Hodge, "'Rational Burning': Milton on Sex and Marriage," *Milton Studies* 13 (1979): 3–33.

48. See Peter Buck's perceptive comments on Graunt's project in "Seventeenth-Century Political Arithmetic: Civil Strife and Vital Statistics," *Isis* 68 (1977): 71–73.

49. Bray, *Homosexuality,* 25. The point about Sodom as a biblical exemplar draws on Warner ("New English Sodom"); Katz ("The Age of Sodomitical Sin, 1607–1740"); and Goldberg's discussion of William Bradford's account of sodomy in colonial America, in *Sodometries,* 223–46.

50. Ovid narrates the death of Orpheus in *Metamorphosis,* trans. Mary K. Innes (London: Penguin, 1955), 246–48. On the implications of maenadic frenzy in Milton, see Richard Halpern, "Puritanism and Maenadism in *A Mask,*" in *Rewriting the Renaissance,* 88–105.

51. Stanley Fish develops this position—that Milton functions as an educator teaching his reader—at length in *Surprised by Sin: The Reader in Paradise Lost* (Berkeley and Los Angeles: University of California Press, 1971).

52. For the identification of this allusion to Ezekiel, see Hughes, *Complete Poems,* 898n123.

53. Adam's dream of a world without women gives voice to and (in his alternative fantasy of male generation) qualifies a Muggletonian song, in which the sectaries imagined that "in heaven we shall be 'All males, not made to generate, / But live in divine happy state.'" Quoted in Christopher Hill, *The World Turned Upside Down,* 314. While Christine Froula recognizes a "rivalry between female and male creativity" ("When Eve Reads Milton," 340), she grounds the contest in a psychoanalytic account of gendered subject formation that attributes to Adam "womb envy" (332 and 347n29). That is, Froula posits an extradiscursive "sex" that is the reality upon which patriarchy establishes monolithic relations of dissymmetry (334), a biological substratum that inevitably determines gender identifications, the psychological structures of lack, and the institutions of female subordination.

54. Even Thomas Browne, who rejected the hermeticist claims to have (like Paracelsus) achieved the ideal of male birth, "yearned," according to Turner, "for the ideal state of masculine self-sufficiency" in generation (Turner, *One Flesh*, 162). On Paracelsus's claim to have propagated a man from his sperm, a recovery of the imagined powers possessed by Adam and held out to the "spiritual adept," see 161.

55. Turner, *One Flesh*, 172–73.

56. Ibid., 172.

57. Ibid., 173.

58. Ibid., 164.

59. I owe this insight to Jonathan Goldberg. On these lines, Bentley—despite himself—is perceptive: "What? all her Progeny to be Female? no doubt he gave it, *Multitudes like* YOUR SELVS" (Richard Bentley, *Milton's Paradise Lost* [London, 1732], annotations to line 4.474).

60. Ovid, *Metamorphosis*, 38–40.

61. William Petyt, *Brittania Languens* (1680), 29.

62. Petty, *Economic Writings*, 278.

63. Ibid., 259.

64. Andrew Marvell, "On Paradise Lost," in Milton, *Complete Poems*, l.42.

65. Malthus, *Essay*, 83.

66. Ibid., 83.

67. Ibid., 71.

68. Ibid., 200–1. See Poovey, *Modern Fact*, 282–95, for a discussion of the vicissitudes of providentialism in Malthus's work.

69. Malthus, *A Summary View of the Principle of Population* (1830), in Flew, 250.

Index

David Glimp is assistant professor of English literature at the University of Miami in Coral Gables, Florida. His work has appeared in *Modern Language Quarterly* and *Criticism.*